MACHINERY AND ECONO

J. I. Mason
Manchester 1986.

Also by Martin Fransman

TECHNICAL CHANGE AND ECONOMIC DEVELOPMENT
TECHNOLOGICAL CAPABILITY IN THE THIRD WORLD
(editor with Kenneth King)
INDUSTRY AND ACCUMULATION IN AFRICA *(editor)*

MACHINERY AND ECONOMIC DEVELOPMENT

Edited by

Martin Fransman

Lecturer in Economics
University of Edinburgh

MACMILLAN
PRESS

First published 1986

Published by
THE MACMILLAN PRESS LTD
Houndmills, Basingstoke, Hampshire RG21 2XS
and London
Companies and representatives
throughout the world

Printed in Hong Kong

British Library Cataloguing in Publication Data
Machinery and economic development.
1. Economic development 2. Machinery
I. Fransman, Martin
338.4′76218   HD82
ISBN 0–333–36391–4 (hardcover)
ISBN 0–333–36392–2 (paperback)

For Tammy

Contents

Notes on the Contributors

Alice Amsden Graduate School of Business Administration, Harvard University.

Toshiaki Chokki Department of Business Administration, Hosei University, Tokyo.

Daniel Chudnovsky Centro de Economia Transnacional/UNCTAD, Geneva.

Fabio Erber Institute of Industrial Economics, Federal University of Rio de Janeiro.

Martin Fransman Department of Economics, University of Edinburgh.

Linsu Kim Korean Advanced Institute of Science and Technology, Seoul.

Ajit Singh Department of Applied Economics, University of Cambridge.

Introduction

There has recently been a renewed interest in the role of the machine-producing sector in economic development. In large part this interest results from the central role that machinery plays in production and technical change. The improvement of production processes and products usually requires the introduction of different and better machinery. Accordingly, the machine sector lies at the heart of the processes involved in the generation and diffusion of technical change. This observation is, of course, not new. Adam Smith, for example, writing at the beginning of the industrial revolution, began his enquiry into the causes of the wealth of nations with an examination of the explanatory factors lying behind the increase in labour productivity. Along with, and related to, the benefits of an increasing division of labour he identified the development of improved machinery as a major cause of greater productivity. The role of machinery was even more central in Marx's analysis of the dynamics of capitalist accumulation. These and other contributions are considered in more detail in the first chapter of this book.

But why is there a renewed interest now in the role of the machinery sector in economic development? As we have just seen, the importance of machinery has long been a fact of life. Several related reasons may be identified for this new concern. The first is that it is only relatively recently that the question of technical change has been put high on the research agenda of the social sciences. This is a point that is elaborated upon in Chapter 1 with particular reference to economics. But, if it is true that the study of technical change has only recently become a priority, then this itself requires an explanation. It may be suggested that a number of related factors are responsible for this. The first is the world recession that began in the latter 1960s and greatly deepened through the 1970s and into the 1980s. This reduced rates of profit and increased the intensity of competition, thus adding considerably to the pressures for change exerted on firms. Innovations in transportation, such as the widespread switch to containerization, increased international competition by substantially reducing transport costs. Within this context Japan's rapid 'catch up' and in some cases overtaking raised a number of fundamental questions about technical and productivity change. How and why, for example, does a technology follower become a technology leader and correspondingly how and why does the leader come to lose its leadership position? In all countries the view was increasingly expressed that the attainment and maintenance of international competitiveness was not only desirable but a matter of survival. The link between technical and productivity change and international competitiveness was a direct and obvious one. In view of the centrality of the machine producing sector in the generation and diffusion of technical change it was hardly surprising that more attention focused on this sector.

At the same time rapid technical change in many areas of machinery, strong international competitive pressures and the corresponding relative decline of parts of the machinery sector in a number of industrialized countries raised fundamental questions about the role of this sector in economic development. In the United States, for examples, these questions were asked when the domestic machine tool industry was faced, if not by extinction, then by a severe challenge by the success of imported Japanese CNC machine tools. Similar questions have begun to be posed in Britain by the increasing dependence on foreign machinery and the increasing elimination of long-standing British machinery producers. Amongst the fundamental questions raised are the following: While no country can or should be entirely self-sufficient in the area of machinery, how important is it for an industrialized country to have a substantial capital goods sector? What are the implications for international competitiveness if this sector is weak? If it is concluded that it is necessary to have an important domestic capital goods sector, then what measures should be taken to encourage its development?

These are also the kinds of questions that are being increasingly asked in developing countries. While the pioneers amongst these countries in the area of capital goods included India with its emphasis on machinery and heavy industry from the 1950s, China with a similar stress, and more recently Brazil, South Korea, and Taiwan, many other developing countries have taken steps designed to encourage the development of the machinery sector. Reflecting the new-found interest in this sector research projects have been initiated in the 1980s by international organizations such as the ILO, UNCTAD and UNIDO. While the first chapter of the present book ranges over broader conceptual issues relating to the role of the machinery sector, the remaining chapters focus on analytical and policy questions that have arisen in some of the newly industialized countries.

In Chapter 1 Fransman provides a conceptual analysis of the role of machinery in economic development. He begins with a discussion of the machinery industry in the two-sector Feldman–Mahalanobis model. The two sectors are the machinery or capital goods sector and the consumption goods sector respectively. The analytical question relates to how resources should be allocated between these two sectors in order to maximize consumption over the planning period. The model is then extended to include a third sector producing export goods. Now it is possible to import machinery by producing export goods. This introduces the make–import decision, which is examined analytically. The make–import decision is one of the most important facing developing countries in the capital goods sector. The discussion reveals the centrality of the level and growth of productivity in the machinery and export sectors. In turn this raises the issue of the determinants of productivity change over time. This leads on to the second part of the paper where it is shown that the question of technical and productivity change was central for Adam Smith and Karl Marx. The pursuit of this question led both these writers to examine in detail the role of the machinery sector. However, with the exception of Joseph Schumpeter, later economists, for a number of complex reasons, tended to ignore the issue of the determinants of technical and productivity change. In the third part of the chapter a novel approach drawing on a biological analogy is suggested for the analysis of the causes of technical and productivity change. This approach is then applied in an examination of the development of machine tools. In the fourth and final part of the chapter, two issues are discussed which are of central importance in developing countries. These are the make–import decision and the development of design capabilities.

In Chapter 2 Chudnovsky takes up the question of how well developing countries have fared in their attempt to develop indigenous capital goods sectors and benefit from the dynamic contributions to technical and productivity change that this sector has made in the developed countries. Confining his attention to three countries with substantial capital goods sectors, namely Brazil, India and South Korea, Chudnovsky summarizes the results of a comprehensive survey undertaken by UNCTAD. This survey examines more than sixty firms in these countries producing machine tools, electrical power equipment, and machinery for the process industries. Particular attention is paid in the survey to the sources of technology, the role of the state in encouraging the development of the machinery sector, and the performance of the sector. The latter includes export performance as well as an attempt to assess the success of these countries in developing the crucial ability to design machinery. This ability enables a country to adapt its machinery to suit local conditions and may also assist in the attainment of international competitiveness in a world with short product life cycles where the rapid introduction of newly designed machinery can provide a considerable competitive advantage. Chudnovsky concludes that, although design capabilities have been developing in the countries surveyed, these tend to be in the area of detail design rather than in the more fundamental area of basic design. As a result design capabilities are still rather limited thus restricting the more dynamic contributions of the machinery sector in these countries. One of the reasons for the limited development of design capabilities is the successful attempt made by foreign companies to restrict the transfer of such capabilities in their licensing agreements.

The question of design capabilities is also central in the paper by Amsden and Kim in Chapter 3. In this paper a more detailed case-study is provided of a number of firms in the general machinery industry in South Korea. This study, based on work undertaken for the World Bank, examines the performance of three large firms in South Korea. While the first is now state-owned (Korea Heavy Industries & Construction Company), the other two are part of large privately owned conglomerates (Hyundai Heavy Industries and Samsung Heavy Industries). The products examined are materials handling, power generating, and earth-moving equipment. In assessing the performance of these firms, Amsden and Kim examine the breadth of their technological capabilities. By a technological capability they mean the ability, embodied in people, to select the appropriate technology; to implement it; to operate the production facilities so implemented; to adapt and improve them, and possibly to create new processes and products. A technology may be purchased but a technological capability is acquired only through the build-up of human capital. In examining the technological capability of these firms they focus on three elements: the initial technology acquisition; operations and maintenance; and design. They conclude that the South Korean firms have made important progress in all these areas and in particular in the first two. With regard to design their conclusion is somewhat more optimistic than Chudnovsky's: despite the difficulties of technology transfer, technological capability has come to include design, at least for a limited subset of products. There are also many signs of progressive improvements in performance. In addition Amsden and Kim examine some of the criticisms that have been made inside South Korea of government policy in the machinery area. These criticisms argue that the machinery sector has been overly subsidized and sheltered from foreign competition with detrimental effects on performance. The authors, however, do not find strong evidence of poor performance. Furthermore they argue that rapid growth in the machinery sector has had a beneficial impact on productivity.

In Chapter 4 Chokki examines the history of one of the world's most successful machinery industries, namely the Japanese machine tool industry. The first part of the chapter traces the development of this industry in Japan from its origins as a supplier of machine tools to state-owned arsenals. As Chokki illustrates, Japan's various wars provided a substantial stimulus for the production of machine tools. However, as discussed in the second part, the situation in this respect changed dramatically after the Second World War with the government, apart from the Japan National Railways, ceasing to become a substantial purchaser of machine tools. Accordingly, the industry was dependent on the private domestic sector, and increasingly later the export sector, for its sales. In his discussion Chokki examines factors such as the role of government, credit, marketing, the internal organization of machine tool firms, as well as the geographical location of these firms in Japan.

The question of the explanation of the international competitiveness of Japan and the Asian newly industrialized countries is taken up in Chapter 5 by Fransman through an examination of machine tool production in Taiwan and Japan. The first part of the paper contains a critical discussion of the most widely accepted explanation of the economic performance of the Asian newly industrialized countries – Hong Kong, Singapore, South Korea and Taiwan. This explanation, based on the concept of comparative advantage, emphasizes the importance of the wage rate in these countries in facilitating the choice of labour-intensive techniques of production and enabling the successful establishment of a labour-intensive export sector. With the passage of time export-led growth results in the exhaustion of labour surpluses, a rise in real wage rates, and to a shift in comparative advantage in line with the changed factor endowments. Fransman argues, however, that, while this explanation may correctly focus on some of the causal mechanisms behind the successful economic performance of these countries, it either ignores or is misleading about some of the other causes. Of particular importance are the process of technical and productivity change and the role of the state, both of which are ignored in the conventional explanation. This argument is elaborated upon in the rest of the chapter, which contains an examination of the determinants of technical change, including the part played by the international diffusion of technology, and the role of the state in the machine tool industry in Taiwan and Japan. The final section contains an account of the sharp differences that have emerged in Taiwan over the question of the policies that are necessary to ensure the establishment and maintenance of international competitiveness in CNC (computer numerically controlled) machine tools. This discussion illustrates the difficulties involved in the 'technology-following' strategy where a country attempts to use the latest technologies without paying the price of developing them.

In the final two chapters attention is shifted to two of the most indus-trialized countries in Latin America - Brazil and Mexico. In Chapter 6 Erber examines in detail the development and contribution of the capital goods sector in Brazil. This sector, which is the most important contributor to manufactured exports, has for some time been a priority for government promotional measures. Largely as a result there has been a rapid expansion of capital goods production and Brazil is now one of the largest producers of capital goods amongst developing countries. Like Chudnovsky, Erber is concerned to establish whether this sector has made the same contribution in Brazil which it has made in the developed countries. Beginning the chapter with a resumé of the importance of the capital goods sector in the wider literature on economic development, Erber goes on to chart the growth, strengths and weaknesses of this sector in Brazil. In his discussion particular importance is attached to the state of the world economy, and to Brazil's role in it, and to the negative effects of a poorly developed network of subcontracting and engineering firms and the inadequate financing of local capital goods producers and users. Furthermore, like Chudnovsky, he stresses that while technological capabilities have been improved in the metalworking sector as a whole (including the capital goods sector), progress is less apparent in the case of complex capital goods: 'the evidence available suggests that the trajectory of technological development is limited and that the Brazilian [capital goods] industry tends to rely on imported technology for new and more complex products'. For these reasons Erber concludes that while the capital goods sector in Brazil has made important contributions to the performance of the economy, significant constraints limit its role. Nevertheless, he points out that this sector has assisted in alleviating the country's foreign exchange difficulties.

It is precisely this question of the potential contribution of the capital goods sector to the balance of payments that is Singh's concern in Chapter 7. In examining the causes of the balance of payments crisis in Mexico, Singh argues that the major cause was the increased penetration of capital goods imports following on liberalization of import control. Although the changed structure of the Mexican economy with the expansion of the oil sector also contributed to the increase in the rate of growth of imports, it was the greater penetration of imports that was responsible for the larger share of the increase. Singh argues that the Mexican government was faced with two clear options. The first was greatly to liberalize foreign trade, thus integrating the Mexican economy more closely with that of the United States and the rest of the world economy. The second, supported by, for example, the Ministry of Industry, was to extend import substitution in the intermediate and capital goods sectors by instituting protective measures. The crisis, in Singh's view, was the result of the failure decisively to follow the second alternative. During the boom period from 1976 to 1981, 90 per cent of imports consisted of intermediate and capital goods. Accordingly, Singh suggests, the capital goods sector should now be expanded and restrictions on the import of capital goods reimposed. This will allow the capital goods sector to expand from its current relatively small size with comparatively low technological capabilities to something more comparable with that existing in other countries like Brazil. Furthermore, Singh argues that this will not result in increased capacity shortages and accordingly reduced growth of output. Presenting data on the growing underutilization of industrial capacity in Mexico since 1979 Singh suggests that reduced imports of capital goods will have the effect of increasing domestic capacity utilization. Examining the potential constraints of market size and technological capacity and skills he argues that Mexico should expand its capital goods sector so that it comes to play as important a role as in comparable countries like India and South Korea.

From this brief introduction, and from the additional details provided in the chapters themselves, it can be seen that the machinery sector plays a central role in economic development. The very least that can be claimed is that, while further research is still required in many related areas, some progress has been made in understanding this contribution and in clarifying the policy issues that are confronted in the attempt to develop the machinery sector.

Edinburgh   MARTIN FRANSMAN

1 Machinery in Economic Development[1]

MARTIN FRANSMAN

I INTRODUCTION

In recent years there has been a renewed interest in the role of the machine-producing sector in economic development, as is evident from the growing number of articles published in this area and the research programmes undertaken by international organizations such as the ILO, UNCTAD and UNIDO. A number of factors account for the generation of new interest. Perhaps the most important is the increasing attention that has been given since the late 1970s to the role of technical change in improving the quantity and quality of national output. Advances in processes and products invariably require improved machinery. Accordingly, the machine-producing sector lies at the heart of the production and diffusion of technical change. A further reason for the new interest in this sector stems from the change in industrial structure that has occurred in many of the more industrialized developing countries. Partly as a result of policies intended to promote the growth of the machinery sector countries such as Brazil, Argentina, India, China, South Korea and Taiwan have become substantial producers, and in some cases exporters, of machinery. This change in industrial structure has prompted questions regarding the benefits provided by the machinery sector.

However, while there certainly has been a renewed interest in the machine-producing sector, this sector has long fascinated both scholars and those more pragmatically concerned with policy. In raising once more fundamental questions about the role of the machinery sector in economic development it is useful to take stock of past analyses and debates. This endeavour is not merely of academic interest since, as we shall see, despite the dramatic improvements that have occurred in the machines themselves,

1

earlier examinations have focused attention on issues that are just as relevant today.

In the 1950s a vigorous debate was sparked off by the application by Mahalanobis of the two-sector Feldman model in examining the role of the capital goods sector in India. Much later the model was systematically extended to include an export sector and thus incorporate the role of international trade. In these analyses the underlying question was one of optimal resource allocation: how should resources be allocated between the machinery sector and other sectors in order to maximize specified objectives such as consumption over the planning period? In Section II these models are discussed together with some of the difficulties that they raise.

While the Feldman–Mahalanobis model has been extended by Cooper (1984) to include learning-by-doing, it is true to say that neither the model itself, nor its subsequent elaborations, has been concerned with the process of technical change *within* the machine producing sector itself. However, this process was of great interest to some of the classical economists who analysed both the *causes* and the *consequences* of technical change. As Rosenberg has shown, some of the classical writings offer important insights into the determinants of long-term improvements in the cost and quality of output. These classical contributions are examined in the first part of Section III, while in the second part of this section some of Rosenberg's ideas are discussed together with Little's observations on the role of the capital goods sector in developing countries.

In the third part of Section III an approach is presented for the analysis of the determinants of technical change in the machine-producing sector. Based on a biological analogy, this approach stresses both the social organization within enterprises as well as the environmental factors which influence its operations and bring about change. The following environmental factors are considered: the relationship of machine producers to users, on the one hand, and component suppliers on the other; the influence of competitive pressures and information flows in both the domestic and export markets; and lastly, the influence of the state. Three related causal factors are stressed in examining the process of technical and productivity change: pressures, incentives, and information flows that are both market and non-market mediated. The approach is qualitative and non-deterministic.

Finally, in Section IV some policy issues are examined confronting developing countries in the area of machine production. The first is the make–import decision which raises the following question: When should a machine be produced domestically and when should it be imported? This question in turn raises other related issues. If the decision is made to make rather than import under conditions where the industry in question does not immediately enjoy international competitiveness, then a further set of questions arise regarding the best way of insulating domestic producers from foreign competition. It is shown in this section that while the conventional approaches adopted by economists in tackling such issues may be a useful starting-point, they are severely handicapped by their *static* examination of resource allocation. With reference to Japan and the Asian newly industrialized countries (particularly South Korea and Taiwan) it is shown that at least some of the economically successful developing countries have not made use of the static techniques currently available, but have rather been concerned with the dynamic determinants of technical and productivity change and with international competitiveness in a rapidly altering international environment. This concern explains the use of policy instruments such as the total prohibition of imports and quota restrictions, instruments which according to conventional economic theory are only third or even fourth best options.

The choice to make machinery domestically does not imply that all inputs will be locally produced. More specifically, this choice does not imply that the machinery will be domestically designed. In the last part of Section IV the issue of the design of machinery is examined. While the use of foreign designs, either purchased through arrangements such as licensing or turn-key projects or acquired via non-market-mediated means such as imitation, may substantially reduce designing costs, it is shown that under some circumstances this option may present further difficulties. In the case of those countries attempting to achieve international competitiveness in areas where the technology frontier is rapidly shifting, total reliance on foreign designs may be unviable. In the case of machine tools of the computer numerically controlled variety, for example, design life-cycles may be as short as two years before they become obsolete. This may cause problems since the sellers of technology will often not provide the latest versions and since there is an inevitable time lag involved in imitation. Under these circumstances it will be necessary for enterprises to strengthen their own design capabilities. However, it is shown that it is the current consensus of opinion that in even the most industrialized developing countries design capabilities are seriously limited.

In the following section we begin by examining the two-sector Feldman-Mahalanobis model.

II OPTIMAL RESOURCE ALLOCATION AND THE MACHINERY SECTOR

The question of optimal resource allocation lies at the heart of the Feldman–Mahalanobis model. The Feldman model had its origin in the Soviet industrialization debates of the 1920s and was later used and elaborated upon by Mahalanobis in the Indian context influencing industrial planning in the 1950s and 1960s.[2]

In the Feldman–Mahalanobis model the objective is taken to be the maximization of consumption over a given planning period. Since machines are required for the production of consumption goods, the model is concerned centrally with the production and allocation of machinery. The main question addressed in the model is the following: how must machines be allocated between the machine-producing sector and the consumption-goods sector in order to maximize consumption. The driving force in the model is investment in machines to make machines since the growth of the capital stock in the consumption-goods sector depends ultimately on accumulation in the capital-goods sector. Accordingly, accumulation in the capital-goods sector is given by the equation

$$dK_1/dt = (\lambda b_1 - \alpha)K_1$$

while the growth of the capital stock in the consumption-goods sector (and hence, through the capital–output ratio, final output) is given by

$$dK_2/dt = (1 - \lambda)b_1 K_1 - \alpha K_2$$

where

K_1, K_2 = capital stock in the capital and consumption goods sector respectively

b_1 = the output–capital ratio in the capital goods sector

λ = the proportion of initial investment devoted to the capital-goods sector, and

α = the physical rate of capital depreciation

At each point in time there is in principle the choice of allocating resources to the machinery sector (producing machines to make machines) in order to produce more consumption-goods in the future, or allocating resources to the consumption-goods sector (producing machines to make consumption goods) in order to produce more of these goods now.

To examine this question it is assumed in the model that the economy is divided into two sectors: a consumption goods sector, C, and a machine-producing sector, I. The economy is assumed to be closed so that either there is no foreign trade, or such trade is negligible. Labour is in abundant supply and it is also assumed that once machines are allocated to one of the two sectors, they cannot be reallocated. The mechanics of the model are shown in Figure 1.1 where machines, produced by the machinery sector, can either be allocated to this same sector in order to produce more machines, or they can be allocated to the consumption goods sector to produce consumer goods.[3]

The conclusion of the model is that consumption will be maximized if in the first stage all machinery is allocated to the machine-producing sector (the 'accumulation stage'), followed by a 'consumption stage' when the total output of machinery goes to the consumption goods sector. The model itself provides a solution to the question regarding the duration of the first stage.

A different set of issues, however, arise if we begin by posing additional questions about foreign trade. If, instead of assuming either that there is no foreign trade or that such trade is negligible, we pose the question about the role of the machine-producing sector where there is an export sector, then, as Harris (1972) shows, the resource allocation problem is now more complicated. As illustrated in Figure 1.2, there are now three sectors in the economy: an *I*-sector producing machinery, a *C*-sector producing consumption goods, and an *X*-sector producing goods that for convenience are assumed to be entirely for export. Machines produced by the *I*-sector can, as before, be allocated to the *I*-sector itself, or to the *C*-sector, but they can also be allocated to the *X*-sector in order to produce exports. Furthermore, machinery needs in all three sectors can now also be met by machinery imported with the foreign exchange earned by the *X*-sector. Accordingly, the importance of the local machine-producing sector is diminished in so far as it is now possible to use imported machinery in each of the three sectors.

In achieving the objective of maximizing the output of consumption goods over the planning period, the planners therefore have a further

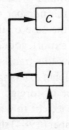

FIGURE 1.1

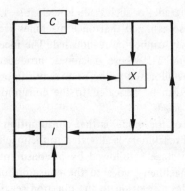

FIGURE 1.2

choice: either to expand the output of the *I*-sector in order to obtain the necessary machines, or to expand the output of the *X*-sector and import machinery. This is the important *make–import decision*.

As we shall see later in this chapter, the make–import decision is one of the most difficult that developing countries confront in building up their machine-producing sector. We shall later examine some of the policy steps that have been taken regarding the import of machinery. However, from an analytically static point of view, the make–import decision is relatively easy to resolve. Since the aim is to end up with as many machines as possible by allocating resources in an optimal proportion between the *I*- and *X*-sectors, it is necessary to calculate the marginal return in each sector, that is the number of machines 'earned' in each sector per unit of resources allocated to that sector. As long as there is a divergence between the two sectors, resources should be allocated to that which yields the higher return. Several factors will determine the number of machines 'earned' and therefore the optimal allocation. The productivity of the *I*-goods sector will determine the number of machines (output) obtained per unit of resource input. In the case of the *X*-sector, productivity levels will determine the output of export goods received per unit of resource input. In order to calculate how this translates into machines, information is needed on the amount of foreign exchange that will be earned by selling the export goods, and the price of foreign machinery. In this way the calculation can be made as to the extent to which machines should be locally produced, or imported.[4] As Cooper (1984) shows, the make–import decision can be expressed in terms of Ricardian static comparative advantage.

However, additional complications arise when further questions are posed about the levels of productivity in the I- and X-goods sectors which until now have been assumed to be exogenously determined. In order to endogenize productivity, Cooper introduces a simple learning mechanism into the Harris model. Following Arrow's notion of learning-by-doing, Cooper assumes that 'learning', and hence productivity increases, are a function of 'doing' measured by cumulative gross investment. If the learning elasticities in the I- and X-goods sectors, that is the responsiveness of changes in productivity in these sectors to cumulative gross investment, are different, then the conclusions of the model will have to be modified. Of particular interest is the case where the learning elasticity in the I-goods sector is greater than that in the X-goods sector. If this differential is sufficiently great, then it will be justified to allocate resources to the I-goods sector even when this violates the Ricardian principle of static comparative advantage. In this case the static 'loss' of machines that results from allocating resources to the I-sector rather than to the X-sector is more than compensated for by the differential increase over time in the productivity of the former sector as a consequence of the 'learning' process.

As is clear from this example, the time dimension is crucial. Depending on the differential in the learning elasticities, different solutions to the make–import decision may be yielded in the short- and long-run cases. However, as always in economic theory, the introduction of a time dimension poses severe analytical difficulties in the *ex ante* situation since it introduces the problems of uncertainty and expectations. In the model discussed these difficulties are not dealt with since determinate learning elasticities are assumed. Accordingly, although the optimal make–import decision becomes more complicated, it is still soluble. From a policy point of view, however, uncertainty and expectations can no longer be held at arm's length. In effect, *different questions* are posed about the make–import decision in the policy context. Here the question is the following: How should the decision be made as to whether a machine should be locally produced or imported, given that uncertainty exists regarding productivities and the other relevant magnitudes over the planning period? Later in this chapter we shall briefly examine how the states of various countries have confronted this question.

We should note, however, that in attempting to endogenize productivity we have come a long way from the initial questions of resource allocation that were posed in the Feldman–Mahalanobis and Harris models. These models, as we saw, are primarily concerned with the question of the optimal allocation of resources among different sectors with given productivities. By opening up the issue of the *causes* of productivity, Cooper introduces a qualitatively different set of questions. At the same time he implicitly makes the important point that in order to satisfactorily resolve the make-import decision it is necessary to ask questions about *both* optimal resource allocation among sectors *and* the causes of productivity change. We shall return later to the policy implications of this point.

Cooper also implicitly (and in places explicitly) admits that there are formidable difficulties in introducing the causes of productivity into the formal analysis. As he rightly states, the productivity-increasing mechanism introduced by the notion of learning-by-doing is simplistic. While possessing the undoubted advantage of its amenability to formal analysis, this particular mechanism fails to capture important aspects of the productivity-increasing process. Cooper notes, for example, that extremely difficult formal problems are raised if we attempt to drop the assumption implicit in the notion of learning-by-doing that productivity increases achieved in this way are costless. Furthermore, it is clearly necessary that any realistic analysis takes account of other productivity-increasing mechanisms.

Nevertheless, it is of interest that questions posed about resource allocation within the context of analyses of the role of the machinery-producing sector have led ultimately to the addressing of further questions about the causes of productivity increases. One of the reasons for the interest in this progression is that some of the classical political economists followed a very different route in their consideration of closely related issues. This is perhaps clearest in the case of Smith and Marx. Rather than beginning with questions of resource allocation, Smith began by posing at the very start of *The Wealth of Nations* questions about the causes of productivity increases which he saw as central to his inquiry into the determinants of the wealth of nations. As we shall see, these questions led him immediately to consider the role of machinery and its contribution to productivity increases. Marx also believed that productivity increases lay at the heart of the process of capital accumulation, and even more so than Smith he felt that the contributions made by the machinery sector were central in raising productivity. Both Smith and Marx were particularly interested in the process of technical change *within* the machine-producing sector.

III THE MACHINERY SECTOR AND TECHNICAL CHANGE

Machinery and Technical Change in the History of Economic Thought

Classical political economy since at least the time of Adam Smith has grappled with the importance of machinery. Although Adam Smith wrote within the context of a primarily agrarian society, and although as Hicks (1965) emphasizes his 'pure theory' of economic growth was based on a single-period corn model where the entire captial stock consisted of circulating rather than fixed capital, he was profoundly aware of the importance of machinery. In the beginning of chapter 1, book 1 of *The Wealth of Nations*, Adam Smith attributes increases in labour productivity to three major causes, the last being the invention of machinery:

> This great increase of the quantity of work which, in consequence of the division of labour, the same number of people are capable of performing, is owing to three different circumstances; first, to the increase of dexterity in every particular workman; secondly, to the saving of the time which is commonly lost in passing from one species of work to another; and lastly to the invention of a great number of machines which facilitate and abridge labour, and enable one man to do the work of many. (Smith, 1910, p.7)

In causal terms Adam Smith saw the development of machinery as the *consequence* of the social division of labour in the factory thus implicitly taking issue with latter-day technological determinists who examine the effects on economy and society of autonomous changes in technology, including machinery. Smith states clearly that 'the invention of all those machines by which labour is so much facilitated and abridged seems to have been originally owing to the division of labour.' (ibid, p.9). However, in elaborating on the link between the social division of labour and the development of machinery, Smith, with great foresight, anticipated the emergence of a specialized capital goods sector and the application of the division of labour to science itself, although he pointed out that 'common workmen' often invented or improved the relatively simple machinery that existed in his day.

> A great part of the machines made use of in those manufacturers in which labour is most subdivided, were originally the inventions of common workmen ... All the improvements in machinery, however, have by no means been the inventions of those who had occasion to use the machines. Many improvements had been made by the ingenuity of the makers of the machines, when to make them became the business of a peculiar trade; and some by that of those who are called philosophers or men of speculation, whose trade it is not to do anything, but to observe everything ... In the progress of society, philosophy or speculation became, like every other employment, the principal or sole trade and occupation of a particular class of citizens ... this subdivision of

employment in philosophy, as well as in every other business, improves dexterity, and saves time. (ibid, pp.9, 10)

Being the astute observer that he was, Adam Smith was also acutely aware of the cumulative importance of incremental changes in the improvement of machinery, a perception that was later to be obscured by the emphasis given to major technological change in the writings of authors like Schumpeter. Smith noted that 'We have not, nor cannot have, any complete history of the invention of machines, because most of them are at first imperfect, and receive gradual improvements and increase of powers from those who use them.'[5]

Writing at a time when the Industrial Revolution was well under way, machinery (or, more generally, fixed capital) was more central for Ricardo than for Adam Smith. Since in his model Ricardo assumed that all accumulation was derived from profits, the question of the distribution of the national product between profit, rent and wages assumed a central significance. In examining the relationship between profit, rent and wages Ricardo abstracted from international trade and technical change. The accumulation of capital, Ricardo argued, would result in an increase in the marginal cost of food as diminishing returns in agriculture set in and less fertile land was cultivated. This in turn resulted in an increase in the share of wages and consequently in a fall in the share of profit. Eventually the point would be reached where total wages equalled total product minus rent, and with profits reduced to zero, the stationary state would be achieved. Writers such as Schumpeter have argued that a pessimistic view of the long-run tendencies of capitalist societies lay at he heart of the work of Ricardo and Malthus. However, a recent reinterpretation (Berg, 1980) has suggested that Ricardo produced his 'pessimistic' model precisely in order to illustrate the optimistic significance of foreign trade and technical change which he excluded from his model. Certainly a closer textual analysis makes it clear that Ricardo believed that both these factors, including 'improvements in machinery', were capable of arresting the long-run tendency of profits to fall:

The natural tendency of profits ... is to fall; for in the progress of society and wealth, the additional quantity of food required is obtained by the sacrifice of more and more labour. This tendency ... is happily checked at repeated intervals by the improvements in machinery connected with the production of necessaries, as well as by discoveries in the science of agriculture which enable us to relinquish a portion of labour before required, and therefore to lower the price of the prime necessary of the labourer. (*Principles*, Sraffa edn, p. 120)

For Ricardo the share of wages in national product was central since it bore an inverse relationship to the share of profits which was the mainspring of accumulation. Accordingly, technical change embodied in machinery would increase the rate of accumulation by reducing the cost of wage goods. 'If ... by the extension of foreign trade, or by improvements in machinery, the food and necessaries of the labourer can be brought to market at a reduced price, profits will rise' (ibid, p.132). Therefore, technical change exerts a positive influence, not directly on output, but through its effect on wages and accordingly profits. Thus a fall in the price of luxury goods will leave the rate of profit and the rate of accumulation unaffected: 'if the commodities obtained at a cheaper rate, by the extension of foreign commerce, or by the improvements of machinery, be exclusively the commodities consumed by the rich, no alteration will take place in the rate of profits' (ibid). More generally:

The rate of profits is never increased by a better distribution of labour, by the invention of machinery, by the establishment of roads and canals, or by any means of abridging labour either in the manufacture or in the conveyance of goods. These are causes which operate on price, and never fail to be highly beneficial to consumers; ... but they have no effect whatever on profit. On the other hand, every diminution in the wages of labour raise profits, but produces no effect on the price of commodities. (ibid, p. 133)

Ricardo was also interested in the direct consequences for the working class of the introduction of machinery and shocked many of his contemporaries when he declared, in a new section in the third edition of his *Principles* published in 1821, that new machinery might be injurious to workers by reducing output for a time and creating unemployment. However, Ricardo was more concerned with the consequences than the causes of technical change. Preoccupied as he was with the effects of changes in the distribution of income on accumulation he accepted, but did not take further, Adam Smith's analysis of the division of labour and its effects on productivity.

This task was undertaken by Marx who, probably more than any other of the great economists, was concerned with productivity, its causes and consequences and the contribution made by the development of machinery. It is for this reason that Rosenberg (1982) has suggested that Marx's formulation of the problem of technological change 'deserves to be a starting point for any serious investigation of technology and its ramifications'.

For Marx the machine-producing sector lay at the heart of the dynamic process of accumulation. Beginning where Adam Smith left off, Marx agreed that the division of labour in manufacture (literally, production by hand without the use of machinery) gave rise to the emergence of a specialized machine-producing sector and hence to 'machinofacture'. Unlike in the period of handicraft production, which preceded manufacture, manufacture in factories led to a process of division of labour which was soon extended to the tools used by workers:

> Manufacture is characterized by the differentiation of the instruments of labour – a differentiation whereby tools of a given sort acquire fixed shapes, adapted to each potential application – and by the specialization of these instruments . . . The manufacturing period simplifies, improves and multiplies the implements of labour by adapting them to the exclusive and special functions of each kind of worker.[6] It thus creates at the same time one of the material conditions for the existence of machinery, which consists of a combination of simple instruments. (Marx, 1976, pp. 460–1)

However, going beyond Smith, Marx argued that the production of machinery led to the undermining of the manufacture form of production itself:

> Manufacture produced the machinery with which large-scale industry [i.e. machinofacture] abolished the handicraft and manufacturing systems in the spheres of production it first seized hold of. The system of machine production therefore grew spontaneously on a material basis which was inadequate to it. (Marx, 1976, p. 504)[7]

According to Marx, the introduction of machinery involves the replacement of subjective, human control of the production process by more predictable and controllable natural forces. In this way the conditions are created for the conscious application of science to production. 'As machinery, the instrument of labour assumes a material mode of existence which necessitates the replacement of human force by natural forces, and the replacement of the rule of thumb by the conscious application of natural science' (ibid, p.508). Paraphrasing Marx, Rosenberg (1982) elaborates on this theme:

> science itself can never be extensively applied to the productive process so long as that process continues to be dependent upon forces the

behaviour of which cannot be predicted and controlled with the strictest accuracy. Science, in other words, must incorporate its principles in impersonal machinery. Such machinery may be relied upon to behave in accordance with scientifically established physical relationships. Science, however, cannot be incorporated into techniques dominated by large-scale human interventions, for human action involves too much that is subjective and capricious. More generally, human beings have wills of their own and are therefore too refractory to constitute reliable, i.e. controllable, inputs in complex and interdependent productive processes. (p. 42)

By applying science in the design and production of machinery, productivity may be increased and hence costs reduced. 'Like every other instrument for increasing the productivity of labour, machinery is intended to cheapen commodities' (Marx, 1976, p. 492). However, it is the relative *price* (i.e. market price rather than value) of labour-power and machinery that will govern the introduction of machinery since it is this that will determine actual costs and hence influence the actions of capitalists under the pressure of competition. Accordingly, production techniques will be expected to differ between countries with different relative prices:

The use of machinery for the exclusive purpose of cheapening the product is limited by the requirement that less labour must be expended in producing the machinery than is displaced by the employment of that machinery ... it is possible for the difference between the price of the machinery and the price of the labour-power replaced by that machinery to undergo great variations,[8] while the difference between the quantity of labour needed to produce the machine and the total quantity of labour replaced by it remains constant. But it is only the former difference that determines the cost to the capitalist of producing a commodity, and influences his actions through the pressure of competition. Hence the invention nowadays in England of machines that are employed in North America. (Marx, 1976, pp. 515-16)

The argument that the introduction of machinery depended on relative factor prices was not original to Marx and had been expressed earlier by Ricardo.[9] Similarly, Marx's statement that the individual capitalist, including the machine-producing capitalist, has 'a motive ... to cheapen his commodities by increasing the productivity of labour' (Marx, 1976, p. 435) was also unoriginal. Marx's observation that the individual capitalist who increased his productivity above the average (social) level 'realizes an extra surplus value' (Marx, 1976, p. 434) is very much in line with Adam Smith's views on the self-interest of producers. However, Marx certainly went beyond his predecessors when he elaborated on the processes whereby more productive methods of production became generalized over time. For it is here that what Marx refers to as a social process, rather than individual motives, are determinant. It is these processes that lie at the heart of Marx's concept of value which differs qualitatively from that of Ricardo.

In order to illustrate this let us take the case of two vintages of machinery, the power-loom and the hand-loom. Marx observed that 'The introduction of power-looms into England . . . probably reduced by one half the labour required to convert a given quantity of yarn into woven fabric.[10] In order to do this, the English hand-loom weaver in fact needed the same amount of labour-time as before' (Marx, 1976, p. 129). However, with the introduction of more productive power-looms (i.e. in terms of total factor productivity) the price of woven fabric will fall. Marx elaborates on how the fall in price comes about. The first capitalist to use the power-loom will find, by assumption, that his unit cost[11] has fallen by one-half. He will, however, attempt to sell his woven fabric at the prevailing price determined by hand-loom costs. But since his total factor productivity has doubled, all other things remaining constant, his total output will have doubled. 'Hence, in order to get rid of the product . . . the demand [for this capitalist's output] must be double what it was, i.e. the market must become twice as extensive. Other things being equal, the capitalist's commodities can only command a more extensive market if their prices are reduced. He will, therefore, sell them above their individual but below their social [i.e. average] value' (Marx, 1976, p. 434). The capitalist will therefore realize an 'extra surplus value' as a result of the introduction of the power-loom. Accordingly, 'there is a motive for each individual capitalist to cheapen his commodities by increasing the productivity of labour' (Marx, 1976, p. 435). As other capitalists voluntarily respond to this incentive, the price of woven fabric will fall. This, however, creates problems for the hand-loom weaver who operates under lower-productivity, higher-cost conditions and therefore feels the pressure of the falling unit selling price.[12] As Marx puts it, the product of the hand-loom weaver's 'individual hour of labour now only (represents) half an hour of social labour, and consequently (falls) to one half of its former value' (Marx, 1976, p. 129). The result is that the hand-loom weaver is *forced*, independently of his will and intentions, to alter his methods of production which have become socially unproductive:

The price of the commodity, therefore, is merely the money-name of the quantity of social labour objectified in it. But now the old-established conditions of production in weaving are thrown into the melting-pot, without the permission of, and behind the back of our weaver. What was yesterday undoubtedly labour-time socially necessary to the production of a yard of linen ceases to be so today, a fact which the owner of . . . money [i.e. the consumer] is only too eager to prove from the prices quoted from our friend's competitors. Unluckily for the weaver, people of his kind are in plentiful supply. (Marx, 1976, p. 202)

Elsewhere Marx expresses the same idea:

The rule that the labour-time expended on a commodity should not exceed the amount socially necessary to produce it is one that appears, in the production of commodities in general, to be enforced from outside by the action of competition: to put it superficially, each single producer is obliged to sell his commodity at its market price. (Marx, 1976, p. 465)

Although Marx refers here primarily to productivity and unit cost, he makes it explicitly clear that product quality is also central. In a discussion of the exchange of commodities for money Marx states that the commodity must be 'socially useful' to the consumer: i.e. meet the needs of the consumer at least as well as other alternative commodities. For if it does not, the consumer will not part with his money. Here Marx explicitly envisages the possibility of new products meeting new needs. The commodity

cannot acquire universal social validity as an equivalent-form except by being converted into money. That money, however, is in someone else's pocket. To allow it to be drawn out, the commodity produced by its owner's labour must above all be a use-value for the owner of the money. The labour expended on it must therefore be of a socially useful kind . . . Perhaps the commodity is the product of a new kind of labour and claims to satisfy a newly arisen need, or is even trying to bring forth a new need on its own account . . . Today the product satisfies a social need. Tomorrow it may perhaps be expelled partly or completely from its place by a similar product. (Marx, 1976, p. 201)

As this discussion makes clear, two or more techniques of production can co-exist at a given point in time only if they fulfil the following necessary conditions: (i) they meet market requirements in terms of product price and quality, and (ii) they generate the average rate of profit. If a technique does not meet both these conditions then either it will become obsolete (its user will over time go bankrupt or have to be subsidized), or total factor productivity obtained in using the technique will have to be sufficiently increased. An attempt to achieve the latter may result in improvements in machinery and/or change in other factors affecting total factor productivity such as changes in the division of labour and the labour process. Marx devoted a good deal of attention to the productivity effects of changes in the organization of labour and these discussions complement the analysis of machinery. However, these analyses have been omitted here since the focus is more narrowly on machinery.[13]

Following Ricardo,[14] Marx agreed that increases in productivity (through improvements in machinery and/or the labour process) would positively effect the rate of accumulation through decreases in the wage share (or, in Marx's terminology, the value of labour-power). This would be achieved through decreasing the real cost of labour. Accumulation achieved in this way was referred to by Marx as the production of relative surplus value. 'In order to make the value of labour-power go down the rise in the productivity of labour must seize upon those branches of industry whose products determine the value of labour-power, and consequently either belong to the category of normal means of subsistence, or are capable of replacing them' (Marx, 1976, p.432). As with Ricardo, increases in productivity in the luxury goods sector will not exert these effects on accumulation.

As Rosenberg (1982) has noted, Marx was particularly concerned with the capital-saving improvements that are made in the capital goods sector (although most accounts of Marx concentrate solely on his discussion of labour-saving technical change). However, while capital-saving innovations increase productivity and accumulation, they may also be a source of economic destabilization. The reason is that improvements in the latest vintages of machinery will cause a depreciation in the value of earlier vintages, a process that Marx referred to as 'moral depreciation'.[15] This may present problems for users who purchased the machinery at its original price and who, due to the improvements in the latest vintages, now find difficulty in recouping the cost of the machine plus the average rate of return. These users, to use the Keynesian terminology, will find their expectations frustrated by the changes in values that result from capital-saving innovations in the machine-producing sector, and accordingly will be in *ex-post* disequilibrium. In this way, technical improvements may be a mixed blessing.[16]

How then do we assess Marx's contribution in the area of machinery and technical change? Marx's main contribution, it may be argued, lies in his examination of the complex *causes* of increases in productivity and in his demonstration that in a system of 'generalized commodity production', where producers purchase *all* their inputs, including labour, and sell *all* their output in exchange for money, there will be extremely strong pressures for all producers to achieve average (social) levels of productivity. While the period of manufacture, and the division of labour on which it was based, created the conditions for the emergence of a specialised machinery sector, and while this in turn created the possibility of applying science to production, the actual rate of technical change is left indeterminate in Marx. Although Marx acknowledges the importance of the motivations of individual capitalists in seeking to improve productivity through various means and thus earn 'extra surplus value', he is more concerned with the way in which productivity increases, caused in various ways, are generalized throughout the system. It is this generalization process that forms the basis of his value analysis. While, as we have seen, market processes, including changes in relative product and factor prices and competition, play a central role in the generalization process, Marx, unlike his neoclassical successors, was concerned to examine the origins of productivity increases within the sphere of production itself. In this examination the development of machinery and changes in the labour process are central and Marx argues strongly that these developments and changes cannot be adequately understood by seeing them simply as responses to market processes. Although the spheres of production and exchange are inter-related, it is not possible to reduce the former to the latter as is implied in neo-classical economies.

The reason for devoting so much attention here to the classical economists, and particularly to Marx, is that, after the birth of neo-classical economics with the advent of the 'marginal revolution' in the latter nineteenth century, attention shifted sharply away from issues relating to the causes of productivity and technical change. The neo-classical economists were far more concerned to integrate a theory of utility into their analysis of price determination and, particularly in the case of Walras and his followers, to examine the interaction between markets which gave birth to the concern with general equilibrium analysis. In his important essay, *The Nature and Significance of Economic Science*, published in 1932, Robbins summarized the prevailing climate of opinion just prior to the Keynesian Revolution:

Instead of regarding the economic system as a gigantic machine for turning out an aggregate product and proceeding to enquire what causes make this product greater or less, and in what proportions this product is divided, we regard it as a series of interdependent but conceptually discrete relationships between men and economic goods ... although Adam Smith's great work professed to deal with the causes of the wealth of nations, and did in fact make many remarks on the general question of the conditions of opulence which are of great importance in any history of applied Economics, yet from the point of view of the history of theoretical Economics, the central achievement of this book was his demonstration of the mode in which the division of labour tended to be kept in equilibrium by the mechanism of relative prices. (p. 68)

A theory of economic development had no place, therefore, in Robbins's 'theoretical Economics'.

While the mainstream of the economics profession either implicitly or explicitly went along with Robbins's sharp separation of applied and theoretical economics, others were less satisfied with this strict distinction. Here particular mention must be made of Schumpeter who was centrally concerned in his theoretical work to understand the processes operating in the economic system that are responsible for increasing the quantity and quality of output. Rather than a harmonious gigantic machine, to use Robbins's terminology, Schumpeter saw a disequilibrating creative-destructive process caused by the efforts of entrepreneurs and, in his later work, the R & D departments of large corporations, to compete through innovation. The improvements that were brought about sent shock waves through the entire economic system, nationally and in some cases internationally, as competing firms were 'compelled' to respond:

capitalist economy is not and cannot be stationary. Nor is it merely expanding in a steady manner. It is incessantly being revolutionized *from within* by new enterprise, i.e. by the intrusion of new commodities or new methods of production or new commercial opportunities into the industrial structure as it exists at any moment. Any existing structures and all the conditions of doing business are always in a process of change. Every situation is being upset before it has had time to work itself out... Possibilities of gains to be reaped by producing new things or by producing old things more cheaply are constantly materializing and calling for new investments. These new products and new methods compete with the old products and old methods not on equal terms but at a decisive advantage that may mean death to the latter. This is how 'progress' comes about in capitalist society. In order to escape being undersold, *every* firm is in the end compelled to follow suit, to invest in its turn and, in order to be able to do so, to plough back part of its profits, i.e. to accumulate. Thus, everyone else accumulates. (*Capitalism, Socialism and Democracy*, pp. 31-2)

However, with his discursive rather than formal mode of analysis, Schumpeter remained something of an outsider. Furthermore, one of his major works, the theory of business cycles, was largely eclipsed by Keynes. Accordingly, the analysis of the causes and consequences of technical change remained off-stage with the spotlights focusing on other directions.

Questions of the determinants of productivity and technical change were beyond Keynes's immediate concerns. Keynes was understandably preoccupied with the situation produced by the Great Depression where machines, which were neither technically nor economically obsolete, lay idle while the workers capable of operating them waited in the dole queues.[17] Keynes's theoretical response to this situation resulted in a short-run model of output and employment in which aggregate demand and expectations featured prominently. As Keynes made clear:

We take as given the existing skill and quantity of available labour, the existing quality and quantity of available equipment, the existing technique, the degree of competition, the tastes and habits of the consumer, the disutility of different intensities of labour and of the activities of supervision and organization, as well as the social structure including the forces, other than our variables set out below, which determine the distribution of the national income. (*General Theory*, p. 245)

Thus by the end of the Second World War, and notwithstanding the exceptional contribution made by Schumpeter as well as some of the more discursive comments made by Marshall, mainstream economics in both the areas of microeconomics and macroeconomics lacked a theory of the determinants of productivity and technical change. The paradox in this situation, arising from the fact that productivity and technical change lie at the heart of the determination of costs, competitiveness, and economic growth, issues that are of central concern in both microeconomics and macroeconomics, went unnoticed.

However, from the 1950s the situation began to change somewhat. While the theoretical branches of economics continued to ignore questions about the determinants of technical change and productivity growth, which did not form part of the growth theories that emerged in the post-war years, with the work of Abramowitz and Solow in the latter 1950s an empirical concern with technical change began to emerge. Working within the context of the neo-classical economics paradigm, economists began to realize that technical change was a significant contributor to growth in output and productivity. Accordingly, a good deal of intellectual effort was invested in the attempt to understand this contribution better.

However, by the early 1980s a number of well-known economists, who had come to specialize in the area of technical change, arrived at the conclusion that the work on technical change inspired by the neo-classical approach in economics had become, in the words of Lakatos, a degenerating research programme. Among the harshest of these critics were Nelson and Winter (1982) who summarized their views in the following way:

> Following upon the discovery that there was a large 'residual' involved in neo-classical explanations of economic growth, and the identification of that residual with technical change, economists undertook a considerable amount of research aimed at pinning down what technical change actually is... But what we now know about technical change should not be comforting to an economist who has been holding the hypothesis that technical change can be easily accommodated within an augmented neoclassical model. Nor can the problem be brushed aside as involving a phenomenon that is 'small' relative to those that are well handled by the theory; rather it relates to a phenomenon [i.e. technical change] that all analysts (or virtually all) acknowledge as the central one in economic growth. The tail now wags the dog. And the dog does not fit the tail very well. The neo-classical approach to growth theory has taken us down a smooth road to a dead end. (pp. 204-5)

The result is that, at a time when issues of technical change and productivity growth are becoming more important, particularly in the area of public policy, economists have tended to find themselves unable to offer a great deal of assistance.[18]

In the following sub-section we return to the machinery sector and begin by examining the views of one prominent scholar, Rosenberg, who sees this sector as playing a central role in the process of technical change.

Rosenberg and Little on the Machinery Sector

For Rosenberg, the relationship between the capital and consumption goods sectors is dynamic with technical change at the centre. The starting-point in the analysis of this relationship is the growth of demand in the capital-goods-using sector. When demand reaches a critical minimum size, then in an Adam Smithian sense the conditions are created for capital-goods-producing firms to reap the benefits, not only of economies of scale, but also economies of specialization. 'The importance of the growth in markets is not necessarily bigness but rather an increased division of labour among firms in the specific sense of a narrowing down of the product range and the ability to concentrate on a limited range of products possessing certain specified properties, performing specific functions, and meeting highly specialized requirements' (Rosenberg, 1976, p. 13). This process of specialization is assisted by an important phenomenon, which Rosenberg refers to as technological convergence. This convergence exists in a dual way. On the one hand a number of industries producing entirely different products are technologically convergent in the sense that they use very similar machinery inputs. As an example Rosenberg documents the growth of the American machine tool industry from 1840 to 1910 which served industries producing the following products: guns, sewing machines, bicycles, motorcycles and automobiles. On the other hand, however, technological convergence also refers to the fact that similar technological processes are characteristic of the entire machinery and metal using sector. Accordingly, the process of specialization and machinery improvement, and later the diffusion of adapted and new machinery, is facilitated by the fact that technological conditions and processes are similar in both capital-goods-producing and -using industries. Convergence 'exists throughout the machinery and metal-using sectors of an industrial economy. Throughout these sectors there are common processes, initially in the refining and smelting of ores, subsequently in foundry work whereby the refined metals are cast into preliminary shapes, and then in the various machinery processes through which the component metal parts are converted into final form preparatory to their assembly as a finished product' (p. 16). Following Marx (see above), Rosenberg stresses that improvements in quality and/or reductions in cost in the capital goods sector constitute forms of capital-saving innovation for the economy as a whole. In this way the capital goods sector creates important pecuniary externalities that benefit using firms as capital goods are diffused. The centrality of the capital goods sector in the process of technological innovation is clear once it is realized that 'All innovations – whether they involve the introduction of a new product or provide a cheaper way of producing an existing product – require that the capital goods sector shall produce a new product (machine) according to certain specifications' (p. 142). For these reasons Rosenberg concludes that 'one of the most propelling forces in the growth of currently high-income countries has been the technological dynamism of their capital goods industries which has maintained the marginal efficiency of capital at a high level' (p. 150). Rosenberg is equally concerned with the importance of the capital goods sector for the development of the under-developed countries. In these countries, however, the major problem is the absence of a capital goods sector and hence of the dynamic benefits which this sector provides:

> underdeveloped countries with little or no organized domestic capital goods sector simply have not had the opportunity to make capital-saving innovations because they have not had the capital goods industry necessary for them. Under these circumstances, such countries have typically imported their capital goods from abroad, but this has meant that they have not developed the technological base of skills, knowledge, facilities, and organization upon which further technical progress so largely depends. (p. 147)

The assertion in the last quotation that less-developed countries face a severe restraint in their ability to generate technical progress will be examined critically later in this introduction in the context of a discussion of design capabilities. Here, however, we note some of the important issues that are raised by Rosenberg's argument. A major question, given the dynamic benefits provided by an indigenous capital goods sector, relates to how far less-developed countries should go in encouraging the local pro-duction of capital goods when there is the possibility of importing these goods. While importing capital goods will not *per se* encourage the develop-ment of local technological capabilities, it will, where the imported capital goods are of a higher quality and/or available at a lower price, provide a capital-saving innovation to the local economy. The question of the social costs and benefits surrounding the make–import decision is not adequately examined by Rosenberg. More generally, the international trade dimension as a whole is not considered in sufficient detail. Thus, for example, in con-sidering the importance of the constraint of local market size in less-developed countries Rosenberg fails to examine the possibilities of exporting capital goods (a failing that is understandable from the perspective of the early 1960s, when Rosenberg wrote, although it is an omission from the point of view of the subsequent adoption of export-oriented policies by some such countries). The question of international trade, however, lies at the heart of Little's (1982) discussion of the capital goods sector. For Little the *sine qua non* for the development of capital goods production is that the capital good in question enjoys a comparative advantage. Little notes that 'A country does not have to travel far down the industrialization road for it to have a comparative advantage in making many kinds of capital goods' (p. 249). However, in the capital goods sector, as elsewhere in the economy, production is in general unjustifiable if there is no comparative advantage. Accordingly, Little concludes that 'A plausible argument can be made for local production of some capital goods, but that is very different from a broad-based industrial development of . . . capital-intensive producers' goods ' (p. 242). In connection with a comparative advantage in capital goods in less-developed countries, Little notes that 'machinery tends to be more skill intensive than capital intensive' (p. 243).

There are two arguments, Little suggests, which have been used to justify the development of a local capital goods sector. The first is that 'indigenous research and development [is] essential for healthy growth in which production is suited and adapted to the factor proportions, indigenous materials, and special needs of the people'. This, he notes, 'is a dynamic form of the argument from inappropriate technology. Appropriate technologies cannot be created once and for all but must be continuously improved and recreated as conditions change' (p. 242). Little points out that this first argument is applicable to the mechanical engineering sector as a whole, and not only to capital goods, and as such he has some sympathy with it. 'There is something to be said for the recent idea that mechanical engineering is a sector that particularly deserves encouragement, for proximity permits easier collaboration between makers and users of equipment and contributes to the possibilities of indigenous adaptation and development' (p. 181). However, as an argument for the widespread development of capital goods production, Little has serious reservations. On the one hand, the production of capital goods in less-developed countries usually amounts to no more than the copying of imported products and therefore is no more appropriate than the latter (pp. 243, 248). On the other hand, there are better ways to encourage the choice of more appropriate (i.e. more labour-intensive) techniques of production, namely by eliminating the bias in favour of capital-intensity and making use of the range of techniques available from abroad. The

recent stress on the inappropriateness of existing technology has been overdone. The earlier version, that one of the great advantages of backwardness is that more modern techniques can be acquired from abroad far more cheaply than they can be developed and invented, is still valid. Indeed, most of the modern methods for making what ordinary people want and need are available for free, and are incorporated in readily available machinery [i.e. since in most cases the technology is non-proprietary]. (p. 181)

The second argument for the development of a local capital goods sector, according to Little, is that in this way less-developed countries will begin 'to capture some of the rents that attach to innovation' (p. 243). While Little delivers 'some warnings' regarding this argument (p. 243), he implies that it may be valid under some circumstances. However, taking both these arguments into account, Little's 'interim view' regarding 'the question whether capital goods production merits special encouragement' and the necessary requirements to facilitate the 'best ways of assimilating technology from more developed countries' is that

for most LDCs the priority is to improve knowledge of the range of world technology and so to improve the choice of techniques . . . Such knowledge also lays the basis for adaptation and even innovation. Some engineering capacity is surely complementary, though that does not imply that any large-scale production of capital goods is a *sine qua non*. (p. 244)

The absence of a substantial capital goods sector in less-developed countries thus appears as less of a problem for Little than it does for Rosenberg. The possibility of intentional trade largely alleviates the problem. Accordingly, Little arrives at a similar conclusion to that of Ricardo. It will be recalled that Ricardo pointed to the positive economic effects of international trade and the introduction of machinery on the cheapening of wage-goods. Similarly, Little points to the beneficial effects in less-developed countries of imported capital goods.

An Approach to Technical Change in the Machinery Sector

Introduction

In order to understand the process of technical change and productivity increase (in terms of both cost and quality) in machinery-producing firms, it is proposed that a biological analogy might prove illuminating.

According to this analogy, 'firms', defined broadly to include public companies and research institutions, are seen as hierarchically structured complex social organisms existing within changing environmental conditions. Before going on to examine in more detail the specific environmental conditions influencing machine-producing firms, a little more will be said about the concept of a 'social organism' and its 'environment'.

Firms are involved in the purchasing of inputs, both material and human, and the transforming of these inputs into outputs. Technology may be conceived of broadly as involving everything related to the transformation of inputs into outputs. Accordingly, technical *change* refers to changes in the ways in which inputs are transformed into outputs. Technical change will often, although not necessarily, result in productivity change which is measured by the ratio of output to inputs. While this is usually not done, attention should also be paid to changes in quality when measuring changes in productivity.

By conceptualizing the firm as a 'social organism' account is taken of the obvious, but frequently ignored, fact that the transformation of inputs into outputs involves the interaction between people.[19] This social intercourse is structured by the organization of the firm which will determine factors such as the functions that are assigned to departments and individuals, and the way in which decisions are made within the firm. The organization of the firm is to a significant degree independent of the firm's environment. Accordingly, there is no reason why two firms producing similar products in the same industry should be similarly organized. Furthermore, there is no reason why such firms should respond in the same way to the same environmental conditions. Different responses might be explained by different organizational structures. However, these responses might also be explained by the existence of uncertainty. In the face of uncertainty different individuals may expect divergent outcomes and therefore suggest different courses of action. Firms may also differ, not only in their decisions made in response to environmental circumstances, but also in terms of the effectiveness with which these decisions are implemented within the firm. The Japanese case, for example, suggests that the quality of the relationship between those higher up, and those lower down, the firm's hierarchy may have an important bearing on the effectiveness of implementation.[20]

Accordingly, the main implication to be drawn from seeing the firm as a social organism is that there will be a wide variation between firms regarding the way in which, and the success with which, they respond to their environment. Some firms, therefore, will earn above average rates of profit and will expand relatively, while others will be less successful and some may even go bankrupt.

In examining the firm's environment it is suggested that the combined effect of three factors constitutes an important influence on the firm. These three factors are: pressure, incentives, and information flows.

Competition from other firms on domestic and/or export markets constitutes an example of an environmental pressure. Strong competition may have the effect of decreasing a firm's profit rate or its market share. However, pressures, with the same consequences for profitability, may also result from other sources such as the increasing price or decreasing quality of inputs. Pressures serve as powerful attention-focusing devices since they point to negative consequences that will have to be faced if the firm does not respond adequately. Pressures must be distinguished from incentives since they may have asymmetric effects. In contrast to pressures, incentives indicate that the firm will be better off if it responds satis-factorily, but not necessarily that its position will deteriorate if it fails to respond. In some cases it may be that a firm attaches a greater weight to a deterioration in its position than to an improvement, with the result that pressures may be expected to be a stronger influence than incentives. Accordingly, in examining a firm's environment it is necessary to identify both the pressures and the incentives that exist.

A third environmental factor that must be examined is information flows. Several points may be made about information flows. The first is that a good deal of work has been done in mainstream economics high-lighting the role played by the price system in the provision of information. Changing prices provide information to the firm about changing demand and/or supply conditions although, following the discussion above, it is not possible to be sure how firms will respond to this information. Informa-tion or, more generally, knowledge, may also be a commodity and there-fore have a price. Information can therefore be purchased through a market transaction and indeed a large amount of research has been done on the operation of the market for information. However, in analysing information flows it is necessary also to take account of non-market-mediated flows of information that may also influence the response of firms. For example, as Schumpeter noted, imitation is an important part of the competitive process. Yet the process of imitation frequently involves the acquisition of information through non-market means. Similar-ly, other activities such as learning from the experience of the users of a firm's products, or obtaining information from sources such as academic and trade journals, may provide important knowledge to a firm.

Two additional points must be made about information flows. The first is that many forms of information are not acquired automatically by a firm but require a conscious allocation of resources in order to be obtained.

In some instances this might be obvious, such as in the case of the acquisition of proprietary knowledge. But in other instances the point might not be so obvious. For example, it is not at all clear that 'doing' (i.e. producing) will lead automatically to the acquisition of information that will facilitate 'learning' and hence improvement. In this sense the notion 'learning-by-doing', at least as conventionally used, may be misleading. Second, and following on from the first point, it is not necessarily the case that information that has been acquired will be effectively used. For this reason if an analysis of information flows is to be used in order to understand the processes of technical and productivity change, it is necessary to simultaneously examine the environmental pressures and incentives that exist.

In the remaining part of this subsection these brief comments on the biological analogy are elaborated upon in the specific case of machine-producing firms. Empirical examples are drawn largely from the area of machine tools. The approach adopted for the analysis of machine-production is presented in Figure 1.3.

Four features of the interaction between machine-producing firms and their 'environment' are highlighted in Figure 1.3. These are, first, the relationship between the users and producer of machinery; second, the interaction between the component suppliers and the producer; third, the competitive relationship between producers on both domestic and export markets; and fourth, the role of the state. Each of these features will be considered in more detail.

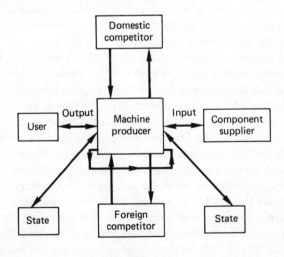

FIGURE 1.3

User–Producer Interaction

The importance of the interaction between the user and producer of
machinery as a major factor shaping the process of technical change in
the machine-producing sector has long been recognized. In 1867 a writer
in the journal *Engineering* observed that

> It is generally known that engineer's tools made in Scotland are some-
> what different in their style and design from the tools made in the
> neighbourhood of Manchester and Leeds, the two great centres of
> machine construction in England. Tool-makers in Scotland, who have
> principally to supply the extensive demands of marine engineers and
> shipbuiilders in their own locality, are, by the nature of the heavy work
> for which their machines are intended, induced to look to great weights,
> massive framings and very large castings in shape of foundations or base
> plates rather than to that elegance of form and that economy of material
> which gives to the modern tools of the first tool-makers in Manchester
> and Leeds their style and characteristic appearance.[21]

Similarly, Rosenberg (1976) has shown how user requirements in the
gun, sewing-machine, and bicycle industries shaped the development of
machine tools. This later facilitated the development of the motor car
industry which in turn prompted further changes in machine tools.
Rosenberg has argued, as we saw earlier, that the technological convergence which existed among these users of machine tools facilitated the
process of the specialization of producers.

User–producer interactions have also had an important bearing on
international competitiveness. Floud (1976) has shown that one of the
factors behind the successful invasion of European markets by American
machine-tool producers from the middle 1890s was the relatively low
unit cost of American machines. Lower costs were influenced by the
production in the United States of standardized machine tools while, on
the whole, British products tended to be custom designed and built.
While Floud argues that this does not necessarily mean that British producers were less efficient, since the purchasers of American standardized
machine tools frequently had to make their own modifications and adaptations, his book suggests that British users were more insistent than their
American counterparts on custom-built machines. In turn this inhibited
standardization and cost-competitiveness (though not necessarily quality-
competitiveness) in the British industry. However, Floud does not provide

a detailed examination of the causes and effects underlying the user–producer relationship in this period.

Ironically, it was precisely in the area of standardized, relatively low-cost machine tools that American producers began to lose market shares to the Japanese in the latter 1970s. The loss in the case of the major products, CNC lathes and CNC machining centres (computer-numerically-controlled), was dramatic. In 1976 Japanese exports of CNC machining centres, for example, were 2.1 per cent of apparent US consumption in value terms, while this rose to 38.2 per cent in 1981. In terms of units of machine tools the figures were 3.7 per cent and 50.1 per cent respectively, reflecting the fact that the Japanese tend to specialize in the medium price and performance range, building standardized machine tools.

However, for present purposes, more important than the fact of Japanese success is the explanation behind it. In this connection Watanabe (1983) has recently advanced the interesting hypothesis that one dimension of the explanation of Japanese international competitiveness in machine tools relates to the specific structure of user demand in Japan. More particularly Watanabe argues that the motor car industry constituted the major user of NC and later CNC machine tools in Japan. Furthermore, in view of the extensive subcontracting network that exists in this industry in Japan, many of the users of these machine tools were relatively small and in total constituted a large number of firms. In addition, the strong competition that existed between motor car producers in both local and export markets meant that they made increasingly stringent demands, in terms of both quality and price, of their subcontracting firms supplying components. Since CNC machine tools are in general better suited to these requirements than conventional machine tools, a large and growing market was created for CNC products. Responding to these 'environmental' conditions Japanese machine-tool producers with, as we shall later see, the assistance of the suppliers of control systems, began to produce high-performance, medium-priced, standardized CNC machine tools. Only *later*, once their products had been developed for the domestic market, did Japanese producers enter more competitive export markets, particularly that of the United States. On the other hand, Watanabe shows that the user structure differed substantially in the United States, where the motor car industry was a relatively small user of CNC machine tools and where rather the aerospace industry constituted the major user. American producers, accordingly, produced more specialized, heavier, and higher-priced CNC machine tools.[22]

Furthermore, Watanabe shows that Japanese users did not simply constitute a 'passive' source of demand for CNC machine tools. The bulk of the firms that he interviewed indicated that users provided the most significant source of information for improvements and R & D. Thus non-market-mediated flows of information, usually ignored in market-oriented studies, were crucial.

It would be wrong to see machine producers being simply 'pulled' by the demands of users. While, as has been indicated, demand is certainly an important influence shaping the process of technical change in the machine-producing sector, the availability and development of new technologies on the 'supply' side have also played a significant role. This is made clear in the next section dealing with the relationship between CNC suppliers and producers of machinery.

A final point that must be made in connection with the interaction between the user and producer of machinery is that, as Rosenberg (1976) has observed, a special feature of some kinds of machine producers, particularly machine tool producers, is that they are at times both producers *and users* of the machinery they produce. This is indicated by the loop in Figure 1.3. Accordingly, user–producer information feed-back is internalized within the same firm, which may result in a more efficient flow and utilization of information.

Component Supplier–Producer Interaction

While a process of specialization within the machinery industry between component suppliers – for example, the producers of castings and machined components – and machine-builders has long been a feature of the industry, in recent years this process appears to have increased. In part this is due to the substantial advances that have taken place in the area of control systems based on microelectronic techniques. In the case of machine tools, for example, the introduction of microprocessors into CNC machine tools and the integration of these machines into broader production systems have given an enhanced role to the producers of electronic components which constitute a substantial proportion of total cost. While 'market pull' undoubtedly played a role in the development of CNC machine tools, even more important was the availability of microelectronic technology developed independently of the machine tool industry.

In the area of machine tools, an important example of the role played by component suppliers is provided by the Japanese firm, Fanuc, a subsidiary of the electronics firm, Fujitsu, which now produces over half of world output of CNC controls. Based originally on information gleaned from the Servomechanisms Laboratory in MIT in the United States which developed the first numerically controlled machine tool, Fanuc together with a Japanese machine tool firm, Makino, produced the first Japanese NC machine tool.[23] From that time on, Fanuc has enjoyed a very close relationship with the major Japanese machine tool producers, eclipsing several other large producers of controls, and has contributed substantially to their international success. Interestingly, Watanabe (1983) suggests that the success of Fanuc is based less on the direct cost of their control units, and more on the quality of their software and servicing facilities (p. 38). Furthermore, as Fransman shows in his paper in the present book, Fanuc has also contributed substantially to the development of CNC machine tool production in Taiwan (not to mention other countries such as South Korea and China) through the sale of control units.

As has been shown in this section, it is clearly necessary to take account of the interaction between component suppliers and producers, a relationship that cannot simply be reduced to one of market-pull, in accounting for the shaping of technical change in the machinery industry.

Competitors

The next 'environmental' factor to be discussed in analysing the shaping of technical change in the machinery sector is the role played by competitors.

In examining the role of competitors in the process of technical change the most obvious factor to take into account is the pressures that they exert on competing firms 'compelling' the latter (in Schumpeter's words) to introduce changes. Such pressures have been extremely important, for example, in the case of Japanese and Taiwanese machine tool producers, as is shown in the studies in the present book.

However, competitors also influence the process of technical change in a number of other ways through both market and non-market interactions. An example of the former are licensing and other know-how agreements which, as all the studies in this book show, have at times been significant sources of technical change. However, competitors unintentionally and unwillingly also provide non-market-mediated flows of information by making their products available on the market. These flows provide the basis for imitation which, as Fransman shows in his chapter in this book, has been an important source of design for both Japanese and Taiwanese machine tool producers.

In the literature on technical change in developing countries it has frequently been claimed that special benefits flow from the firm's activities in export markets. To begin with, at least in the larger export markets, competitive pressures are often greater than on the domestic market, with the result that firms are forced to become more efficient in terms of criteria such as price, quality, delivery time, after-sales service, etc. Not only will the most efficient firms tend to compete on these markets, but users will also tend to be more sophisticated. These users, as was seen earlier, may be an important source of information feed-back thus facilitating a process of 'learning-by-exporting'. Accordingly, it has been suggested by writers such as Krueger and Findlay that dynamic considerations such as these, rather than the conventional neo-classical trade model based on static resource allocation, provide an important part of the explanation of the economic success of the export-oriented newly industrialized countries.[24]

However, while it is certainly correct that these advantages associated with exporting have accrued, for some countries at least an important question of sequencing arises. In the case of Japanese machine tools, for example, it is clear that the major capabilities were first built up in connection with production for the domestic market and a little later for relatively undemanding regional markets in East and South East Asia. This was followed some time later by exports to the most sophisticated United States market. The same sequencing has been observed in other newly industrialized countries. Teubal (1984) observes that in Brazil capital goods exports, which have recently constituted the most significant export category, occurred only after a learning process had taken place through production for the local market. In South Korea the sequencing is somewhat different with the state providing important incentives, and indeed exerting substantial pressures, for machine-producing firms to begin exporting immediately, and therefore benefit from the 'export externalities' discussed as well as earn foreign exchange. However, one of the major incentives provided by the state is guaranteed easy access to the domestic market as a result of the imposition of protective measures such as outright prohibition of imports and the imposition of quota restrictions where 'similars' are available locally. In the present book this is documented by Amsden and Kim. Japan at an earlier period and Brazil currently have also imposed similar protective measures in order to benefit local machine-producers. Taiwan and Singapore have followed to a greater extent an export-oriented approach to the building of technological capabilities in the machinery sector. Since the 1960s in Taiwan protective measures for local machine-producers have been relatively limited although attempts are made by the state to encourage local purchase where possible. In the 1970s Taiwanese machine tool producers shifted as rapidly from South East Asian markets to the United States market as did Japanese firms. Singapore, on the other hand, is different from the other Asian countries discussed here in two respects. First, this country has only relatively recently become a significant machine tool producer, and second, its major firms are foreign ones which already possessed, before entering Singapore, internationally efficient technological capabilities.[25]

Accordingly, it must be concluded that, although the evidence is somewhat mixed, there does not exist firm support for the contention that what we have referred to here as 'export externalities' provide a necessary condition for the initial emergence of international competitiveness among machine-producers, although in later stages such 'externalities' may help to maintain and strengthen competitiveness.

The State

The state may be an important influence on machine-producing firms, on both the input and output sides, as is indicated in Figure 1.3. In this section, attention is focused on the state's role as a procurer, as a protector of domestic industry, as a restructurer of domestic industry, and as a possible protector of foreign markets.

(i) The state as a procurer. State-owned arsenals have been an important influence on the development of the machine tool industry as, for example, Rosenberg (1976) demonstrates for the case of machine tool producers in the United States in the nineteenth century, and as Chokki (present volume) documents for the earliest period of the Japanese industry in the late nineteenth and the early twentieth centuries. Similarly, the state's role as procurer was a significant influence in the development of numerical control for machine tools in the 1940s in the United States. Numerical control, that was to revolutionise machining practices, was developed initially by the Servomechanisms Laboratory of MIT in order to machine helicopter blades for the United States airforce. As we saw earlier, Watanabe (1983) has suggested that the dominance of the aerospace industry as the major user of CNC machine tools in the United States has been an important factor influencing the production in that country of specialized, large-sized, high precision machine tools. This is contrasted with the production in Japan of standardized, medium-sized machine tools largely for the subcontractors of the motor car industry.

To the extent that the state is a procurer and user of machines its needs will influence the production of this machinery in the same way as the needs of other users. However, the state is a user with special characteristics.

To begin with it is often an extremely large user relative to other users and therefore may be expected to carry a good deal of 'weight' with producers thus constituting an important influence in the shaping of design characteristics in the machinery industry. This has often been the case in connection with the production of machinery for military uses. Second, the state is not a profit-motivated commercial user as are most other users of machinery. The relationship between the state and machine producers is often qualitatively different from that existing with commercial users. To the extent that machinery is being developed for purposes regarded by the state as 'sensitive', competition between producers for state contracts may be limited to a few firms that have already established 'trustworthy' ties with the relevant state departments. Furthermore, in these cases state contracts are frequently awarded on a 'cost-plus' basis with the result that the pressures and constraints are likely to be different as compared with the case of a normal commercial user. In producing for the state, at least in instances such as military production, it might be that the quality–price trade-off tends to be biased in favour of quality, whereas in the typical commercial case relatively greater weight is given to price. To the extent that such differences exist, the trajectory of design development of machinery will be influenced by the state's role as a procurer. This may have important implications for the international competitiveness of a country's machinery industry.[26]

(ii) The state as a protector of domestic industry. In various countries at different points in time the state has exerted a substantial influence on the development of the domestic machinery industry as a result of the measures it has taken to protect local producers from international competition. For example, Floud (1976) has documented the high levels of protection imposed in the infancy stages of the development of the machine tool industry in the United States in the late nineteenth century. High levels of protection were still in existence when United States machine tools successfully swept into European markets in the 1890s. Similarly, as discussed further in the following section and in the chapter in the present book by Fransman, import restrictions of various forms were imposed in Japan, South Korea, and Taiwan where 'similars' were locally produced. While the implications of these measures for the economic theory of the effectiveness of various policy instruments are considered below, here it is simply noted that the insulation by the state of local producers from international competition can have significant short- and long-term consequences for the machinery industry.

(iii) The state as a restructurer of domestic industry. In this section various examples will be discussed of measures that have been taken by different states in order to restructure the domestic machinery industry. The examples are intended to be illustrative rather than exhaustive.

In both Japan and South Korea attempts have been made to prevent 'excessive' competition in the machinery industry. In Japan, as discussed by Chokki and Fransman in the present volume, attempts were made by the Ministry of International Trade and Industry (MITI) to put pressure on producers through the Japan Machine Tool Builders Association in order to concentrate the production of machine tools. In this way it was hoped to reap additional economies of scale and specialization. Further-more, efforts were made to prevent 'excessive' competition in export markets by getting producers to agree on 'orderly' pricing and marketing arrangements. In South Korea, as Nagao (1983) shows, the state has gone even further in the case of electrical power equipment and allowed only a small number of producers to make certain kinds of equipment. This has been justified in terms of the small size of the domestic market and the consequent necessity to concentrate production in order to achieve economies of scale and specialization.

State subsidization has also been used in Japan and the Asian newly industrialized countries as an important instrument to restructure the machinery industry. Three forms of subsidization may be distinguished: the direct provision of subsidized credit; the indirect provision of sub-sidized technology inputs; the subsidization of users of locally produced machinery. Japan, Singapore, South Korea and Taiwan have all provided credit at subsidized rates of interest to machinery producers for specific purposes. Furthermore, in some cases export subsidies of various kinds have been given. In Japan, South Korea, and Taiwan specialized state research institutions have been established in order to assist machinery producers with design work and, in the case of Japan, more basic research. The institutions include MITI's Mechanical Engineering Laboratory in Japan which played an important role in the development of NC (numerical control) and later CNC (computer numerical control); the Korea Advanced Institute of Science and Technology; and the Mechanical Industries Research Laboratory in Taiwan. The latter two institutions have assisted local firms with the design and development of CNC machine tools. Finally, Japan has in the past subsidized the users of locally produced machine tools and this substantially boosted demand for domestic producers. In addition to these measures, various tax incentives have been introduced to encourage the modernization of the equipment of machine tool producers as well as their R & D efforts.

In view of the large technology gap that existed between advanced country producers and their Japanese counterparts in the 1950s and 1960s and the similar gap between South Korean and Taiwanese producers and their competitors in the highly industrialized countries (including Japan) in the present period, the activities of the state in encouraging the process of restructuring have been important. In this area the state has often intervened to bring about positive changes that, while in the interest of the industry as a whole, could not be expected to be introduced by private firms themselves. For example, it is conceivable that a state of 'excessive' competition may result from firms following what they regard to be their own best interests. Under such circumstances it may be impossible for firms to agree privately on the concentration of resources in the production of different types of machinery. Indeed this is the situation that existed in the 1950s and 1960s in the Japanese machine tool industry, and the various restructuring plans introduced by MITI (and documented in the chapter by Fransman) provide evidence of the tensions that existed between private producers and the state over the question of the concentration of production. This may be thought of as a special case of 'market failure' requiring state intervention.

(iv) The state as possible protector of foreign markets. Under some circumstances the state may successfully intervene in order to maintain access to foreign markets. One recent example is the action reportedly taken by the Japanese state to ensure access by Japanese machine tool producers to the United States market. Faced with the inflood of Japanese machine tools, particularly CNC lathes and CNC machining centres referred to earlier in this chapter, United States producers attempted through legal and other means to persuade the American government to protect its domestic market against Japanese producers. The main argument put forward by United States machine tool producers was that the Japanese government had subsidized its own producers and encouraged them to take part in collusive actions, thus giving them an unfair advantage over their American competitors. It was argued, furthermore, that these steps, had they been taken in the United States, would have violated the law. In March 1982 a large American machine tool producer, Houdaille Industries Inc., submitted a petition to the President of the United States providing detailed support for the argument regarding unfair Japanese competition.

According to a lengthy front-page article in the *Washington Post* on 15 August 1983, titled 'Trade Battle With Japan Shows Policy Confusion', the Houdaille petition brought out the ambiguities in United States trade and industry policy. The petition was apparently discussed at a number of

Cabinet meetings with sharp differenes of opinion being expressed by those taking a 'hard' free trade line on the one hand, and on the other those more amenable to some form of protection. According to the newspaper, the tide was beginning to turn in favour of the protectionists when the Japanese Prime Minister Nakasone, receiving information about the change in attitudes, personally intervened. According to the *Post*:

> The Japanese lobbying effort was personally headed by Nakasone, who sent the same message through two channels to Reagan. The essence of the Nakasone message, administration and private sources agreed, was that Tokyo would consider a finding of unfair trade practices as akin to branding Japan, which is America's foremost Pacific ally, as an enemy. Nakasone also was reported to have stressed the importance of up coming parliamentary elections to his party's program of increased support for the U.S. defense strategy in the Pacific.

This pressure was apparently successful in getting Reagan to back down and ultimately oppose the implementation of protective measures against Japanese machine tool producers. This example serves as a reminder that the political economy of trade policy is at times a profoundly political matter, with the result that the policies that are ultimately introduced are frequently as much a reflection of political considerations as they are a calculation of economic costs and benefits.

Conclusion

In this section it has been suggested that a biological analogy is helpful in understanding the process of technical and productivity change in machine-producing firms. According to this analogy 'firms' are seen as complex social organisms existing within changing environmental conditions. In examining the interaction between the firm and its environment, particular attention has been paid to pressures, incentives and information flows. A number of specific relationships influencing the process of technical and productivity change in machine-producing firms were identified and discussed. These were the relationship between the producers of machinery on the one hand and users and component suppliers on the other, domestic and foreign competition, and the role of the state. While it was stressed that it is necessary to see 'firms' as complexly structured social organisms, very little was said about this in the case of machine-producing firms. This omission, however, is the result of the absence of analyses of the relationship between social and organizational structure in firms and technical and productivity change. By implication it is suggested that further research is urgently needed in this area. Similarly, very little has been said about the causal significance of these relationships in influencing the processes of technical and productivity change in specific instances. Once again more research is needed here.

IV SOME POLICY ISSUES CONFRONTING DEVELOPING COUNTRIES

The Make–Import Decision

When should a machine be produced domestically and when should it be imported? The general answer is that that option should be chosen which will provide the greatest net benefit to society. But this raises a further question: how is the policy-maker to decide in practice which option will yield greatest net benefit?

In Section II above we noted some of the considerations that must be taken into account in answering this second question. To begin with, we saw from the Harris model that it is necessary, even if in an indirect way, to calculate the productivity levels in both the local capital goods sector and the export sector, since the latter is a potential source of imported machinery. In short, it is necessary to examine whether it is possible to obtain more machines by allocating resources to the export sector and importing machinery than by devoting these resources to the domestic capital goods sector. As we saw, this examination will require an analysis of the external terms of trade, that is the price of exports relative to the price of foreign machinery.[27]

However, a number of further complicating factors must also be taken into account in the make–import decision. The first is the question of 'extraordinary output' or externalities. In calculating the net benefit provided by the capital goods sector compared with other sectors in the economy it is necessary also to take account of the positive and negative externalities that are produced in all the sectors. For example, it has been argued, in an attempt to justify the development of a domestic capital goods sector, that this sector tends to be more 'externality intensive' than other sectors in the economy. More specifically, it has been suggested that this sector produces both pecuniary externalities (which are paid for by other firms) in the form of machinery that has been adapted, modified and improved to take account of local conditions, as well as non-pecuniary externalities in the form of manpower which has been trained to bring about such changes in machinery. Since the capital goods sector uses machinery in order to produce more machinery, as opposed to other sectors which simply use machinery, it is argued that the capital goods sector will be more efficient at training skilled workers to change production processes. In other words, since the *output* of the capital goods sector consists of the *means of production*, and since this output is constantly being modified in response to influences examined in the previous section, it is suggested that this sector is more efficient than others in producing the skills required to improve methods of production.[28] The supply of skills 'produced' in this way by this sector thus constitutes an extraordinary output which is made freely available to other firms through the mobility of labour. It should accordingly be taken into account in the calculation of net benefits, along with the externalities generated by other sectors.

A second complicating factor in taking the make–import decision, which was discussed in Section II, relates to *future* improvements in productivity (including both price and quality changes). We saw that Cooper's extension of the Harris model took account of productivity improvements by assuming a simple learning-by-doing mechanism. In the previous section, however, we saw that a large number of additional factors must be taken into account as determinants of technical change and productivity improvement. In view of the complexity of the processes involved it will not be possible to make *ex ante* predictions with certainty regarding future improvements in productivity. Quite clearly though, such improvements are central in the evaluation of the future stream of net benefits to be provided by the capital goods sector. The injection of a considerable degree of uncertainty thus greatly complicates the make–import decision.

Where does this leave the policy-maker confronting this decision? Here a number of comments may be made. To begin with, it will be useful, and indeed perhaps essential, to start with a static analysis of the costs and benefits of the alternative options. Such an analysis, based on *existing* productivities (costs and qualities), will provide an initial indication of the kinds of capital goods which might be suitable candidates for local production. Local production will be contraindicated in those cases where there is a substantial difference between the higher local cost of producing the capital good and the cost of importing it. It is at this stage that widely used techniques such as the domestic resource cost of foreign exchange may prove helpful. The static analysis will enable the identification of areas, possibly including grey areas, where the local production of capital goods may be feasible.

However, it will also be necessary to go beyond the static analysis in order to take account of local future productivity improvements, externalities, and advances in the price and quality of foreign capital goods. While it will not be possible to include these factors with certainty, it is nevertheless necessary that they be incorporated in the analysis. The history of the Japanese machinery industry, for example, shows that these factors have been central determinants of the long-term viability of this industry. However, this does raise the difficult problem of false optimism or pessimism. The impossibility of being very sure about realizing local productivity increases, and about improvements in the price and quality of foreign machinery, leaves the door open to false optimism or pessimism. The many examples that have been documented in the literature of permanent infant industries that have failed to live up to expectations (or perhaps, more accurately, hopes) of increasing productivity over time testify to the difficulty of this problem. Unfortunately, however, there is no way round this dilemma in view of the irreducible uncertainty involved. The most that can, and should, be insisted upon is that the analyses which form the basis for decision-making must be as explicit as possible regarding the reasons why any assumed productivity increases are likely to occur. Similar reasoning must be supplied in the case of assumed externalities. Evidence from similar plants operating under similar conditions in the same or other countries may provide some indication, although the wide variation in observed inter-firm rates of productivity change implies that this information must be used with due caution. The requirement to make explicit the reasoning behind the assumptions made in evaluating the project, particularly where the final decision is sensitive to these assumptions, makes it possible for other observers to form an opinion regarding the adequacy of these assumptions. The ultimate policy decision will in most cases inevitably involve a leap of faith to some degree, but this is no reason for not trying to ensure that the decision is made on the basis of an information set that is as complete as possible. The decision to produce motor cars in Japan in the 1950, proposed by the Ministry of International Trade and Industry (MITI) but opposed by the Bank of Japan on the grounds that this would run counter to the country's comparative advantage, shows how difficult such a decision might in practice be. Most analysts would argue, with hindsight, that the decision was a correct one. Furthermore, the motor car industry has stimulated through its linkages other industries such as machine tools which have also become internationally competitive with the passage of time. However, from an *ex ante* point of view the optimum course is never certain.

Where the decision is made to make rather than import, and where the particular capital goods industry is not immediately internationally competitive, a further decision will have to be taken regarding the most appropriate way of insulating domestic producers from international competition. The instruments available for this purpose include the total prohibition of competing imports, quota restrictions on imports, tariffs, and subsidies attaching either to output or to various inputs. How does the policy-maker decide which of these instruments, or which combination, is most appropriate?

The first point to make is that only limited guidance will be provided by conventional economic analysis. The reason is that conventional analysis is typically based on a static examination of resource allocation. For example, in comparing the social costs and benefits of subsidies versus tariffs (see, for example, Corden, 1971, 1974, 1980) the conventional mode of analysis involves identifying the production or protective effect as well as the by-product distortionary effects. Corden defines the latter as divergences in marginal private and marginal social costs and benefits introduced as a result of government intervention. On this basis the conventional conclusion is that sudsidies are to be preferred to tariffs, since the latter, by putting up prices, will introduce a consumption distortion entailing a loss in consumers' surplus while both measures will have an identical production or protective effect.[29]

The major advantage of such partial analyses, and of similar general equilibrium analyses, is that they identify in a rigorous way the consequences of using various instruments on the basis of the static assumption that technology and productivity remain constant. (To the extent that the latter vary, it is assumed that their change is exogenously determined.) Once again this static analysis is a useful starting-point. For example, in imposing a tariff in order to protect machine producers it is essential to take account of the implicit tax that is thereby imposed on the users of machinery. The effects of this tax will be negative and must be weighed against any positive consequences of the tariff.

However, policy-makers have seldom been concerned with the static effects of the use of such instruments on resource allocation. For example, in those countries where policy-makers have been concerned to rapidly achieve international competitiveness, such as Japan and the Asian newly industrialized countries, of far greater concern has been the effects of the use of various instruments on technical and productivity change. In these countries there is no evidence that policy-makers have undertaken, or been influenced by, the kinds of static analyses referred to here. Rather they have been concerned with the dynamic processes bringing about improvements in technology and productivity. At times this point has been made explicit as, for example, in this statement by a Vice-Minister of the Japanese MITI:

> The Ministry of International Trade and Industry decided to establish in Japan industries which require intensive employment of capital and technology [in the early post-war years], industries that in consideration of competitive cost of production should be the most inappropriate for Japan, industries such as steel, oil refining, petrochemicals, automobiles, aircraft, industrial machinery of all sorts, and electronics, including electronic computers. From a short-run static viewpoint, encouragement of such industries would seem to conflict with economic rationalism. But, from a long-range viewpoint, these are precisely the industries where income elasticity of demand is high, technological progress is rapid, and labour productivity rises fast. (OECD, 1972, p. 92)

The case of machine tools serves as a specific example. In South Korea, for instance, the government has made selective attempts to promote the machine tool industry as part of the increased emphasis given from the early 1970s to heavy and chemical industries. In the latter 1970s several plans were introduced dealing specifically with machine tools. Two major instruments have been used to encourage the machine tool sector. The first involves the total prohibition of imports where locally produced 'similars' are available. In fact the Korean Machine Tool Manufacturer's Association is empowered to decide whether domestic 'similars' are obtainable, and hence whether imports will be restricted, an arrangement that has drawn some criticism from within the country. The second instrument, used in conjunction with the prohibition of imports, is the granting of large amounts of subsidized credit to machine-tool producing firms. In the case of the largest firm, subsidized loans of 44 million US dollars were given. An important feature of these instruments is that the benefits which they provide to firms are made contingent on export performance. This forces firms to immediately confront the issue of international competitiveness even while enjoying subsidized credit and protected conditions on the domestic market, although the possibility of cross-subsidizing exports from the proceeds of domestic sales does exist as a way of alleviating the pressure to some extent. With the use of these instruments the government is attempting to rapidly move resources into those parts of the manufacturing sector where it is believed an international competitiveness can eventually be established. In order to achieve this

objective a combined system of incentives and pressures has been introduced. The incentives, in the form of large amounts of subsidized credit
and guaranteed certain access to the domestic market, have been combined
with strong pressures to export. The competitive pressures from international producers are intended to ensure that the industry is compelled to
keep up with improving international standards. The effect has been that
firms have made substantial efforts to upgrade their design capabilities in
order to keep up with the rapidly shifting frontier in the area of CNC
machine tools. Design assistance has also been provided by the government-owned Korean Advanced Institute of Science and Technology
(KAIST). (For further details see Jacobsson, 1984.)

Taiwanese authorities have been equally concerned with the dynamic
processes of technical and productivity change. However, although a
20 per cent tariff is levied on imported machinery, and the import licensing
system is used to restrict the import of 'similars' (the ultimate decision
resting in government hands rather than with the producers), the Taiwanese
authorities have been far more reluctant than their South Korean counterparts to use the protection instrument. Similarly, they have allocated
smaller sums in the form of subsidized inputs than in South Korea. By
mid-1983 fifteen machine tool firms had been given subsidized loans
amounting to 10 million US dollars. Furthermore, subsidized design
inputs were provided by the state-owned MIRL. (See the paper by Fransman
in Chapter 5 of the present volume for further details.) However, in
Taiwan, as in South Korea, state policy in this area was concerned primarily
with achieving international competitiveness in designated priority industries, and exports were continually stressed.

Accordingly, it may be concluded that more important than the traditional static analysis of the effects of policy instruments are the dynamic
effects on technical and productivity change. There is no evidence that
these countries have been at all concerned with conventional static analyses,
either in their selection of products and industries for specialization, or in
their choice of policy instruments. Far more useful, it may be suggested,
is an analysis of the kind proposed in the previous section which examines
the question of the choice of policy instruments in terms of the effects of
these instruments on the incentives, pressures and information flows
which together influence change at the level of the firm. Such an analysis
would also help to explain the successful use in these countries of instruments such as the prohibition of imports and quota restrictions, which
according to the conventional analysis are third- or even fourth-best
policies. It must be acknowledged, however, that an analysis of the kind
suggested here leaves a good deal of uncertainty in choosing the 'best'
mix of policies. But this is unavoidable.

Design Capabilities

Over time, pressures will mount for the local capital goods sector to improve its productivity in terms of both price and quality. This is most obviously the case where strong pressures exist for this sector to become internationally competitive, as in the instance of South Korea and Taiwan referred to above. But some degree of pressure is also likely to be exerted even where no attempts are being made to render the industry internationally competitive. Quite apart from the pressures resulting from domestic competition, it is likely that capital goods users in the private and/or public sectors, aware to a greater or lesser extent of improvements occurring in the rest of the world economy, will encourage local producers to introduce similar changes. This focuses attention on the design of capital goods.

It has long been realized that the contribution of the capital goods sector stems largely from the ability to design improved capital goods. Referring to the benefits of specialization in this sector, Rosenberg (1976) has argued that:

The importance of this specialization must be conceived, not only in a static sense, but in a dynamic sense as well. For there is an important learning process involved in machinery production, and a high degree of specialization is conducive not only to an effective learning process but to an effective *application* of that which is learned. This highly developed facility in the designing and production of specialized machinery is, perhaps, the most important single characteristic of a well-developed capital goods industry and constitutes an external economy of enormous importance to other sectors of the economy. (p. 17)

However, it is necessary to distinguish between the decision to *make* capital goods locally and the decision to *design* capital goods. The making of capital goods does not necessarily imply the designing of such goods. In fact, in the newly industrialized countries of Asia and Latin America, capital goods design tends on the whole to be imported from the highly industrialized countries. These range from market-mediated imports such as the purchase of turnkey projects and licensing agreements, to non-market-mediated imports such as imitation. As with the make–import decision, an evaluation will have to be undertaken regarding the costs and benefits of designing locally as opposed to importing foreign designs. In many cases it will be judged that foreign designs available in one form or another are less costly than local designing. The importation of designs may also reduce uncertainty regarding production and marketing.

Nevertheless, particularly where an industry is intending to become internationally competitive, and where the technology frontier is shifting rapidly, serious problems may be presented by the absence of local design capabilities. In general, the greater the speed of the product cycle, the lower the benefits of pursuing a 'technology-following' strategy. Since there is an inevitable time-lag between the point at which the innovator introduces a new technology and the follower adopts it, rapid innovation will reduce the benefits of following. This has posed severe strategic problems for followers in industries such as computers and telecommunications where the rate of technical change is rapid. In the case of CNC machine tools the life-time of a design may be as short as two years before it becomes obsolete. This has forced both enterprises and state-owned research institutes in countries like Taiwan and South Korea to develop indigenous design capabilities. The increasing complexity of the product, as CNC machine tools become a part of flexible manufacturing systems, adds to the design difficulties.

In the literature some pessimism has been expressed regarding the development of design capabilities in the newly industrialized countries. In the present volume, for example, Chudnovsky, on the basis of firms surveyed for an UNCTAD study in India, Brazil and South Korea, concludes that

the evidence is far from conclusive about the progress made by firms surveyed in mastering design...technology. All firms [surveyed] rely on licensors for design technology and most of them have not been able as yet to use licensing agreements to learn design methodology. One reason is the reluctance of licensors to provide recent designs. In any case basic design and, in some cases, even detail designs for complex capital goods are not yet mastered by leading producers in the countries studied. Accordingly, they suffer from a major handicap which affects their ability to fulfill their role as eventual generators of technological innovations.

A similar point is made also in this volume by Erber, who notes that a large number of studies of the Brazilian capital goods sector have concluded that the

Brazilian capital goods industry has acquired considerable mastery over the full set of design and manufacturing technological activities for a range of products, based on the tradition of metalworking in Brazil and on processes of copying and adapting. None the less, the evidence available suggests that such a trajectory of technological development is limited and that the Brazilian industry tends to rely on imported technology for new and more complex products.

However, Amsden and Kim in the present book suggest that important improvements in design capabilities have occurred in the general machinery subsector in South Korea. They conclude that 'Despite the difficulties of technology transfer, technological capability has come to include design, at least for a limited subset of products. There are also many signs of progressive improvements in performance... although there remains a heavy dependence on foreign licenses, those which are renewed tend to be for more complex models or to satisfy dubious customers.'

More research is clearly needed on the costs and benefits of developing specific indigenous design capabilities. More specifically, the major factors constraining such capabilities must be identified in order to evaluate the costs and benefits of overcoming them.

V CONCLUSION

In this chapter we began by discussing the two and three sector models that have been used to analyse the question of the optimum allocation of resources to the local machinery sector. This discussion revealed the centrality of the productivities existing in the different sectors and led on to consideration of the role of the machinery sector in the process of technical and productivity change. The latter question was pursued, first through an examination of the analysis of machinery in the history of economic thought, and second through the construction of a biological analogy in order to examine the determinants of technical and productivity change in the machinery industry. However, far more research, of both a conceptual and empirical kind, is needed if we are to adequately understand the causal processes shaping technical change in this and other industries.

APPENDIX

In order to compare the effects of subsidies and tariffs, Corden (1974), p. 12 uses the following diagram:

PP' is the foreign supply curve for imports of the product under the usual 'small country' assumption, DD' is the domestic demand curve for the product, and GG' is the supply curve of the domestic import-competing producers. In the absence of state intervention, domestic produc-

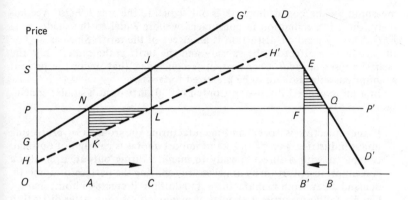

APPENDIX 1.1   Quantity of the importable

tion of *OA* would take place with *AB*, the excess of demand over local production, being imported.

We now assume that the local industry generates external economies that need to be taken into account through state intervention. From the point of view of social accounting, the value of these benefits must be deducted from the costs. In so doing, curve *HH'* is derived showing the marginal social cost of production. Local production, however, should continue up to the point where the marginal social cost of production is equal to the marginal cost of imports, that is to *OC* . (At outputs lower than *OC* the marginal cost of imports is greater than the marginal social cost of production implying that it is preferable to produce the product locally rather than import it.) Accordingly, state intervention is justified in order to increase locally produced output by *AC*.

This can be done either with a subsidy or a tariff, both of which will increase output by protecting the industry. A subsidy at the *ad valorem* rate of *SP/PO* will raise the price received by producers, thus inducing them to raise output to *OC*. The cost to society of the additional output *AC* is given by *AKLC*, the area under the social marginal cost curve. However, the cost of the imports that are replaced by local production is *ANLC*, the area under the marginal cost of imports curve. The difference between the two areas, *KNL*, represents the gain to society brought about by the subsidy.

The same production or protection effect can be brought about by imposing a tariff at the rate *SP/PO*. This raises the domestic price of the product to *OS* with the result that domestic output increases to *OC*, with the social gain the same as in the case of the subsidy, namely *KNL*. However, unlike with the subsidy there is now also a *consumption effect* resulting from the increase in price to consumers. At the higher price of *OS* consumption falls by *BB'*. In terms of the notion of 'consumers' surplus' the value to consumers of the *B'B* units is *B'EQB*. However, the cost, measured by the cost of imports, is only equal to the area $B'FQB$. Accordingly, there is a reduction in consumers' welfare equal to the shaded area FEQ. This by-product distortion is an effect of the tariff. Since as we saw the production effect of the subsidy and the tariff is the same, while the tariff imposes an *additional* cost, it is concluded that under the present assumptions subsidies are to be preferred to tariffs.

In a more general discussion Corden (1980) arrives at a similar conclusion:

> If the objective is to expand manufacturing on grounds of protecting infant industries, a tariff and set of import quotas is clearly not optimal. Compared with a direct subsidy to manufacturing output, it creates a consumption distortion by unnecessarily shifting the pattern of domestic demand away from manufactures. In addition, it creates a home-market bias by failing to protect exports of manufactures. The latter distortion could be eliminated by supplementing the tariff with export subsidies. (p. 64)

Where does this leave a country like South Korea which, as we see in the text, has chosen to use a combination of total prohibition of imports and subsidies in order to protect various kinds of machine production? According to conventional theory prohibition should be a third- or even fourth-best option. However, the problem with the conventional analysis is that it is static in the sense that technology and productivity are assumed to be exogenously given and unchanging. The concern of policy makers in South Korea, on the other hand, has been to *increase* productivity and international competitiveness. Rather than assuming *given* cost curves like PP' and GG' in the diagram above, and attempting to minimize by-product distortions, the South Korean state has attempted to *reduce* costs (and increase product quality) in the effort to become internationally competitive. The following diagram more accurately depicts their concern.

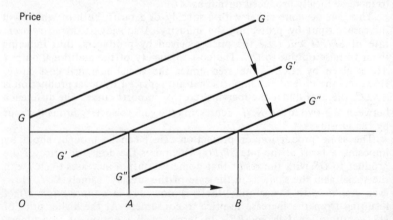

APPENDIX 1.2   Quantity of the importable

The diagram shows the supply curve of the domestic import-competing producers shifting rightwards as productivity increases and costs fall. Curve *GG* represents the infant industry case with domestic costs above the import price. Here the objective of government policy is to shift the curve to *G'G'* and later to *G"G"* by making local production internationally competitive. This is precisely what the South Korean government is attempting to do, for example, in the case of CNC machine tools and more complex electrical power equipment. A major weakness inherent in the diagram, however, is its inability to portray the mechanisms whereby productivity increases. From the point of view of the South Korean policy-maker, as emphasised in the text, policy instruments such as the prohibition of imports, the subsidization of output or inputs, and the insistence on exports by making discretionary benefits contingent upon export performance, are important largely as a result of the combination of incentives and pressures that they create thus facilitating technical and productivity change in the local firms. From this perspective the *dynamic* effects of the instruments on production are more important than their distortionary effects. This therefore explains the use in countries like South Korea of instruments that in the conventional theory appear to be sub-optimal.

NOTES

1. I would like to thank Frances Stewart, Staffan Jacobsson and members of the Research Policy Institute, Lund University in Sweden for comments on various parts of this chapter. None of them bears any responsibility for the present contents.
2. The interested reader seeking further details about the model may consult the original articles themselves as well as the growing secondary literature in this area. For this secondary literature see, for example, Stewart (1977, Ch.6), Taylor (1979, Ch.8), and Cooper (1984). The present sub-section draws heavily on the extremely helpful paper by Cooper.
3. This, and Figure 1.2, come from Cooper (1984).
4. This may be expressed symbolically in the following way. Machinery should be locally produced rather than imported if and only if

$$\beta_I > \beta_X P$$

where

β_I, β_X = capital productivities of the I and X sectors
P = external terms of trade

$$= \frac{P_X}{P_I} \text{ (where } P_X = \text{price of 'our' exports, } P_I = \text{price of}$$

foreign-made machinery)

5. Adam Smith, *Lectures*, quoted in Rosenberg (1982).
6. Here Marx refers to Darwin and the biological analogy of natural selection. For a more recent attempt to apply the same analogy to economic growth see Nelson and Winter (1982) *An Evolutionary Theory of Economic Growth.*
7. Marx was no doubt correct in characterizing Smith as 'the quintessential political economist of the period of manufacture' (ibid, p. 468). However, Marx went on to argue, without justification, that 'Smith also confuses the differentiation of the instruments of labour, in which the specialized workers of the manufacturing epoch themselves took an active part, with the invention of machinery; in the latter case it is not the workers but men of learning, artisans and even peasants . . . who play the main role' (Marx, 1976, p. 468).
8. For example, between regions and countries.
9. For example: 'We here see why it is that old countries are constantly impelled to employ machinery, and new countries to employ labour. With every difficulty of providing for the maintenance of men, labour necessarily rises, and with every rise in the price of labour, new temptations are offered to the use of machinery. This difficulty of providing for the maintenance of men is in constant operation in old countries' (*Principles*, p. 41).
10. That is, including both the direct labout input provided by workers and the indirect labour input provided by the machinery, and raw material.
11. Marx, of course, calculated in terms of average rather than marginal cost.
12. The reasonable assumption here is that the hand-loom weaver purchases inputs, including labour-power, on the same markets as the power-loom weaver and therefore pays the same price.
13. See chapters 7, 14 and 15 of volume 1 of *Capital* and the more recently published appendix 'Results of the Immediate Process of Production'.
14. See quotation from Ricardo, p. 14.
15. Here again we see Marx's concern with demand-side factors. The value of a machine is not determined solely by the amount of labour-time embodied directly and indirectly in it. Every commodity must be 'socially useful'. An old vintage machine that does not satisfy user needs as well as a newer vintage will accordingly lose some of its value.
16. See the quotations from Marx, *Capital*, vol. III, in Rosenberg (1982) p. 50.
17. James Meade, who was one of a small group including Richard Kahn, Joan and Austin Robinson, and Piero Sraffa which met in 1930/1 to develop Keynes's analysis in the *Treatise on Money* put the issue in the following way: 'I am one of that generation of young men and women who in the 1920s and 1930s in the United Kingdom turned to economics because of the prevailing mass unemployment. We believed that it was both stupid and wicked to do nothing about poverty in the midst of potential plenty, that is to say, to allow

resources of men and machinery to rust in involuntary idleness when there were so many real needs to be satisfied. We fell under the spell of Keynes. We believed that effective demand would be stimulated, and the production of useful things thus be restarted' (Meade, 1983, p. 2).

18. However, like the process of technical change itself, the conceptual study of technical change is not static but continuously alters. Faced with the inability to offer convincing explanations in the area of technical change, some economists have begun to create new conceptualizations. Examples are the work of Nelson and Winter and Rosenberg. In view of the space limitations, these new conceptualizations will not be discussed here.

19. For a recent interesting attempt to take this into account in a formal model of the determinants of productivity change, see Gordon, Bowles and Weisskopf (1983).

20. For a fascinating account see the classic by Dore (1973), *British Factory–Japanese Factory*.

21. Quoted in Floud (1976, p. 54).

22. For further details of how military demand affected the long-run international competitiveness of the American machine tool industry, see Melman (1983).

23. Accordingly, 'market pull' played a more important role in the development of NC than CNC in both the United States and Japan.

24. See, for an elaboration, Fransman (1985) 'Conceptualizing Technical Change in the Third World in the 1980s: An Interpretive Survey', *Journal of Development Studies* vol. 21, no. 4, July 1985.

25. For a more detailed account of the Singapore case, see Fransman (1984).

26. Melman (1983) argues that the international competitiveness of the US machine tool industry has been detrimentally influenced by this industry's involvement with military production.

27. Of the Asian newly industrialized countries only one, Hong Kong, has left this decision entirely to market forces. Singapore, South Korea and Taiwan have all made selective attempts to encourage the growth of the machinery section which is seen as a priority sector. Of the four, Hong Kong has the smallest capital goods sector.

28. It must, however, be noted that this hypothesis has not been seriously examined.

29. This is considered in more detail in the appendix.

REFERENCES

Arrow, K. J. (1962) 'The Economic Implications of Learning by Doing', *Review of Economic Studies*, vol. 29, June, pp. 155–73.

Berg, M. (1980) *The Machinery Question and the Making of Political Economy, 1815–1848* (Cambridge: Cambridge University Press).

Cooper, C. (1984) '"Learning-By-Doing" in an Open Economy Version of the 'Feldman Model': paper given at the Fourth EADI General Conference, Madrid, September.

Corden, W. M. (1971) *The Theory of Protection* (Oxford: Oxford University Press).

Corden, W. M. (1974) *Trade Policy and Economic Welfare* (Oxford: Oxford University Press).

Corden, W. M. (1980) 'Trade Policies', in Cody, J., Hughes, H. and Wall, D., *Policies for Industrial Progress in Developing Countries*. Sponsored by UNIDO and World Bank (Oxford University Press).

Dore (1973) *British Factory – Japanese Factory. The Origins of National Diversity in Industrial Relations* (London: Allen & Unwin).

Floud, R. (1976) *The British Machine Tool Industry, 1850–1914* (Cambridge University Press).

Fransman, M. (1982) 'Learning and the Capital Goods Sector Under Free Trade: The Case of Hong-Kong', *World Development*, vol. 10, no. 11.

Fransman, M. (1984) 'Explaining the Success of the Asian NIC's: Incentives and Technology, *I.D.S. Bulletin*, April.

Fransman, M. (1984) 'Promoting Technological Capability in the Capital Goods Sector: The Case of Singapore', *Research Policy*.

Fransman, M. (1985) 'Conceptualising Technical Change in the Third World in the 1980s: An Interpretive Survey', *Journal of Development Studies*, vol. 21, no. 4, July.

Fransman, M. (1985) 'International Competitiveness, International Diffusion of Technology and the State: A Case Study from Taiwan and Japan' (forthcoming).

Fransman, M. and King, K. (eds) (1984) *Technological Capability in the Third World* (London: Macmillan).

Gordon, D. M., Bowles, S. and Weisskopf, T. (1983) 'Hearts and Minds. A Social Model of Aggingate Productivity Growth in the United States. 1948–1979', *Brookings Papers on Economic Activity, 1*.

Harris, D. K. (1972) 'Economic Growth with Limited Import Capacity', *Economic Development and Cultural Change*, vol. 20, no. 3.

Hicks, J. R. (1965) *Capital and Growth* (Oxford: Oxford University Press).

Jacobsson, B. S. (1984) 'Technical Change and Industrial Policy: The Case of Numerically Controlled Lathes in Argentina, Republic of Korea and Taiwan', PhD. Dissertation, University of Sussex.

Keynes, J. M. (1961) *The General Theory of Employment, Interest and Money* (London: Macmillan).

Little, I. M. D. (1982) *Economic Development: Theory, Policy and International Relations* (New York: Basic Books).

Marx, K. (1976) *Capital*, vols I, II and III (Harmondsworth: Penguin).

Meade, J. (1983) 'A New Keynesian Approach to Full Employment', *Lloyds Bank Review*, October, no. 150.

Melman, S. (1983) 'How Yankees Lost Their Know-How', *Technology Review*, October.

Nagao, M. (1983) 'Technology Unpackaging in the Power Plant Sector of the Republic of Korea', Technology Division, UNCTAD. (Mimeo).

Nelson, R. R. and Winter, S. G. (1982) *An Evolutionary Theory of Economic Change* (Boston, Mass: The Belknap Press of Harvard University Press).

OECD (1972) *The Industrial Policy of Japan* (Paris).

Ricardo, D. (1951) *On The Principles of Political Economy and Taxation*, edited by P. Sraffa with the collaboration of M. H. Dobb (Cambridge: Cambridge University Press).

Robbins, L. (1932) *The Nature and Significance of Economic Science* (London: Macmillan).

Rosenberg, N. (1976) *Perspectives on Technology* (Cambridge: Cambridge University Press).

Rosenberg, N. (1982) *Inside The Black Box: Technology and Economics* (Cambridge: Cambridge Univeristy Press).

Schumpeter, J. A. (1943) *Capitalism, Socialism and Democracy* (London: Allen & Unwin).

Smith, A. (1910) *An Inquiry into the Nature and Causes of the Wealth of Nations* (London: Dent) (Everyman edition).

Stewart, F. (1977) *Technology and Underdevelopment* (London: Macmillan).

Taylor, L. (1979) *Macro Models for Developing Countries* (New York: McGraw-Hill).

Teubal, M. (1984) 'The Role of Technological Learning in the Export of Manufactured Goods: The Case of Selected Capital Goods in Brazil', *World Development*, vol. 12, no. 8.

Watanabe, S. (1983) 'Market Structure, Industrial Organization and Technological Development: The Case of the Japanese Electronics-based NC Machine Tool Industry', WEP 2–22/WP.111 (Geneva: ILO).

2 The Entry into the Design and Production of Complex Capital Goods: The Experiences of Brazil, India and South Korea[1]

DANIEL CHUDNOVSKY

INTRODUCTION

The manufacture of capital goods, and particularly of industrial machinery, has been a fundamental instrument in generating and diffusing technological innovations. For this reason, it has been argued that 'creating a capital goods industry is, in effect, a major way of *institutionalizing* internal pressures for the adoption of new technology'.[2]

In contrast to the historical evidence and convincing analytical explanations provided by Rosenberg in support of the case for creating a capital goods sector in industrializing countries, relatively little is known about the actual experience of those few countries like Brazil, India and South Korea (hereafter referred to as Korea) in which the capital goods sector has already achieved a considerable development.

In this connection, it is pertinent to inquire whether these countries are able to satisfy to any considerable extent not only their needs for capital accumulation through indigenous production of capital goods but also the technological requirements of such investments in cases where the manufacture of complex machinery and equipment is already taking place. In other words, it is worth examining whether the countries in question have largely overcome 'the structural incapacity to produce the capital goods required for growth' that has been considered as a key feature of technological dependence.[3]

As the entry into the design and manufacture of complex equipment in the countries under study has been carried out with considerable reliance on imported product designs and technical assistance from abroad for the fabrication process, and in some cases through the activities of foreign subsidiaries, it is very important to investigate the extent to which this way of entry has affected the function that machinery producers are supposed to perform not only as carriers of foreign technology but also as agents in adapting, diffusing and eventually generating innovations. In other words, although the physical manufacture of complex capital goods on the basis of imposed technology has certainly been a step forward towards the creation of a capital goods industry able to fulfil its historical role as an instrument in generating and diffusing technological innovations, that alone is not a sufficient reason for assuming that the physical manufacture of such equipment has *ipso facto* endowed indigenous machinery producers with an endogenous technological capacity (i.e. a capacity 'which undertakes technical change and adaptation as a matter of course and routine').[4] It is worthwhile, therefore, to assess progress made not only towards the formation of a capital goods sector but also towards the creation of an endogenous technological capacity to design and manufacture complex equipment and the extent to which elements of imported technology and indigenous efforts have been used for this purpose. It is with the object of answering this important question that leading capital goods producers in Brazil, India and Korea are studied in this paper[5] drawing on the results of research carried out by the UNCTAD Secretariat.

For a sound analysis of the experience of these producers it is important to first have an idea of the economic context in which the firms concerned have been operating. Hence, Section I describes the main features and indicates the recent performance of the capital goods sector in these three countries, and Section II discusses some government policies which have encouraged the development of the capital goods sector. The profile of leading capital goods makers in these countries is shown in Section III, and the economics of technology acquisition by these firms is discussed in Section IV. Although Section IV deals with a number of issues concerning manufacturing and design technology, it concentrates on the extent to which the various elements of imported technology have contributed, or have failed to contribute, to the development of an endogenous capability in the firms under examination.

In the light of the discussion in those sections, a final section sums up some conclusions that may be drawn about the experiences of these countries.

TABLE 2.1 Selected indicators of the development of the capital goods sector

		India	Brazil	Korea
1.	Number of establishments[a] engaged in capital goods manufacturing (thousands)	18.3	15.8	6.0
2.	Number of workers engaged[b] in capital goods manufacturing (thousands)	1283	1031	417
3.	Gross output[c] ($ billion)	8.0	16.9	7.2
4.	Imports[d] ($ billion)	1.4	4.0	6.1
5.	Exports[e] ($ billion)	0.5	2.4	2.4
6.	(5): (3) (per cent)	6.2	14.2	33.3
7.	(5) as per cent of all manufactured exports (SITC 5 to 8 − (67 + 68)	13.3	29.0	19.7
8.	Apparent consumption of capital goods ($ billion) ((3) + (4) − (5))	8.9	18.5	10.9
9.	Domestic supply ratio ((3) − (5) as % of (8))	84.3	78.4	44.0
10.	Value added[f] ($ billion)	2.1	7.2	2.7
11.	Production of machine tools[g] ($ million)	165	315	135
12.	of which exports ($ million)	25	71	26
13.	Imports of machine tools[h] ($ million)	76	175	344
14.	Apparent consumption of machine tools ((11) + (13) − (12)) ($ million)	216	419	453
15.	Domestic supply ratio for machine tools ((11) − (12)) as per cent of (14)	65	58	30
16.	Number of scientists and engineers[i] (thousands)	698	541	800
17.	Number of engineering graduates[j] (thousands)	13.6	18.1	32.3
	(per cent increase over 10 years earlier)	14	148	539

NOTES AND SOURCES The data are not strictly comparable owing to differences in coverage of years, number of establishments and goods produced and traded. For details see following notes.

a Brazil, Korea: establishments employing five or more workers; India: establishments with 10 or more workers using electrical power, or 20 or more workers not using power; the information relates to 1979

(Korea), 1978 (India), 1977 (Brazil). SOURCE: United Nations *Yearbook of Industrial Statistics*, 1980 edition, vol. 1. Establishments making radio and TV sets (ISIC 3832) were excluded in India and the Republic of Korea but not in the other countries.

b Same coverage as for *a*.

c Excluding electrical appliances and passenger cars in Brazil, India and Korea. The information relates to 1979 for Korea and Brazil and 1978 for India.

d Imports are SITC 7, Rev. 1 for India and Korea. For Brazil data concerning capital goods imports were taken from the Brazilian case study (*op. cit.*). The information relates to 1979 for Brazil and Korea and 1978 for India.

e Exports are SITC7, Rev. 1 for India, SITC 7 minus (761+762+763+781), following SITC, Rev. 2 for Korea. For Brazil they were taken from the case study (*op. cit.*). The information relates to the same year as for imports (see note *d* above).

f Value added for India, Brazil and Korea refer to the same coverage as gross output. For Brazil, value added has been estimated on the basis of the share of value added in gross output of ISIC 382 to 385 and 390 in 1977 (as reported in the *United Nations Yearbook of Industrial Statistics*), applying it to the 1979 figure (reported in the Brazilian case study). The information relates to 1979 for Brazil and Korea and 1978 for India.

g Revised estimates for 1980 as shown in *American Machinist*, February 1982.

h 1980 for India, Korea and Brazil, as shown in *American Machinist* (*op. cit.*).

i The number of scientists and engineers is taken from *Statistical Yearbook of UNESCO*, 1982. Data are given for following years: 1977 (India and Korea), 1970 (Brazil).

j The information relates to 1979 for Korea, 1978 for Brazil and 1976 for India. *Statistical Yearbook of UNESCO*, 1972, 1975 and 1981 editions.

I THE CAPITAL GOODS SECTOR IN BRAZIL, INDIA AND KOREA

General Features

The present capital goods sector in these three countries reflects the progress made in the development of the sector. At the same time, the main indicators in Table 2.1 show important differences among these countries.[6]

Although India has the second largest sector (after China) among developing countries in terms of employment and number of establishments, it has been surpassed by Brazil and Korea in terms of value added (see Table 2.1). The share of the value added by capital goods industries in India's total manufacturing value added was 22 per cent in 1973. This country's exports of capital goods are far lower than those of Brazil and Korea, though they have been growing in the 1970s. (Exports accounted for 6.2 per cent of India's total production in 1978 as compared with 2 per cent in 1970.)

Brazil has the second largest capital goods sector (after China) among developing countries in terms of gross output. The share of capital goods in its total manufacturing output is similar to the Indian one (i.e. 23 per cent). Brazil's exports of capital goods figure prominently in the country's manufactured exports, accounting for 29 per cent of such exports in 1979.

Although the manufacture of capital goods in Korea has a long history, it was in the 1970s that the production of these goods really gained momentum. However, the share of capital goods in the country's total manufacturing value added is the lowest among the countries studied in this chapter. It was 14 per cent in 1979.[7] Exports of capital goods from Korea accounted for 33 per cent of the gross output, which is the highest ratio among the three countries studied.

Recent Performance

In Brazil, capital goods production increased almost sevenfold in the period 1970–79. Since 1976 growth rates have been lower and a fall of 10 per cent occurred in 1981. Capital goods production declined by 14.4 per cent in the year to November 1982, after a fall of 16 per cent in the previous twelve months.[8]

Starting from a very low base, capital goods production in Korea increased 15-fold in real terms in the period from 1970 to 1979.[9] Even in the period 1977–9, the annual rate of growth of the output of capital goods averaged 19.2 per cent. After a period of high growth, capital goods production decreased by 15 per cent in 1980 and not until the end of 1981 did it again reach the level of 1979.[10]

The cyclical nature of the capital goods industries and particularly of the machine tools business is well known,[11] and the experience of the machinery industries in Brazil and Korea was not unlike that of their counterparts in industrialized countries. It is worth noting that the production of machinery and transport equipment fell 4 per cent in developed market economy countries in 1982.[12] However, the magnitude and the length of the recession in these two countries and its coincidence with the international recession are unusual. Such a situation not only affects the current position of many producers, especially the indigenous ones, but may also affect the prospects for these countries.

India's production of capital goods grew at high rates until the mid-1960s (e.g. 19.7 per cent per year in 1961-5) but since then has been growing rather slowly (5.4 per cent per year in the 1970s), as compared with that of the other countries under study.[13] In contrast to the experience of Korea and Brazil, the Indian capital goods sector did not this time suffer the impact of the worldwide recession. In 1980 it grew by 4.6 per cent and in 1981 by 7.4 per cent.[14]

Domestic Supply and Internal Composition

The countries under study have been increasingly meeting their domestic requirements of capital goods through local production. In the case of Brazil the share of local production (less exports) in total apparent consumption grew from 72 per cent in 1970 to 78 per cent in 1979. In Korea the corresponding proportion rose from 33 to 44 per cent in the same period, while in India it remained at about 84 per cent in the 1970s. However, while in electrical machinery and transport equipment the self-sufficiency ratio was 90 per cent in India, in non-electrical machinery it was 74 per cent.

Self-sufficiency ratios are lower in the case of machine tools, reflecting the need to import sophisticated machines that are not yet produced in the three countries in question. It has been estimated that local production (minus exports) satisfied 65 per cent and 58 per cent of total apparent consumption in 1980 in Brazil and India, respectively. In Korea the proportion was 30 per cent.[15] Admittedly, the domestic production of machine tools is more recent in Korea than in the other two countries, and the apparent consumption in that country has been very high (Table 2.1). This gives an idea of the increase in the machine building capacity that has been taking place.

The production of capital goods in the countries under study not only grew greatly in the 1970s but also changed its internal composition. The most striking feature is the growing share of the non-electrical machinery branch in the capital goods sector. In the case of Brazil, non-electrical machinery increased its share from 45 per cent in 1970 to 52 per cent in 1979, mostly at the expense of transport equipment.[16] In India, the share of non-electrical machinery was 40 per cent in 1977 (as compared with

31 per cent in 1970) and in Korea was 25 per cent in 1978 (as compared with 22 per cent in 1970).[17]

As in industrialized countries, a feature of the engineering production in these three countries is the importance of military items. In the case of Brazil, the annual production of the arms industry was valued at $4.8 billion in 1979, which represents 36 per cent of the total production of capital goods in that year; there are about 350 enterprises in that industry, employing about 100 000 workers.[18] In India, the defence industry employs almost 250 000 workers[19] and its production is mostly intended for the domestic market. The arms manufacturing consists of some thirty-six ordnance factories and nine defence undertakings, all completely state-owned and managed.[20] In the case of Korea, the defence industry's production does not seem to be very significant.

Skilled Manpower

The development of the capital goods industries in the three countries would not have been possible without the training of manpower. Although no precise information is available on the availability of manpower for the engineering sector, the data on the number of scientists and engineers and the number of engineering graduates offer some guidance. As shown in Table 2.1, Korea, despite a much smaller population, had a larger stock of scientists and engineers than India and Brazil. The annual number of engineering graduates in recent years was also higher in Korea than in Brazil and India. However, while in India 4.1 per cent of the country's stock of scientists and engineers are employed in R & D activities, the comparable ratio in Korea is only 1.8 per cent. This suggests a relative underdevelopment of R & D activities in Korea, as will be shown again later on.

The Entry into the Manufacture of Complex Capital Goods

The capital goods industries in the three countries have been gradually entering into the design and manufacture of relatively complex machinery and equipment.[21] This can be illustrated by some examples drawn from the machine tools and heavy electrical equipment industries.

In Brazil, for example, the following types of lathes which were not being produced in 1970 were made in 1980: multipurpose, frontal, vertical and with numerical control.[22] In 1980, out of 11 428 lathes made in

Brazil, 630 weighed more than 3 000 kg.[23] In India, whereas in the 1960s hardly any automatic, capstan and turret lathes were made in the country, these complex lathes have since been produced and their output was growing at a higher rate than that of all machine tools in India by the late 1970s. HMT, the leading machine tool producer, has also been manufacturing numerically controlled machine tools including machining centres, though in small quantities. Korea has recently started to manufacture high-speed precision tools and NC lathes. In 1982, 222 NC lathes were made in that country.

The size of power generation units made in India increased from 30 MW to 60 MW and then to 100 MW in the 1960s. In the 1970s, steam units of 120 MW and 200 MW were made, and orders have already been placed for thermal sets having a unit rating of 500 MW. The largest units are being produced under licence agreements.

Brazil has made substantial progress in the manufacture of hydroelectric generating equipment with a relatively high degree of local integration[24] but with considerable participation by subsidiaries of transnational corporations. In the Korean case, the degree of local integration of the manufacture of complex electrical equipment, e.g. turbine generators for thermal power plant of 400 MW, was about 40 per cent in 1978.

The information cited above should be taken with caution. While the data certainly indicate that the countries in question are increasingly producing complex equipment (as compared with the situation in the 1960s), no intercountry comparison can be made on the basis of such information. Furthermore, complex equipment has been generally made with the collaboration of foreign technology suppliers, as explained below.

Exports

Another noteworthy feature is the composition and destination of capital goods exported by the countries under study. Korea and Brazil exported machinery and transport equipment to almost the same value in 1980 (i.e. $3.4 billion), whereas Indian exports are far smaller (less than $0.5 billion in 1978). A considerable share of these exports consists of consumer durables. More than $1 billion of Korea's exports of such goods, for example, is accounted for by radio and TV sets, household appliances and passenger cars. These consumer goods account for a smaller share of exports of Brazil, equivalent to about $0.5 billion[25] and for an almost insignificant share in the case of India. Accordingly, the value of

Brazilian exports of capital goods was more than one third higher than that of Korea's exports of such goods in 1980.

The analysis of capital goods exports by Brazil, India and Korea discloses some contrasting features. First, non-electrical machinery represented more than half of the Brazilian exports of these goods, 42 per cent of the Indian exports,[26] and only 15 per cent of those of Korea. Power machinery, agricultural machinery and especially tractors, office machines, machinery for special industries, and metalworking machinery are prominent among Brazilian exports. Second, electrical equipment exports (even excluding consumer goods) are more significant in Korea than in the other two countries. Transistors are by far the largest Korean export item in this category of goods. Third, as regards transport equipment (excluding passenger cars), ships and boats account for more than half of the Korean exports, lorries are the largest item in Brazil, and motor vehicle parts constitute the biggest export item in India's trade in capital goods. Fourth, military items have become substantial among Brazilian exports of engineering goods. In 1979 exports were estimated at $300 million[27], or 12 per cent of total exports of capital goods. Military equipment does not seem to be significant in the exports of India and Korea. Lastly, the composition of the export trade seems to suggest that relatively more complex products have started to be exported by Brazil and, though to a lesser extent, by India than by Korea.

As regards the destination of the exports, it is noteworthy that a high proportion of Indian and Brazilian exports of machinery and transport equipment is shipped to other developing countries (81 and 66 per cent respectively), whereas Korea exports these goods mainly to developed market economy countries (64 per cent). It is also worth noting that almost no trade has taken place among these three countries.

II GOVERNMENT POLICIES

The development of the capital goods sector in the three countries could not have taken place without explicit government policies aimed at fostering the domestic manufacturing of capital goods.[28] Although some indigenous manufacturing of capital goods was carried on for many years in these countries, it was only when the governments had formally decided in their development plans to give priority to this crucial sector that the accelerated development of the capital goods production actually occurred. This was precisely the case with the Second Five-Year Plan in India (1956–61) and the launching of the Heavy and Chemical Industries

Development Programme by Korea in 1973. In Brazil, though the government had been heavily influencing the development of the capital goods sector through a variety of policies relating to imports, exports, public investment and the external financing of projects for many years, it was from 1974 onwards that several specific measures were introduced to foster local production of capital goods and reduce imports.[29]

India

The priority given to the manufacture of capital goods in the Indian industrialization strategy recognizes its origin in the approach followed in this respect by the USSR.[30] In the planning model followed in the Indian Second Five-Year Plan (i.e. that of Mahalanobis), emphasis was given to the heavy industry and to the attainment of self-sufficiency in the machinery sector.[31] Moreover, public sector companies were actually given responsibility for initiating the indigenous manufacture of capital good with the technological assistance of both socialist and market economy countries at least in two important sub-sectors: machine tools and electrical equipment.

In pursuing the import-substituting manufacture of capital goods India has been following a protectionist policy not only with regard to imports of goods but also with regard to overseas investment and, to a lesser extent, to intangible technology imports. Indigenous manufacture of capital goods has been protected by an import control policy pursuant to which import licences are granted for those goods which are considered essential and not available from indigenous sources.[32] In this way the domestic manufacture of capital goods has been protected, although the intensity of protection has not always been the same. In 1968/9 the effective rate of protection was estimated to be 119.6 per cent in the case of electrical equipment and 87.8 per cent in the case of non-electrical machinery.[33]

Although more recent estimates of the effective rate of protection in India are not available, it is likely that the protection is now lower than it was in the past. If so, the lower rate of protection may be the result of various factors, such as the learning process in the industries in question as reflected in their growing competitiveness, the liberalization of certain imports in the case of capital goods required for export industries, including exports of engineering goods, and a simplification of procedures for imports of machinery and parts and components.

Foreign collaboration agreements have been heavily used in the Indian capital goods sector, especially for making complex equipment. In the period 1971-80, 550 agreements covering industrial machinery, 604 agreements covering electrical equipment and 181 contracts for machine tools were approved. If all agreements relating to capital goods are taken into account (1 759 agreements), they represented 58 per cent of all collaboration agreements approved in India in 1971-80 (3 030 agreements). This is a much higher proportion than the share of capital goods production in total manufacturing output.

Foreign collaboration agreements are subject to government approval in India. The system of evaluation and approval of such agreements is complex, the main purpose being to reduce the incidence of restrictive conditions in those agreements and to limit the explicitly stipulated payments to reasonable amounts. The Foreign Exchange Regulation Act (1973) was enacted with the object, among others, of reducing the foreign control in local enterprises to a maximum of 40 per cent of the voting stock. As a result of this Act, foreign controlled companies are now dominant in only four product lines in the capital goods sector. In contrast, in 1964, foreign companies were dominant in fifteen product lines.[34]

To encourage research and development activities in the capital goods sector not only were a number of research institutes created in India (such as the Central Machine Tool Institute and the Central Power Research Institute) but fiscal incentives and foreign exchange concessions under the technical development scheme are also granted to facilitate R & D activities in the firms themselves.

Brazil

In the case of Brazil, imports of capital goods, which were formerly favoured by exemptions from tariff rates,[35] internal tax exemptions, the overvaluation of the cruzeiro and access to foreign suppliers' credits, have generally been discouraged since 1974. At the same time, the indigenous manufacture of capital goods has been fostered by several instruments, such as non-tariff barriers applied to imported equipment; incentives by the Industrial Development Council to increase the proportion of locally supplied equipment in all approved investment projects; fiscal and financial incentives to domestic producers of capital goods; and other measures. This modification in the government's policy has probably increased the effective rate of protection of domestic capital goods production, although the precise incidence of this protection depends on the administrative procedures used, which differ from case to case.[36]

While Brazil's policy governing imports of capital goods has been rather protectionist since 1974, the same is not true of its policy on direct foreign investment. Foreign firms have participated strongly in the development of the capital goods sector, especially in electrical and in transport equipment.

Imports of intangible technology for Brazil's capital goods industries have taken place under contracts for industrial co-operation (a category especially created for the capital goods sector since 1975) and in the form of technical services. While the former are usually for a duration of five years and may cover a range of products, technical service contracts are for less than two years and each such contract relates to one product only. In 1980 and 1981, 499 agreements were approved in the mechanical sector and 116 agreements were authorized in the electrical and communications sector.[37]

The agency responsible for screening contracts for technology transfer, the National Institute of Industrial Property (INPI), has been controlling the terms and conditions of the agreements with the aim of reducing the incidence of restrictive practices, supervising the duration of the contracts and avoiding excessive payments for the imports of technology.

In order to strengthen the competitive power of indigenous producers of capital goods special funds for technological development were created. The mandate of these funds covers not only a variety of activities related to technological development but also imports of technology. Although specific research institutes for the capital goods sector have not been established in Brazil, some of the leading institutes, like the Institute for Technological Research (IPT) in Sao Paulo, has been very active in the machinery sector.

Korea

In Korea, capital goods imports were strongly favoured in the 1960s and early 1970s by tariff exemptions, overvaluation of the won, suppliers' credit, and in other ways. As from 1973 the bias in favour of imported capital goods was modified. Exemptions from tariffs on imported machinery and equipments are granted only when the imported capital goods are essential to the manufacturing process, embody the latest technology and are not domestically produced.[38]

The indigenous manufacture of capital goods has been fostered through the provision of medium- and long-term credit funds for domestically made capital goods and the imposition of quantitative controls on competing ('similar') imports immediately upon the initiation of domestic production. The effective protection for the machinery sector was estimated to be 47.4 per cent on average in 1978.[39] This rate is lower than the Indian one and probably than the Brazilian one after 1974. However, because selective measures other than tariffs for the protection of the industry are applied in Korea, the effective rate of protection is less relevant as an indicator of the protection actually enjoyed by Korean industry.

In sharp contrast to the experiences of India and Brazil, Korea's capital goods industries have been exporters almost since the beginning. Export expansion has been facilitated by subsidies and preferential access to credit and by the fact that 'many of these industries are either monopolized or operate as cartels'.[40] It is precisely the major role that conglomerate business groups known as *chaebul*[41] have been playing in the economy and in the capital goods industries that is another distinctive feature of the Korean experience. Private indigenous companies generally belonging to the *chaebul* are those which have entered into the manufacture of capital goods through a process of diversification of production and have clearly the leadership in this sector. Foreign companies have been relatively unimportant and their participation has taken mostly the form of joint ventures. Public companies are of only limited importance.

The technology needed for facilitating the development of indigenous producers of capital goods has been mostly obtained through licensing agreements. In 1977–80, 332 agreements were approved in the machinery sector which alone accounted for 34 per cent of all agreements (974) approved in Korea in that period.[42]

To encourage the technological development of the capital goods industries the government has established major research institutes such as the Korea Institute for Machinery and Metals (KIMM) and the Korea Advanced Institute for Science and Technology (KAIST). To facilitate the technology efforts of indigenous firms the government has created several schemes, such as long-term loans at low interest rates, fiscal concessions, etc.

Concluding Remarks

It is clear that in these three countries, which have followed different industrialization strategies and have very different socio-political systems, the recent development of indigenous manufacturing of capital goods was made possible not through market forces but through explicit government decisions. Import-substituting manufacture of capital goods has been the common objective of the policies applied in this field. However, it seems that differences are more pronounced than similarities in the means used to achieve this objective.

Protection against similar imported products has been used in Brazil, India and Korea to foster the indigenous manufacture of machinery and equipment. This protection was achieved mostly through quantitative restrictions rather than through tariffs in India and Korea, and through administrative devices in Brazil. While in the case of Brazil and Korea the effective protection before 1973 or 1974 was clearly lower than in India, the present situation is more difficult to assess, although it seems that in Korea the effective protection is the lowest among the three countries. However, the import-substituting manufacture of capital goods in Korea has been protected against imports through a selective system of financial incentives, both to producers and to users of domestic equipment which is not well reflected in the average rate of effective protection.

Exports of capital goods have been favoured in Korea since the beginning of local production and have been promoted recently in both India and Brazil. However, no specific incentives beyond those available for all manufactured exports are granted in these three countries for the promotion of capital goods.

The part played by public, private and foreign enterprises likewise differs materially in the three countries. In India the public enterprises are those responsible for capital goods manufacturing, followed by private firms and some foreign controlled firms. In Brazil and Korea the private domestic sector has been very active in the manufacture of capital goods. Foreign subsidiaries have played an important role in the Brazilian case, especially in the non-mechanical sectors, and are unimportant in Korea. In the case of Korea the importance of the large business conglomerates to which most leading capital goods establishments belong to should not be underestimated.

Imports of intangible technology have been substantial in the three countries, especially at the stage of entry into the design and manufacture of more complex capital goods. Firms based in industrialized countries have been the main source of technology for these countries, licencing agreements being the basic tool used for this purpose.

III PROFILE OF FIRMS SURVEYED

In order to study the technology issues arising in the manufacture and design of complex capital goods, three subsectors (machine tools, equipment for process industries, and electrical equipment) which include a relatively high proportion of complex products, were selected. These subsectors were not chosen because of their statistical importance in the capital goods sector, although their shares are not negligible. Machine tools were chosen because they are the basic components of the capital goods sector and are leading carriers of technological innovation throughout the economy. Machinery for the process industries provides part of the equipment needed for some basic industries like steel, paper and pulp, chemical and petrochemicals.[43] Heavy electrical equipment[44] is the key capital goods item in electrical machinery and has an obvious importance in electricity generation.

Leading firms making complex products[45] in Brazil, India and Korea were analysed in detail for the purpose of assessing their strategy, particularly in relation to the acquisition and development of technology.

Although the enterprises surveyed were not chosen at random, the fact that they are leading firms ensures a relatively good coverage of the situation prevailing in the upper end of these subsectors. The firms surveyed accounted for almost two-thirds (and for more than 70 per cent of electrical equipment and machine tools produced in India) of the total output of the subsectors concerned in Korea and India. The industry coverage of the firms surveyed also seems very high in Brazil, though no precise estimates were available.

The high participation of the firms surveyed in their subsectors in India and Korea suggests a high degree of suppliers' concentration in the capital goods sector in those countries. In the case of Korea this is clearly in line with the picture given by recent estimates of concentration ratios of three firms at eight digits ISIC levels. The weighted average concentration ratio was approximately 60 per cent in the capital goods sector for 118 subbranches.[46] In contrast, in India, cases of three firms accounting for 60 per cent or more of the relevant output were found in eight out of twenty-two subbranches in non-electrical machinery and in five out of thirteen subbranches in electrical machinery. Furthermore, highly concentrated subbranches were fewer in 1978/9 than in 1964, as a result of the entry of new firms and product diversification by existing firms.[47] In Brazil, the four largest establishments produced, on average, 40 per cent of the value of capital goods output in 1973. Concentration ratios were very different, from as low as 10 per cent in machine tools to 90 per cent in tractors.[48]

Altogether, 63 producers of capital goods[49] were surveyed, almost two-thirds (40) of them being domestic enterprises (Table 2.2).[50] Of the firms surveyed, 20 per cent (13) were subsidiaries of transnational enterprises,[51] mostly concentrated in Brazil. In contrast, no foreign subsidiary has been operating in the subsectors under study in Korea. It is in this country that the relatively few joint ventures (10)[52] among the firms surveyed are mostly located.

The low share accounted for by foreign subsidiaries in the number of firms surveyed should not necessarily be taken as an accurate representation of the situation of those firms in the capital goods sector as a whole in the countries studied. Foreign firms are important in some capital goods subsectors not considered in this study, such as tractors or electronics. At the same time, it is possible that in joint ventures foreign partners are able to exercise technological control over the whole enterprise. However, given the explicit policy followed in India and Korea of not allowing direct foreign investment (through majority ownership) in this sector, the picture emerging from Table 2.2 does not seem to be very far from the reality of the sector.[53] In the case of Brazil, the extent of foreign firms participation is probably greater than that suggested in the table.

It is noteworthy that domestic enterprises are predominant in machine tools and equipment for process industries, while their presence is more limited in electrical equipment. These domestic enterprises are all private firms in Brazil and mostly private in Korea and India. However, in India, the two biggest firms making machine tools and electrical equipment are public undertakings,[54] while in Korea the manufacture of electric power equipment is dominated by a public firm. Two other public firms are also active in the production of equipment for process industries in Korea.

Leading domestic enterprises in these subsectors have relied on licensing agreements, as is shown in Table 2.2. Only 11 (all private firms) out of 40 domestic firms and mainly making machine tools, are not using such agreements for technology acquisition. As shown below, the reliance on licensing is important enough to draw a distinction between firms operating with and those operating without licensing agreements.[55]

The fact that the firms surveyed all manufacture complex capital goods does not mean that they make only this type of product. Many of these firms have entered into a more sophisticated range of products while continuing to make less-complex goods as well. The share of custom-order equipment[56] in total output and the value of output under licence in relation to that of total output (see below) roughly indicate as well the importance achieved by complex equipment in the activities of the enterprises studied.

In the case of the Brazilian domestic firms, the practice of concluding licensing agreements relating to the manufacture of mostly complex capital goods started relatively late in their lives, on average 23 years after

TABLE 2.2   Ownership characteristics of firms surveyed in the sample (number of firms)

Country and ownership	Sector			
	Machine tools	Equipment for process industries	Electrical equipment	Total
Brazil	8	6	8	22
Wholly domestic firms	1	–	1	2
Domestic firms with foreign technical collaboration	3	5	3	11
Foreign subsidiaries	4	1	4	9
India	7	7	6	20
Wholly domestic firms	2	3	2	7
Domestic firms with foreign technical collaboration	2	3	1	6
Joint ventures	1	1	1	3
Foreign subsidiaries	2	–	2	4
Korea	7	8	6	21
Wholly domestic firms	2	–	–	2
Domestic firms with foreign technical collaboration	5	5	2	12
Joint ventures	–	3	4	7
Above three countries	22	21	20	63
Wholly domestic firms	5	3	3	11
Domestic firms with foreign technical collaboration	10	13	6	29
Joint ventures	1	4	5	10
Foreign subsidiaries	6	1	6	13

SOURCE   Country case studies (see note 5 to this chapter).

their foundation and mostly in the mid-1960s. No similar information is available for the other countries, though it seems that licensing started at an early stage or even at the time of the establishment of the firms, as in the case of some leading firms in India.

IV ECONOMICS OF TECHNOLOGY ACQUISITION

Introduction

The entry of the three developing countries studied into the design and manufacture of complex capital goods has called not only for considerable manufacturing experience on the part of the firms surveyed but also for substantial technological efforts. These efforts were indispensable for the purpose of designing and making products of high quality and reliability for very demanding users.

The general organization of the plant and the organization of the production process become more complex as firms make increasingly complex capital goods.[57] Activities like quality control in each shop in addition to final quality control, methods of fabrication, time studies of different operations, control of inventories, etc. require specific efforts by specialized personnel. At the same time, the organization of the plant becomes more complex and the management of procurement of materials, production, quality control, sales and after-sales service decisively effect the performance, quality and reliability of the products.

The fact that the firms in question have been in this business for a considerable number of years does not necessarily imply that they have mastered all the aspects of design and manufacturing technology. In a recent study of some cases in Latin American, Katz has shown that the process of acquiring such technological knowledge is a slow one and can take decades.[58] Another study of machinery producers in developing countries (including India and Korea) has shown that task-level and plant-wide productivities in these firms are much lower than in industrialized countries, because of certain shortcomings in the organization of the process of production, including poor working conditions, the use of poor cutting tools and tool holders; absence of jigs, poor plant layout, poor scheduling, etc.[59]

Information collected among firms surveyed in Korea has confirmed some of the shortcomings. Modern techniques of internal scheduling are seldom used. The plant layout in most capital goods firms is arranged on function basis and is not suitable for operation on a product-line basis. Despite the modern equipment recently incorporated by many firms, there is a shortage of specialized machine tools and of special purpose jigs.

Information available from the firms surveyed does not make it possible to say how far and how these shortcomings have been remedied.[60] In some cases, firms have relied on their own efforts to solve these problems or have requested the assistance of research institutes. Several firms have used licensing agreements to deal with manufacturing problems or to strengthen quality control. However, licensing agreements generally relate to specific products and therefore fall short of disposing of difficulties in processes of production or of organizational difficulties which affect a number of products. Licensors may not be interested as such in improving the overall efficiency of licensees. In fact, the licensor is often financially better off when the licensed product is sold in a protected local market at a high price in those frequent cases in which technology payments are calculated as a percentage of sales. In the case of capital goods, design activities are particularly important and it is in this area that licensing agreements have been widely used by the firms surveyed.

Technology Transfer Agreements

Reliance on Technology Transfer Agreements

The firms surveyed have generally relied on transfer of technology agreements in order to meet their technological requirements. These agreements have been used not only by almost three-quarters of the 40 indigenous enterprises studied but also by all joint ventures and most foreign subsidiaries. Altogether 208 agreements have been signed by the 49 enterprises surveyed that have used such agreements for importing intangible technology.

The number of contracts is a limited indicator of the degree of reliance on licensing. The value of the goods produced under licence as a percentage of the value of total production is a better indicator. Unfortunately, this percentage ratio is only available for Indian firms and to some extent for Brazilian ones. Indigenous manufacturers in India and Brazil produce half or more of their total output under licensing agreements, this proportion being lower in the case of Brazilian firms making machine tools. Joint ventures in India also rely on licensed products for a considerable share of their total output.

Although the information available for Indian firms indicates a relatively heavy reliance on licensed products, it is fair to mention that the percentage shares of their production under collaboration agreements in total production are now somewhat lower than they were in 1975. It is also fair to point out that domestic firms without any licensing agreements in force are active in the three subsectors in India (Table 2.2). However, four of these seven firms have purchased designs and drawings on the basis of lump sum payments.

Content of the Agreements

Licence agreements relating to capital goods are used mainly for obtaining the basic design of the product, detailed design for the manufacture of parts and components and technical assistance for specific manufacturing processes. These three items are often specified in the text of the agreements and are not always transferred together.

While basic design (and in most cases design methodology) is the item more often included in licensing agreements entered into by Indian firms, this is not the case with detailed designs. It seems then that Indian firms have achieved a considerable capacity for making detailed designs for the manufacture of parts and components. Licensing agreements have been used to obtain in some cases, especially as regards machine tools, technical assistance for the manufacturing process and for the training of personnel.

In the agreements concluded by Brazilian firms, detailed design has almost the same weight as basic design. In fact, all firms making electrical equipment have received the three main technical items together. In the case of firms making equipment for process industries the majority of the 40 agreements cover the three main items. This is not the case as regards machine tools, where basic and detailed design seems relatively less important, whereas assistance for manufacturing has been frequently received under those agreements.

Although the information collected on Korean sample firms is not strictly comparable, most of their technology import contracts contain provisions concerning product design, production know-how and training. As regards designs it seems that Korean firms rely completely on licensors for the drawings and specifications, and hardly any transfer of design technology has been taking place.

The evidence collected from the terms of the contracts in the countries studied suggests a heavy reliance on foreign suppliers for the technology used in making capital goods. However, while a more selective process of importation is apparent in Indian domestic firms and to some extent in Brazilian firms, this does not seem to be the case in Korea.

However, the information collected in India about the age of designs transferred through collaboration agreements is significant.

Firms surveyed in India have been mostly receiving designs more than six years old, and in the case of equipment for process industries the majority of designs are more than nine years old. Even foreign subsidiaries are not better off than their domestic counterparts as regards the age of designs received from their parent companies. It is not clear whether this age structure of designs is due to the reluctance of suppliers to provide more recent technology or to the policies of recipient firms that were prepared to import such designs in the light of Indian domestic conditions.

The study of Brazilian enterprises makes it clear that an important learning process has been taking place regarding manufacturing know-how and, in some cases, regarding detailed designs. Design capability is still underdeveloped, specially in firms making equipment for process industries, and for this reason basic and detailed design is mostly imported.

Information collected in Korea corroborates the point often made in Brazil and India that technology suppliers are not prepared to provide particulars of the methodology of recent basic design. In the case of numerically controlled machine tools as well as in the electrical equipment sector, technology suppliers are only prepared to provide designs of an older vintage. This policy is partly explained by the requirements of the recipient companies to have adequate guarantees for the technology to be transferred.

Foreign subsidiaries usually receive the whole technological package from their parent companies and carry out only some adaptive work regarding detailed designs and manufacturing technology in order to take account of local conditions. This seems to be the case of foreign subsidiaries in India and Brazil, the exception being subsidiaries making electrical equipment in Brazil. Given the importance of the Brazilian market for electrical equipment and the long time that foreign firms have been operating in that country, it is not surprising to find an important process of learning and hence a certain degree of technological autonomy regarding production know-how. However, these subsidiaries still rely upon their parents for the basic design of complex products, like turbines and generators.

Costs and Benefits of Importing Technology

(i) Direct payments. Reliance on licensing agreements involves costs for the firms surveyed as well as important advantages. Payments under licensing agreements are usually made either in the form of royalties and/or fees calculated as a percentage of sales or in the form of lump sum payments. Sometimes a combination of both methods is found. Where joint ventures and subsidiaries are concerned, dividends to the technology supplier for its equity investment (sometimes technology capitalization) can also be considered a payment to that supplier.

In examining payments for technology it is important to bear in mind that in each of the countries studied the government has been participating in the negotiation of the terms and conditions of technology transfer agreements and, therefore, resulting royalty payments are affected by this intervention. Furthermore, recipient firms carry on business in concentrated market structures and sell products of a high unit value generally facing an inelastic demand. Hence, it is reasonable to assume that part of the explicit costs incurred in importing technology can be passed on to their customers.

Information collected in India and Korea gives some idea of the total payments for licensed technology made in 1980 by the firms surveyed. Such payments, expressed as a percentage of the total production of the firms having agreements, range from a low of 0.03 per cent in the case of joint ventures making equipment for process industries in India to a high of 2.6 per cent in the case of Korean joint ventures. The percentages are higher in the latter than in the former country, particularly for machine tool makers. This is to be expected, given the age of the design transferred to Indian firms and their export performance.

The corresponding information about Brazilian firms is not comparable to that concerning India and Korea because the Brazilian information relates not to total payments made in one year but to royalties and/or lump sum payments agreed in the approved text of licensing agreements. Royalty payments as a percentage of licensed sales have amounted under many agreements (in 17 out of 25 contracts) to about 4 or 5 per cent, and sometimes other payments are also included.

(ii) Implicit costs. In addition to the explicit payments for receiving foreign technology, which do not seem to be very high except in Brazil,[61] implicit costs have to be taken into consideration. These implicit costs are usually reflected in contractual clauses like those stipulating export restrictions, tied imports of parts and components, grant back provisions, etc.

In the case of the Korean firms surveyed, 37 per cent of the agreements signed by domestic machine tool makers and 26 per cent of the contracts entered into by domestic firms making electrical equipment contained restrictive conditions regarding the purchase of parts and components. Restrictions on exports were found in 41 per cent of the contracts. Such restrictions were particularly severe in the case of contracts concluded by domestic firms making chemical equipment (90 per cent of the contracts). It is noteworthy that most technology import contracts were amended in the course of the government's examination prior to approval. Hence, the restrictions mentioned above are those remaining in force after the government intervention in the negotiation process.

Among the agreements concluded by the firms surveyed in Brazil, tied-in import clauses were found in half of the contracts relating to process industries and electrical equipment. Formal restrictions of exports were found in 17 per cent of the agreements, and provisions requiring the licensor's formal authorization for the introduction of modifications of the products were found in 11 per cent of the contracts. The relatively smaller incidence of restrictive clauses in the contracts as compared with the situation in the early 1970s can be attributed to the policy of the government body responsible for monitoring licensing agreements, the National Institute of Industrial Property (INPI), of not authorizing such clauses in the agreements. It also reflects the stronger bargaining position of the licensees as a result of the 'learning to license' process which has taken place in Brazil. None the less, the relatively small incidence of these clauses in the text of the contracts does not exclude the existence of 'gentlemen's agreements' or their implicit acceptance in cases in which licensees prefer to avoid disputes with the licensors (e.g. the licensee may informally consult the licensor about changes to be introduced or exports to be made, even where the licensee is nominally free to make these changes or exports under the terms of the contract). In this connection, tied-in imports, which are relatively the most frequent subject of restrictive clauses, can also facilitate unauthorized payments through over-invoicing of imports.

Although restrictive clauses (export restrictions, tied-in imports, etc.) are still in force under many agreements entered into by Indian firms, they are now less frequent and less comprehensive than in the early 1970s. This can be attributed to both the government policy in regulating licensing agreements and the 'learning to license' process which has taken place in India as well. However, restrictions on exports and on adaptations to be made in the imported design or affecting the scope of patent rights in the product specification have been reported by some Indian firms. The lower proportion of products made under collaboration agreements which is exported as compared with the share of licensed products in total sales for the internal market is indicative of the effect of the first restriction.

(iii) Some implications. Licensing agreements have brought both advantages and costs to the firms surveyed. For example, as far as Brazil is concerned, in addition to transferring the design and manufacturing know-how, all agreements relating to electrical equipment, 86 per cent of those relating to machine tools and one-fourth of those relating to equipment for the process industries have given exclusive rights to the licensee in the Brazilian market. This is a very important clause for the licensee, not only with a view of preventing competition from other would-be licensees but also with a view to stopping the licensor from setting up a subsidiary in the country during the duration of the agreement.[62]

Another advantage is that conferred by the clause providing for access to innovations, a clause included in all agreements relating to machine tools and in half of the contracts relating to the other two sectors signed by domestic firms in Brazil. In the case of the Korean firms surveyed, 58 per cent of the contracts relating to machine tools, 82 per cent of those relating to equipment for process industries and 56 per cent of those relating to electrical equipment contained a similar clause. However, although this clause is also included in the agreements signed in the other two countries, licensees sometimes find that they cannot obtain updated technology unless additional payments are made.

Licensing contracts have still another important private benefit for the recipient firm. Even if a trade mark is not covered by the contract, the possibility of mentioning that the product is made under licence of a recognized international firm is a fundamental marketing tool. Users have sometimes virtually forced domestic firms to manufacture under licence as a condition for submitting bids, and this is especially the case in procurement policies followed by State companies both in India and Brazil. In any case, a licence is a powerful means of competing with imported products and with goods made in the country by foreign subsidiaries.

These private advantages to the recipient firms do not necessarily constitute social benefits. The divergence between private and social benefits is less wide now than it used to be because explicit and implicit costs under licensing agreements seem to be lower than they were before government intervention in the market for imported technology. However, a basic divergence between private advantages and social benefits still remains, particularly where the licensee has obtained exclusive rights of sale and manufacture in the country in question. On the one hand, the diffusion of the technical innovation covered by the agreement to other indigenous producers is retarded and the buyers of the product have often to bear the price of the exclusivity clause. On the other hand, when imports of similar technologies by other domestic firms take place, it will lead to repetitive imports of a technology which is already available in the country.

Summarizing the foregoing discussion, it may be said that indigenous manufacturers have relied to a significant extent on transfer of technology agreements in order to obtain design and manufacturing technology for entering into the field of complex capital goods. While in the case of Korean firms most contracts provide for the transfer of all elements of design and of production know-how, a more selective process of importation is visible in Indian and some Brazilian firms. In the latter case, detailed designs and production know-how are generally the responsibility of the recipient company while basic design is provided by the licensor. In some cases, the agreements in question may also facilitate the development of a basic design capacity in the recipient parties, although the available evidence is far from conclusive about how licensors behave in this respect. Of course, a great deal depends also on the efforts made by licensees, a point dealt with below.

Local Resources Allocated to R & D Activities

The firms surveyed have not relied solely on licensing agreements in order to meet technological requirements involved in the design and manufacture of capital goods. They have also devoted resources to the strengthening of their technological capabilities in this field. The efforts made in that connexion are not always well reflected in the expenditures on R & D. However, these expenditures could provide a first indication of the financial and human resources involved.

Level of R & D Expenditures by Firms

It is difficult to measure the magnitude of these resources and to determine what they consist of, for the available information does not specify the breakdown of technological activities (e.g. quality control, adaptive work, applied research, development work, testing activities). Further, where fiscal concessions are granted in respect of expenditures on R & D [63] the resulting figures may be expected to be somewhat inflated. For these reasons, the following data, obtained in India and Korea on R & D expenditure, have to be treated with caution.

Average expenditures on R & D, in absolute terms and as a percentage of output or sales are shown in Table 2.3. In analysing this table, it is important to bear in mind that R & D expenditures by the Korean firms surveyed were incurred in connection with the manufacture of all their products and not only the product lines which were studied for the purposes of this research.

When compared with the direct payments for imported technology, it is apparent that R & D expenditures by firms studied in Korea have been low, in the three sub-sectors, being somewhat higher the expenditures made by joint ventures.

In the case of India, R & D expenditures are higher than in Korea especially in the machine tool industry. They are also higher than payments devoted to imported technology. Furthermore, in India indigenous firms have allocated relatively more resources to R & D than have joint ventures and foreign controlled firms, the exception being the producers of equipment for process industries. Among indigenous firms, those without foreign collaboration agreements have devoted more to R & D (in relation to sales) than their domestic competitors that operate under

TABLE 2.3 R & D expenditures of the sample firms in 1980 (in thousands of dollars and as percentage of output (India) or sales (Korea)

	Machine tools		Equipment for process industries		Electrical equipment	
	Value	*(%)*	*Value*	*(%)*	*Value*	*(%)*
Korea	*378*	*0.4*	*306*	*0.7*	*672*	*0.5*
Wholly domestic firms	124	4.2	–	–	–	–
Domestic firms with foreign technical collaboration	480	0.4	283	0.5	565	0.3
Joint ventures	–	–	343	1.3	726	0.7
India	*673*	*3.4*	*424*	*2.0*	*3624*	*2.5*
Wholly domestic firms	748	3.4	512	2.7	280	2.9
Domestic firms with foreign technical collaboration	1159	3.0	237	1.4	13760	3.2
Joint ventures	218	1.3	725	3.8	27	1.0
Foreign subsidiaries	335	2.5	–	–	106	1.1

SOURCE   As for Table 2.2

foreign collaboration agreements relating to machine tools and equipment for process industries. Among electrical equipment producers, domestic firms with foreign collaboration agreements have spent relatively more on R & D than their competitors without licensing agreements.

In contrast to Korea, it is remarkable that considerable sums have been devoted to R & D in India not only by indigenous firms without foreign collaboration agreements but also by domestic firms that have relied on licensing agreements. It is also remarkable that foreign subsidiaries and joint ventures in India spend relatively less on R & D. In their case, it seems that the benefits of centralized R & D at their headquarters out-weigh the advantages derived from the lower cost of local research personnel.

No comparable information is available about the Brazilian firms. However, half of the domestic firms[64] have used government loans for technological development which are granted on very favourable terms and are not available to foreign subsidiaries. These loans were used mainly for product development, including the expenditures for importing and absorbing foreign technology.

The R & D expenditure by machine tool makers in India and by some firms in Korea - 3 to 7 per cent of sales - is very high by international standards.[65] In Brazil, the leading domestic firm is devoting a similar proportion of sales to R & D (5-6 per cent). In contrast, these expenditures are relatively low in the electrical equipment sector, an industry in which the ratio of R & D to sales is high in industrialized countries.[66] The reason for the relatively high expenditures on R & D by domestic machine tool manufacturers is probably that it was relatively easier to obtain tangible results in product development in this area of the mechanical industry, at least before the diffusion of NC machine tools.

In the case of the electrical equipment sector, however, where technical progress is very much linked to pure and applied research, particularly in the area of materials, the fruits of the R & D effort are more difficult to obtain.[67]

R & D Activities by Research Institutes

A growing collaboration between the firms and research institutes has been noted in Brazil. In the case of equipment for process industries, local manufacturers in Brazil have been using research institutes for the design of equipment; in one case of reverse engineering a firm producing equipment for process industries has been helped by an institute to find the parameters of design. In Korea, the firms surveyed tend to rely on research institutes, especially in the machine tool sector. In India, indigenous firms have been in close contact with research institutes like the Central Machine Tools Institute and the Central Power Research Institute for their technological requirements. In the case of subsidiaries and joint ventures a similar process has taken place only in the machine tool sector. In addition to being concerned with design, R & D efforts in Brazil and India have related to a variety of operations arising in product engineering and process of production engineering (building up prototypes, quality control systems, better testing facilities, development of specific pieces of equipment, redesigning of jigs and fixtures, etc.

Adaptation of Imported Designs

The object of most of the design activities has been so far to adapt received designs, to use more local materials and to rely less on imported ones (especially as regards detailed designs for parts and components in India and Brazil). As regards adaptations made with a view to using more unskilled labour, it is worth pointing out that in India only two domestic firms without foreign collaboration agreements (one making machine tools and another producing equipment for process industries) and one with licensing agreements relating to equipment for process industries are reported to have made such adaptations. It is clear, therefore, that machinery producers in India have not been concerned with modifying received designs in order to take account of the abundance of unskilled labour in their country.

Some Results of Research Efforts

Although the results of research efforts – both through formal and informal activities – undertaken by the firms surveyed are not easy to quantify, the new products added by surveyed firms in India can be used as proxy indicator.[68] Out of 64 new products introduced by firms surveyed in India since 1975 (i.e. 3.2 products per firm), 18 product additions were made possible by the assimilation of already imported technology along with reliance on intramural research and on research institutes. Wholly domestic Indian firms were responsible for 14 out of these 18 products.[69] The remaining products resulted from licensing agreements (40 products, of which 21 were added by domestic firms with licensing agreements) and from imports of designs (six products).

In the case of Korean sample firms several products in the machine tool industry were the result of the firms' own development and of collaboration schemes with research institutes. However, for most products introduced in recent years imports of technology have been widely used.

Some Implications

The large number of new products originated by licensing agreements in the case of India, and also the limited resources generally allocated to R & D in Korea and Brazil, are strong indicators that reliance on foreign technology and investment tends to substitute rather than complement local design efforts in the sample firms.

However, the fact that a considerable number of engineers are devoted to design in indigenous firms using licensing agreements and to a lesser extent in joint ventures in India cannot be overlooked. Furthermore, the efforts made by some indigenous machine tool firms in the three countries to assign important human and financial resources to technology development as well as their relations with research institutes should be acknowledged, even if they are more the exception than the rule. While in the short term reliance on foreign design technology tends to substitute for indigenous efforts, this may not be the case in the long run in those few firms which are making their own efforts to develop a design capacity in order to consolidate their entry into the design and manufacture of complex capital goods. In the long run, it is only by developing such a capacity that these domestic firms will be able to make their own designs, to compete in domestic and export markets, to obtain more modern designs from licensing agreements and, eventually, to enter into cross-licensing agreements with the leading firms in this industry at the international level. This is not, of course, the strategy followed by foreign subsidiaries, and hence it is understandable that they allocate a relatively small share of their efforts to design activities.

The target of developing an endogenous technological capacity can only be achieved by increasing engineering efforts in order to gain greater acceptance among capital goods users, with the help of appropriate government policies. In order to increase the efforts in this field, the training of design personnel should receive priority. So far, specialized design staff have mostly received limited training under licensing agreements and relatively little use has been made of other schemes (like individual design assistance from foreign experts, sending personnel abroad for design training).

Computer aided design (CAD) is a technology that could help the firms surveyed to overcome some of their difficulties in this field. Although most firms are using computers for engineering calculations, few of them have a CAD system. These systems are sometimes part of the technology transferred under licensing agreements. Although CAD raises the productivity of design engineers, the technology is still not fully developed, especially in its software aspects, and for this reason its potential contribution to strengthening the design capacity of the firms surveyed is still limited.

Summary of Findings

In the light of the information gathered in the course of the survey of producers of capital goods in the three countries studied, the findings may be summarized as follows:

1. In relying on licensing agreements for some of the technology needed to make complex capital goods and despite the limitations of the agreements mentioned above, the firms surveyed in Brazil, India and Korea have been able to initiate their entry into vital segments of this sector. This entry has been facilitated first by the age, size, modernity of the equipment, adequate skill profile and experience of these firms in making standard capital goods, some of which are already exported in sizeable amounts, and, second, by the support given by their governments to the indigenous manufacture of capital goods.

2. While in the case of the Korean sample firms, the evidence of the terms of the technology agreements suggests that these firms have tended to import all elements of technology, in some Brazilian and most Indian firms a more selective process of importation is visible. Although these findings would imply that the latter firms have made more progress in mastering detailed designs and production technology than the Korean firms, the evidence concerning Korea is not strong enough as to corroborate such a conclusion.

3. Formal R & D expenditures by the firms surveyed have been higher in India than in Korea, where both human and financial resources devoted to R & D are rather low. None the less, in some firms surveyed, especially in the machine tool sector, resources devoted to R & D are considerable

and have led to the generation of new products in the countries under consideration.

4. In the case of foreign subsidiaries, the technological impact on the host country is far more limited than the impact made by indigenous makers. Subsidiaries have been committing relatively fewer resources to R & D, they are less linked to local research institutions, and have less technological autonomy in manufacturing than their domestic competitors.

V CONCLUDING REMARKS

Although the capital goods sector in these three countries has a long history, starting from repairs and maintenance of imported equipment and graduating to the production of relatively simple machinery and equipment, it is apparent that the accelerated development of the capital goods sector has been the result of explicit government policies instituted in the case of India in the 1950s and in the case of Korea in the early 1970s. While in Brazil it is more difficult to find a clear-cut change in government policies, a more pronounced orientation in favour of indigenous manufacture of complex capital goods has been visible since 1974.

The progress made in substituting domestic for imported capital goods has been impressive in India and Brazil, where the ratios of domestic production in total apparent consumption are not very different from those of the large industrialized countries.

Domestic manufacturing of capital goods has been fostered in these countries under protection of tariff and non-tariff barriers against similar imported goods. Although the form and nature of the protection have changed in the course of time, available estimates suggest that effective protection has been higher in India than in Korea and Brazil. Korea has also been promoting the import-substituting manufacture of capital goods but in a selective manner and mainly by recourse to financial incentives. At the same time, Korea is the most export-oriented country among the three considered here, although Brazil is making progress as an exporter and has a more diversified composition of capital goods exports than Korea.

The current recession has severely affected the Brazilian and Korean capital goods industries and is responsible for high rates of idle capacity and serious financial problems in some firms. The Indian capital goods industries, however, did not this time suffer the impact of the recession. Although the cyclical nature of the capital goods industries is well known, the length and severity of the recession seem unusual and could have long-term negative consequences for the capital goods industries in both Brazil and Korea.

By contrast with the situation in the chemical or automobile industries, for example, subsidiaries of transnational corporations have not dominated the development of the capital goods industries in the three countries studied, with the notable exception of the electrical equipment sector in Brazil. Indigenous firms have been the driving force behind the development of the capital goods sector in these countries, particularly in the mechanical engineering branches. In the case of India the leaders in two crucial sub-sectors, i.e. machine tools and electrical equipment, are public companies. Private domestic firms, many of them belonging to large conglomerate groups, have dominated the development of the machinery sector in Korea. In Brazil, private domestic companies are very important in the mechanical branches, whereas public companies are active in certain branches only, e.g., aircraft production.

Indigenous firms are older, bigger and more export-oriented than foreign subsidiaries among the enterprises surveyed for the purposes of this study. In fact, a number of these indigenous firms are big even if compared with their counterparts in industrialized countries, and they have been in the business for quite a long time. This is clearly an asset when these firms enter into the more complex segment of the capital goods industries. However, the size of these firms is, to some extent, a reflection of the high degree of vertical integration prevailing in the capital goods sector in the countries studied. This integration creates a heavy burden on the efficiency of leading producers *vis-à-vis* their counterparts in industrialized countries.

The entry of leading producers into the design and manufacture of complex capital goods in order to satisfy the demanding requirements of machinery users has become possible largely through licensing agreements. From the terms of these agreements, it is possible to discern a more selective process of importation on the part of Indian firms, and to some extent of Brazilian ones, than in the Korean firms surveyed. This is apparently a reflection of the progress made by the former firms in learning detailed design and manufacturing technology.

Explicit costs arising from the use of licensing agreements do not seem to be very high, except in Brazil, and restrictive conditions in the contracts are now less frequent than in the past. This is a result both of the experience acquired by the licensees in dealing with their suppliers and of government intervention in the negotiation process. However, the evidence is far from conclusive about the progress made by firms surveyed in mastering design and manufacturing technology. All firms rely on licensors for design technology and most of them have not been able as yet to use licensing agreements to learn design methodology. One reason is the reluctance of licensors to provide recent designs. In any case basic design and, in some cases, even detailed designs for complex capital goods are not yet mastered by leading producers in the countries studied. Accordingly, they suffer from a major handicap which affects their ability to fulfil their role as eventual generators of technological innovations.

As regards manufacturing technology, licensing agreements normally make provision for assistance in the manufacture of specific products according to the quality standards laid down by the licensor. Although this assistance is of great help in improving manufacturing standards linked to specific products, the organization of the production process, relations with sub-contractors, process engineering, organization and methods, etc. are not generally covered by these agreements. Dealing with these matters not only requires considerable time and experience but also calls for specific engineering skills that are not always at the disposal of the firms in question. Handicaps in these areas are, of course, aggravated by the more general deficiencies of the organization of the capital goods sector as a whole in these countries. Needless to say, these handicaps in manufacturing technology affect the performance of machinery producers and hamper their efforts to supply the user industries with capital-saving innovations.

Resources devoted by firms surveyed to R & D are not very substantial, except in the case of India, and generally it is in the machine tool industry that R & D efforts have been greatest. The efforts in question are mostly geared to the adaptation of imported designs to the local conditions. As many engineering initiatives in capital goods industries are not reflected in formal expenditures in R & D, it is not possible to conclude that reliance on foreign design and manufacturing technology has generally been a substitute for rather than a complement to intensive indigenous R & D activities in the countries studied.

None the less, an asymmetry is visible between the progress made in the physical manufacture of complex capital goods on the basis of foreign technology and the development of an endogenous technological capacity in this sector. The human and financial resources devoted to creating such a capacity in the leading producers of capital goods, especially in sectors like electrical equipment, have not been commensurate with the technological requirements. It is for this reason that the entry of the three countries in question into the design and manufacture of complex capital goods is still rather fragile. This fragility is certainly aggravated by some more general deficiencies of the organization of the capital goods sector, like lack of specialization for domestic and export markets, bias in procurement policies of capital goods users in favour of machinery with imported designs, etc.

Policy instruments designed to strengthen indigenous technological capacity in the capital goods sector are needed in order to consolidate the entry of these countries into the complex segments of the machinery industry. The protection given by the State to foster the domestic manufacture of capital goods and the general policies aimed at expanding the educational system, specially in the area of engineering, at strengthening research institutions, at encouraging R & D expenditures through fiscal or financial incentives and at regulating the transactions for the transfer of technology in this field are steps in the right direction. However, as the available information suggests, in the countries studied more progress has been made in substituting domestic for imported capital goods than in substituting domestic for imported technology needed for designing and making those goods; it is clear, therefore, that specific policies are called for. These policies can only be made at the level of the various branches of the capital goods sector and in the light of the trends at the international level regarding the technology to be used, and of the specific circumstances of the country in question.

NOTES

1. This is an abridged version of chapter 3 of D. Chudnovsky and M. Nagao with the collaboration of S. Jacobsson, *Capital Goods Production in the Third World. An Economic Study of Technology Acquisition* (London: Pinter, 1983).
2. N. Rosenberg, *Perspectives on Technology* (Cambridge: Cambridge University Press, 1976) p. 164.
3. See M. Merhav, *Technological Dependence, Monopoly and Growth* (Oxford: Pergamon Press, 1968) p. 30.
4. Rosenberg, *Perspectives*, p. 99.
5. See *Technology Issues in the Capital Goods Sector: A Case Study of Leading Industrial Machinery Producers in Brazil*, study prepared by Mr F. Erber, at the request of the UNCTAD secretariat (TD/B/C.6/AC.7/6) Geneva 1982 (hereafter referred to as Brazilian case study); *Technology Issues in the Capital Goods Sector: A Case Study of Leading Industrial Machinery Producers in India*, study prepared by the Sardar Patel Institute of Economic and Social Research in co-operation with the UNCTAD secretariat (forthcoming) (hereafter referred to as Indian case study); and 'Technology Issues in the Complex Capital Goods Industry in Korea', a study prepared by Young Woo Kim, 1982 (mimeo).

6. The Chinese case is discussed in chapter 4 of Chudnovsky and Nagao.
7. If consumer durables such as radio and TV sets and passenger cars are included in capital goods production, the share of capital goods in total manufacturing value added was 24 per cent in 1979.
8. See *Financial Times*, 22 February 1983.
9. See Kosami, *Korean Machinery* (Seoul, 1981) table 1. These rates refer to ISIC 38 as a whole. Subsector 382 has grown 5.5 times, subsector 383 25 times and subsector 384 13 times.
10. See Bank of Korea, *Monthly Economic Statistics*, no. 12 (1981) p. 105.
11. United States production of machine tools (in contrast dollars) decreased 27 per cent in 1976 as a result of the 1975 recession and not until 1979 were production figures higher than in 1975 in the United States. See National Machine Tool Builders' Association, *Economic Handbook of the Machine Tool Industry 1981–1982* (Westpark Drive, McLean, Virginia) p. 42.
12. See United Nations, *Monthly Bulletin of Statistics*, New York (May 1982) special table A.
13. This slowdown reflects, among other things, the lower rate of growth of the whole Indian economy (3.3 per cent per year) as compared with Korea (10.3 per cent) and Brazil (8.7 per cent) in 1970–79. It is important to bear in mind that industrial production in general, and particularly that of capital goods, grew at a high rate in India until the mid-1960s.
14. *Economic and Political Weekly* (9 October 1982) p. 1634.
15. The corresponding proportions in 1980 were 76 per cent, 68 per cent, 91 per cent and 71 per cent in the United States, Federal Republic of Germany, Japan and Italy, respectively. Except for the United States, the other countries have a positive trade balance in these items.
16. See Brazilian case study, table I.7.A.
17. In the case of India and Korea it is the share of ISIC 382 in ISIC group 38 excluding 3832 and 3843. In the United States, Japan and the Federal Republic of Germany the share of ISIC 382 in ISIC group 38 excluding 3832 and 3843, was 39, 38 and 24 per cent respectively.
18. Stockholm International Peace Research Institute (SIPRI), *World Armaments and Disarmament, SIPRI Yearbook, 1980* (London: Taylor and Francis, 1980) p. 88.
19. Ibid, p. 169.
20. Ibid, p. 89. If it is assumed that the output per employee in the defence industry is the same as in equipment production (ISIC 38), defence industries could be estimated to account for around 20 per cent of the total production of equipment in India.
21. See chapter I, section A, of Chudnovsky and Nagao, for a discussion on complexity in the case of capital goods.
22. See Helio Nogueira da Cruz *et al.*, 'Observaçoes sobre a mudança a technológica no setor de máquinas ferramentas do Brasil' (March 1982) BID/CEPAL/CIID/PNUD Monografia de trabalho No. 47.
23. See Abimaq, 'Máquinas ferramentas para trabalhar metais e carbonetos metálicos', Brazil 1978–80.

24. The following indexes of local integration (as calculated according to FINAME criteria for equipment made in the country) were reported by Electrobas in 1978: Turbines Francis: 75 per cent; Turbines Kaplan: 65 per cent; Transformers 525KV, 200 MVA: 95 per cent; Switches up to 500 kv: 96 per cent. See also Brazilian case study, table II.13.
25. Among Brazil's exports, SITC 724 and 725 amounted to $179 million and passenger cars to $267 million in 1980.
26. In the case of India, industrial plants (for textiles, sugar and cement) accounted for 22 per cent of the exports of capital goods reported by the Engineering Export Promotion Council in 1977/8 (which amounted to $246 million).
27. SIPRI, *World Armaments*, p. 88.
28. In the discussion of the role of such government policies attention will be concentrated on the more recent experiences. No attempt will be made here to discuss the role of government policies in the early development of the capital goods sector in these countries.
29. See Brazilian country case study, paragraph 43 onwards.
30. See 'Experience of the USSR in Building Up Technological Capacity' (TD/B/C.6/52), study prepared by Prof. G. E. Skorov at the request of the UNCTAD secretariat, 1980.
31. See F. Stewart, *Technology and Underdevelopment* (London: Macmillan, 1977) ch. 6, for an excellent discussion of the issue.
32. See J. M. Bhagwati and T. N. Srinivasan, *Foreign Trade Regimes and Economic Development: India* (National Bureau of Economic Research, New York, 1975) ch. 2).
33. Ibid, table 13.1.
34. See Indian case study.
35. See Brazilian case study, paragraph 41.
36. See World Bank, *Brazil: Protection and Competitiveness of the Capital Goods Producing Industries* (Washington, 1980) Report No. 2488-BR, ch. 3, for an extensive discussion and information on this issue. Effective tariff protection in 1973 for capital goods was estimated to be on average 40 per cent. See W. G. Tyler, *Manufactured Export Expansion and Industrialization in Brazil* (Tübingen: J. C. B. Mohr, 1976) p. 246.
37. INPI, *Relatorio de 1981*, Rio de Janeiro.
38. See A. Amsden and L. Kim, 'Korea's Technology Exports' (World Bank, 1982) (mimeo).
39. See Chong Hyun Nam, 'Trade and Industrial Policies and the Structure of Protection in Korea', in W. Hong and L. B. Krause (eds), *Trade and Growth of the Advanced Developing Countries in the Pacific Basin* (Korea Development Institute, Seoul, 1981) table 5. The figure refers to the Balassa method.
40. See L. Westphal, 'Empirical Justification for Infant Industry Protection', World Bank Staff Working Paper No. 445 (1981).
41. See Leroy, P. Jones and Il Sakong, *Government, Business and Entrepreneurship in Economic Development: the Korean Case* (Cambridge, Mass: Harvard University Press, 1980) ch. 8.

42. After machinery, electronic and electrical equipment, which formed the subject of 17.6 per cent of the agreements, and petroleum refining and chemical engineering (16.1 per cent) were the two largest sectors in terms of contracts. If the communications, electricity and metals sectors are included, capital goods industries as a whole accounted for 84 per cent of all agreements on technology transfer.

43. Equipment for process industries comprises instruments and machinery for chemical and petrochemical plants in the countries studied. However, in the case of India some equipment for sugar, cement and paper plants, and in the case of Brazil some steel equipment, mining and oil refining and offshore equipment, are also taken into account.

44. Electrical equipment includes main and auxiliary equipment for the generation and distribution of power. It also includes mechanical equipment for electrical power generation and, in the case of India, power cables.

45. From the fact that all these firms make complex goods, it should not be deduced that these products are of comparable complexity in each subsector in the three countries. The information collected in the field work is not sufficient for making an inter-country evaluation of the products' complexity.

46. See Amsden and Kim, 'Korea's Technology Exports'.

47. See Indian case study, table I.7.

48. See Brazilian case study, paras 15–18 for information on concentration ratios in the Brazilian capital goods sector.

49. As most of the firms surveyed have a diversified product mix, it has been difficult to observe a clear delimitation of their activities, especially between electrical and process industries equipment, and, therefore, to collect appropriate data only for the selected products. However, it is possible to say that, although not strictly covering products which fall in the three selected subsectors, the output of the firms surveyed consists largely of capital goods.

50. Domestic enterprises are those wholly owned by residents. In the tables in this chapter they are divided into domestic enterprises with foreign technical collaboration and into wholly domestic enterprises (i.e. not drawing on foreign technical collaboration).

51. 'Subsidiaries' means firms which are wholly or majority-owned by foreigners, generally transnational firms in the case of Brazil. In India, foreign subsidiaries were those under effective foreign control, though the non-resident equity share does not exceed 40 per cent in conformity with the Foreign Exchange Regulation Act.

52. 'Joint ventures' means firms in which foreign partners have a minority equity participation.

53. In the case of India, the reduced participation of foreign firms is a result of the Foreign Exchange Regulation Act of 1973. See Indian case study, para. 22.

54. The participation of the public sector is very important in India. Public sector units accounted for 57 per cent of the total output of machine tools, 100 per cent of hydrosteam turbines, 95 per cent of boilers and 19 per cent of transformers in 1977/78.

55. Some of the domestic firms operating without licensing agreements had such agreements in the past and are now relying on purchases of designs (e.g. India).
56. Custom-order equipment is equipment not made for stocks, as is the case of the goods manufactured for expected demand. Most but not all custom-order equipment is made to the specifications of users and, therefore, requires modifications in design. The higher design requirements can be considered as an indication of higher complexity of the product.
57. For an analysis of these questions see A. Castaño, J. Katz and F. Navajas, 'Etapas históricas y conductas tecnológicas en una planta argentina de máguinas herramienta', IDB/UN/ECLA/IDRC (Research Programme on Scientific and Technological Development in Latin American) Working Paper No. 38 (Buenos Aires, January 1981).
58. See J. Katz, 'Cambio tecnológico en la industria metalmecánica latinoamericana. Resultados de un programa de estudios de casos', IDB/UN/ECLA/IDRC (Research Programme on Scientific and Technological Development in Latin American) Working Paper No. 51 (Buenos Aires, July 1982).
59. See H. Pack, 'Fostering the Capital Goods Sector in LDC's', *World Development*, vol. 9, no. 3, pp. 229–34.
60. A study of these problems requires several visits to the firms and to the different shops in which the firm is organized. In the visits made to firms surveyed, attention was mostly paid to the general technological strategy and to design problems. However, this does not mean that problems related to the process of production and to the organization of the plant are not important or that they have already been solved in the firms surveyed.
61. As compared with explicit payments in other manufacturing industries and with resources devoted to R & D in the case of India (see Table 2.3).
62. This possibility can arise where the regulation of direct foreign investment is not co-ordinated with the regulation of foreign technology agreements, as is the case in Brazil.
63. In India, there is a tax rebate on equipment purchased for R & D use and 100 per cent depreciation on such equipment within one year is allowed. In addition, the Technical Development Fund may make available the foreign exchange required for some imports of goods and/or technology needed for technological upgrading.
64. One firm making electrical equipment, two enterprises making machine tools and three firms manufacturing equipment for process industries.
65. In the case of firms making machine tools in the United States, R & D expenditures as a proportion of sales in 1981 was 1.9 per cent. See *Business Week*, 5 July 1982.
66. In the electrical equipment sector the R & D sales ratio was 2.9 per cent in 1981 in the United States. (Ibid.)
67. See M. R. Bhagavan, 'Technological Innovations in Indian Industry', *Seminar*, no. 258 (February 1981, New Delhi) for similar conclusions covering innovations in the machine tool and electrical equipment industries in India.

68. This is a proxy indicator because no information is available for measuring the relative complexity of each product addition.
69. It seems that only three of these products were of a complexity similar to that of the products resulting from foreign collaboration or imports of design.

3 A Technological Perspective on The General Machinery Industry in the Republic of Korea

ALICE H. AMSDEN[1]
LINSU KIM

INTRODUCTION

There is nothing extraordinary about the fact that countries classified as less developed produce a large fraction of their general machinery requirements. In the mid-1960s, when the Republic of Korea (hereinafter South Korea or just plain Korea) had paved over the final cracks of its civil war but was only beginning to launch its development drive, it was producing over half its requirements of general machinery (ISIC 382, which includes such items as prime movers, metal working equipment, special industrial machinery, general machinery parts, etc.) (KTA, 1966). At the time, the machinery sector at large (ISIC 38) accounted at most for only about 10–15 per cent of manufacturing value added (EPB, 1966).

The reason the self-sufficiency ratio in general machinery was so high at the time is simple. The entire machinery sector is defined broadly to include fabricated metal products (ISIC 381), general machinery (ISIC 382), electrical machinery (ISIC 383), transport equipment (ISIC 384) and precision machinery (ISIC 385). But even within the general machinery and fabricated metal subsectors – the concerns of this paper – there exists a heterogenous mix of both rudimentary and complex products. As industrialization and its concomitant demands for more complex general machinery increase – phenomena which *are* fairly rare among developing countries – the self-sufficiency ratio tends to fall. If industrialization unfolds successfully, it tends to rise again. In Korea it fell from 52 per cent in

1966 to 13 per cent in 1971, and was up again to 33 per cent a decade later (KOSAMI, 1980, 1982).

The manufacture in Korea of sophisticated metal structures and general machinery has not evolved organically; that is, from simple to technically demanding models in shops which scrimped and saved to grow from small to large. Rather, the modern machinery sector exploded jumbo-size on the industrial scene following the Korean government's turn to heavy and chemical industries in the early 1970s. This left the machinery sector with a dual structure. Integrated machinery affiliates of large *chaebul*, or Korean conglomerates, leap-frogged over small machinery enterprises; if they did not flatten them altogether. We do not, however, concern ourselves with a comparison of the two forms of industrial organization and only juxtapose them when we discuss subcontracting. Rather, our preoccupations and the organization of our paper are as follows.

The first three parts focus on large-scale production of metal structures and general machinery (ISIC 381 and 382). In Section I we air the difficulties of conceptualizing 'performance' in machinery building. We argue that notions of efficiency and the misuse of resources may differ at the aggregate and firm levels. Then we argue that firm-level performance may be grasped in a rough sort of way by assessing the process and extent to which different elements of a *technological capability* have been acquired. We then present in Section II the evidence which we have collected on the acquisition of a technological capability in three integrated machinery works.[2]

In Section III we suggest why performance has been fairly successful in these enterprises. We hang our argument on two of the most striking facts of Korean industrialization. One is that the rate of growth of output of general machinery and metal structures has been phenomenally rapid by historical and world standards. Fast growth of demand has allowed firms to invest a lot and thereby quickly introduce foreign technologies embodied in capital goods; to move rapidly down their learning curves which, in turn, has provided positive feedback for the build-up of their design capabilities; and finally, to reap the benefits of economies of scale. The second fact is the high level of human capital and skills in Korea. It has enabled fast growth policies to be translated into higher productivity rather than higher prices or white elephants.

Because we believe that the rate of growth of output has mattered in the performance of large, Korean machinery works, we devote Section IV to arguing that the rate of growth of output itself has accelerated in no small part due to the high-speed promotional policies of the Korean government.

In Section V we discuss the small-scale machinery sector and sub-contracting.

I THE PERFORMANCE OF LARGE-SCALE MACHINERY SHOPS

Aggregate and Firm-Level Efficiency

The Korean government's turn to heavy industry has come in for a large amount of criticism. True enough, as time has elapsed the chorus of censure has taken on an element of countercyclicality. When capacity utilization and demand were down during the deep world depression of 1979–82, criticism was up. With the first swallow of recovery, however, criticism has dwindled and the government is now even being congratulated for having had the foresight to undertake massive investments in machinery at a time when both interest rates and demand were bottoming during the downswing of 1974–5. Our observations of the machinery sector suggest that some real problems remain but that there are also real achievements to be recognized.

The focus of most criticism is an alleged misallocation of resources at the macro level. At one extreme, one can imagine an argument to the effect that the government has had no business interfering at all in the quantity and quality of investment, the result of which has been too little output per unit of input due to excessive capital-intensity. Further along the spectrum are arguments to the effect that the government has merely gone too far: too much heavy industry and neglect of small firms, too little selectivity in the choice of industries to protect, and too little flexibility in correcting past mistakes (see, for example, Westphal, 1981).

The allocation of resources at the level of the firm, however, has tended to be ignored. Presumably this is because the undeniable presence of excess capacity throughout the machinery sector is taken as glaring proof of the government's flat-footedness. There also appears to be the presumption that if comparative advantage is being violated at the macro level, overly capital-intensive production processes in capital-scarce countries are likely to end in bungling at the firm level as well. This, however, we have not encountered.

Nor do we find this line of reasoning particularly compelling in the most general case. Given the national capital structure, it is perfectly possible for firms to use existing resources efficiently. Assume, for example, one extreme wherein production occurs with only one input, capital. In such a situation, there would be no reason, following plant start-up, to expect a firm in a less developed country (LDC) to produce at lower efficiency than a firm in a developed country (DC). W. A. Lewis (1965) makes an argument to this effect: that firms in LDCs will do better relative to firms in DCs the more process-centred or machine-paced the industry. That is, the more capital-intensive the production technique in labour-abundant countries, possibly the greater the chance for misallocation of resources at the macro level but the lesser the chance for inefficient use of resources at the level of the firm.

Even sectors which utilize highly mechanized or automated production processes, however, have not succeeded in dispensing altogether with inputs of human judgement. Even the most codified and replicable technologies appear subject to unforeseen contingencies which require skills and art to solve. If therefore, we compare two extremes - highly capital-intensive technologies on the one hand, where firms must manage the *attention* of their workers, versus highly labour-intensive technologies on the other, where the task of management is largely limited to policing workers' *physical effort* - then some case might be made that firms in LDCs will be closer to (or above) the efficiency level of firms in DCs in the latter types of operations.

None the less, as we move away from an oversimplified industrial landscape with only two factors of production - raw labour and capital - and add a third - skills - then even more caution is needed about making extrapolations from the macro to the firm level about misuse of resources. If, for example, we understand skills to mean the exercise of discretion by workers which are developed both through formal training and on-the-job experience, then many of the more developed of the developing countries - the so-called NICs[3] - with long industrial histories and large numbers of trained workers, may be said to be gaining a comparative advantage in some products of high skill content. Yet the technologies involved might be the most difficult to transfer because, being skill-intensive, they are the least codified and the most difficult to replicate and master at the level of the firm.

We address this issue below. Suffice it to say here that when we talk about firm-level 'performance' in the South Korean machinery sector, we conceptualize it as a rough, first approximation: not in terms of the marginally efficient use of resources (which our data do not permit us to do) but rather in terms of how far along Korea has moved relative to a rather idealized world technological frontier. In our view, the evidence we present suggests that the performance of the three leading machinery firms we have observed does not fulfil dire expectations of comparative advantage gone awry at the macro level.

The Measurement of Performance

One method to gauge performance is to determine the degree of localization of a commodity (percentage of value added produced by domestic firms). The higher the percentage, presumably the greater the technological mastery. This method, however, tends to be disfavoured for it implies that high local content (rather than specialization) is a good thing. Further, pricing policies rather than technological prowess may overwhelm both make/buy decisions at the firm level and local content percentages nationally. Not surprisingly, a semi-official study of Korean heavy industry which includes data on local content presents a patchy picture (the study is restricted to major producers of power generating, iron and steel, and petrochemical plant equipment; heavy electrical machinery, and marine diesel engines) (KIET, 1982). In some cases, localization was found to be quite high, due allegedly to minimal technological requirements, although factors such as high demand might also have been at play. In the case of other types of machinery (or parts thereof) localization was said to be nil. According to another source of information, 1980 input–output tables, the domestic content of general machinery procured by the government averaged roughly 21 per cent (Seung Jin Kim, 1983).

Many types of general machinery have yet to be produced in Korea. Figure 3.1 puts the progress of the Korean general machinery subsector in a sobering international perspective. As indicated, the general machinery subsector as a percentage of total machinery output in Korea lags considerably behind that of Japan, the United States, and Germany, and even a bit behind that of the other Asian NICs. The percentage accounted for by electrical machinery leads the developed countries, because it includes consumer electronics.

Another approach is to take exports as presumptive evidence of satisfactory performance. The World Bank has favoured this approach in its multi-industry study of the acquisition of a technological capability in four NICs (see note 2). If we look at what are called 'technology exports' (TEs), which for our purposes include steel structures and plant exports (either entire plants or significant parts thereof), then the Korean machiney industry has done quite well (Amsden and Kim, 1982). Although it has exported few full-fledged turnkey plants (save a $200 million cement mill to Saudi Arabia – with the help of Fuller, USA – and an $80 million tyre plant to the Sudan – with the help of Dunlop), exports of steel structures (onshore and offshore) and customized machinery have skyrocketed. Plant exports, very broadly defined, increased at an average annual rate of 123 per cent between 1975 and 1980 and came to account for roughly a quarter of total machinery exports (FKI, 1980). The ratio of plant exports

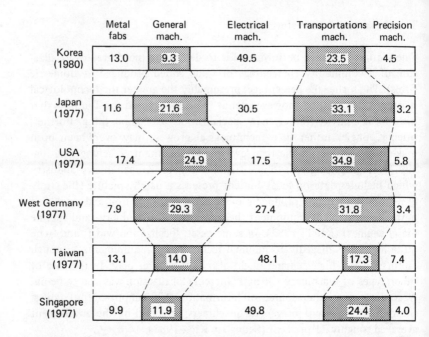

	Metal fabs	General mach.	Electrical mach.	Transportations mach.	Precision mach.
Korea (1980)	13.0	9.3	49.5	23.5	4.5
Japan (1977)	11.6	21.6	30.5	33.1	3.2
USA (1977)	17.4	24.9	17.5	34.9	5.8
West Germany (1977)	7.9	29.3	27.4	31.8	3.4
Taiwan (1977)	13.1	14.0	48.1	17.3	7.4
Singapore (1977)	9.9	11.9	49.8	24.4	4.0

SOURCES   Economic Planning Board, *Mining and Manufacturing Census Report*; Association of Machinery Industries, *Report of Machinery Industries*; Japan Association of Machinery Industries, *Outline of Machinery Industries Statistics* (as cited by Jae Hak Kim, 1982).

FIGURE 3.1   An international comparison of the structure of the machinery industry

to total commodity exports reached 7 per cent (the comparable figure for Germany is over 20 per cent).

Conventional production and export statistics of general machinery in Korea reveal both weaknesses and strengths. Production of general machinery between 1975 and 1981 rose at an astounding average annual rate of roughly 40 per cent.[4] By 1980, 25 per cent of total general machinery output was being exported. The industrial machinery branch within general machinery has had almost as impressive a performance. The manufacture of industrial machinery is often regarded as one rough indicator of a country's technological stature in so far as innovativeness and high productivity throughout the industrial sphere are functions of it. The manufacture of industrial machinery grew at an average annual rate of 27.5 per cent between 1975 and 1981. If one omits the depressed years of the 1980s, then industrial machinery manufacture rose sevenfold between 1975 and 1979. In part this was due to the growing availability of producer goods, as Korea's integrated steel mill came on stream. It was also due to the government's massive investments in infrastructure, which boosted the production of construction and mining machinery. In 1980, over 20 per cent of industrial machinery was exported. Nevertheless, the manufacture of industrial machinery accounts for as little as 20 per cent of total general machinery and contributes to its relatively low self-sufficiency ratio. In 1980, there was an almost $2 billion trade deficit in the general machinery industry. This amount was 2.9 times the $660 million deficit for the rest of the machinery sector. It accounted for as much as 40 per cent of the deficit of total merchandise trade (Jae Hak Kim, 1982).

Exports are an imperfect gauge of a country's competitiveness if they are highly subsidized. None the less, the competitiveness of general machinery depends only in part on price. Quality is critical and depends on skill, manufacturing know-how, and design; which can be subsidized, but only very indirectly.

The approach we use in Section II to gauge performance is to discover the breadth of firms' technological capabilities. In industries undergoing import substitution such as general machinery, whose firms have barely begun to move down their learning curves, we believe this to be a telling measure of performance. By a technological capability we mean the ability, embodied in people, to select the appropriate technology; to implement it; to operate the production facilities so implemented; to adapt and improve them, and possibly to create new processes and products. A technology may be purchased but a technological capability is acquired only through the build-up of human capital. A technological capability involves an understanding of the principles behind what is brought in from outside and an ability to introduce modifications in order to get better results (Dahlman, 1982).

Although many elements comprise a technological capability – including, say, feasibility studies, start-up, modifications and improvements, expansions, and R & D – our study of fabricated metals and general machinery manufacture focuses on only three elements: the initial technology acquisition, operations and maintenance, and in particular design (the creation of new products). The capability of the three firms we examine to undertake expansions has been untested because all have suffered from excess capacity; there has been no question of expansion. As for the capability to modify and improve process and product, this is constantly occurring in job shops which make customized equipment. Most of the more subtle deviations in production techniques from, say, those of the USA or Japan eluded us and remain to be studied.

II THE ACQUISITION OF A TECHNOLOGICAL CAPABILITY

The major source of technology of large, modern firms in the general machinery subsector has been foreign licenses. The machinery industry in the aggregate (ISIC 38) has accounted for a disproportionate share of Korea's total foreign technology licenses. Between 1962 and 1981, it accounted for almost half of all technology imports (by number) but barely 10 per cent of total domestic value added, even toward the end of the period (figures supplied by the Ministry of Finance). Of the total number of technology licenses purchased by the machinery sector at large, the general machinery subsector[5] purchased more than half, despite the fact that it accounted for less than 10 per cent of the value added of total machinery production (see Figure 3.1).

There are several reasons why the general machinery subsector is so foreign license-intensive. It produces a multitude of differentiated products. Most of these involve a long string of distinct processes, each of which may be licensed: from casting and forging to fabrication, testing, subassembly, and assembly. No two products may be alike so that no two processes or technologies may be alike.

The fact that the general machinery subsector accounts for a large fraction of foreign licenses, purchased from a multitude of sources, and used for a diversity of purposes, we take as indicators of the difficulties of technology transfer.[6] Given these difficulties, we now suggest that the subsector has performed relatively well.

The three machine shops we examine are highly integrated – in terms of both product and process – so that it is not surprising that they, too, are foreign license-intensive.

The largest and most integrated of them is the Korea Heavy Industries and Construction Company (KHIC), which employs some 12 000 people. Once under private ownership, it was bought out by the state when it ran into financial difficulties. Capital investment is estimated by KHIC to amount to as much as $560 million, financed primarily by foreign loans. For some, KHIC has come to symbolize the excesses of government-promoted import-substitution in heavy industry. At one time KHIC had as many as 50 foreign licenses to gain technology for items as diverse as castings and forgings, boilers and steam turbines, fork lifts and bulldozers, and spinning and paper making machinery. The number of licenses has declined to roughly 30 due to deficient demand. KHIC specializes to a certain extent in equipment for power generation, over which it has a state granted monopoly for the domestic market. It also subcontracts castings and forgings to smaller machinery firms.

Hyundai Heavy Industries (HHI), the next largest integrated machinery manufacturer, employs some 10 000 people. It has 30–35 foreign licenses both for general machinery and shipbuilding, which are undertaken at the same site (the largest shipbuilding site in the world).

The smallest integrated machinery builder we study is Samsung Heavy Industries (SHI), which employs some 2000 people. The way it has acquired its technology has differed from the above in so far as the Samsung Group's machinery and shipbuilding divisions are part of a joint venture with the Japanese giant Ishikawajima-Harima Heavy Industries (IHI). SHI received much of its original technology from IHI. A licensing agreement between the partners has called for assistance from layout to start-up and beyond. Even so, SHI has a long list of foreign licenses with unaffiliated companies: six, for example, with MESTA (USA), now bankrupt, for steel equipment (primary, plate, hot strip, structural, cold strip and billet and bar mills).

The fact that HHI and SHI are members of two of the largest *chaebul* has aided their acquisition of a technological capability; and has possibly given them an edge over KHIC (the five largest *chaebul*, which include Hyundai and Samsung, account for as much as 21.5 per cent of total manufacturing sales) (Lee Kyu Uck, forthcoming). First, *chaebul* membership has enabled the two machinery divisions not only to weather years of excess capacity and possibly negative returns but even to take a longer view and to plough money from other divisions into learning, human capital development, and R & D. KHIC could only do this under heavy public attack.

The *chaebul* also tend to attract the best among Korea's pool of relatively well-educated people. Both HHI and SHI then subject new recruits to fairly extensive in-house training. Large numbers of both salaried and *non-salaried* personnel are dispatched overseas for further training. Finally, the latest step HHI has taken to build up its human resources is to hire seven foreign engineers directly. KHIC has been unable to follow suit for lack of cash to pay the extremely high salaries which such personnel command.

HHI and SHI have also benefited from intra-corporate technology transfers. Both *chaebul* have divisions (electronics and automotive, for example) whose own technological progress raises the standards of general machinery manufacture.

Intra-corporate technology transfers have also bolstered sales. The exports of a turnkey cement mill by what was then the construction arm of Hyundai pooled the know-how of Hyundai Cement and Hyundai Engineering (HHI now supplies cement-making equipment as well). Most important, when the derived demand for general machinery crashed in the late 1970s, both machinery shops competed for metal fabrication jobs (ISIC 381). Steel structures came to account for as much as 50 per cent of SHI's output in a typical recession month. The know-how to fabricate onshore and offshore facilities came from each *chaebul's* shipbuilding division, one of the first heavy industries to arrive on the scene; and engineering arm, whose apprenticeship was largely served on local, Vietnamese, and Middle Eastern construction projects.

Even in the absence of technical linkages, intra-corporate demand has played an important role; in rewarding the first contract in a subsector where the Catch 22 is reputation; and in sheer volume of demand – the Samsung Group has tended to account for roughly 20 per cent of SHI's orders (with IHI tending to account for another 10–15 per cent).

The build-up of high-calibre personnel, both technical and administrative, has helped in the management of the day-to-day problems of production. The management systems of the three firms appear quite distinct, with Samsung at one end learning heavily towards the Japanese model and Hyundai at the other dominated by its founder. But whatever the system, in large integrated job shops, functions such as scheduling, operations, maintenance, and materials, production, and quality control, are quite difficult to manage. This is indicated by the development pattern as late as in 1982 of the nine Japanese engineers from IHI stationed at SHI. None, for example, was in R & D. Rather, one was in the Welding Development department (an indication of the importance of steel structures in SHI's output), one was in production control, two were in quality, and the rest were in operations on the shop floor. All three firms agree that the management of production remains as difficult as the management of technology.

Typically, a foreign license in the general machinery subsector involves an exchange of personnel and technical assistance for *manufacturing engineering*: production methods, standards, tool designs, route sheets, quality specs, etc. This means that ultimately a design capability can be acquired only through trial and error or experimentation. *Small* machinery manufacturers in Korea typically acquire their original technology through reverse engineering. The more successful of them go on to buy foreign licenses when it becomes necessary to upgrade product and process (Amsden and Kim, forthcoming). Machinery firms which are large simply invert this sequence and begin with foreign licenses and end with something akin to reverse engineering. They possibly also apply a more scientific approach to learning. But foreign licenses cannot substitute for a 'hands on' approach to design.

We turn now to the acquisition of a design capability for three products: materials handling equipment, power generating equipment, and heavy construction equipment, although mention is made of other products where appropriate. The three firms we study emphasize design because of its intrinsically higher profitability. First, a good design is a competitive advantage. Second, it can mean considerable savings on raw materials and machining time. Third, it can be used again and again, if need be with minor modifications, whereas fabrication always requires renewals of labour and raw materials. In other words, value added in design is higher than in other project stages. Fourth, some foreign licenses restrict exporting.

Materials Handling Equipment

Of all subdivisions of machinery in HHI, materials handling has perhaps advanced the furthest technologically. HHI began making overhead cranes for its engineering division without a foreign license. It got a foreign license about seven years ago at the insistence of an overseas client. The license was with Delattre-Levivier (DL) of France for overhead cranes, special cranes for steel plants and jib cranes. DL provided drawings and went much further than simply providing technical assistance for manufacturing engineering. It also provided instructions on how to calculate designs and computer design programs. Even so, HHI continued developing its own designs for small overhead cranes based on its own computer programs. It imported technology on computers from the United States and modified programs for special cranes.

One of the US engineers who now works for HHI formerly worked for Exxon. According to the American, the capability of HHI in materials handling is far higher than anticipated and the capabilities of the basics (maths and science) are as good or better than in the United States. What HHI lacks is experience. Materials handling is not high-tech but there is no one way to design electrical codes, structural systems, etc. The American engineer estimates that HHI is two years behind, say, Exxon or McDonnell Douglas, in learning how to put materials handling systems on the computer. Customer specifications change and CAD/CAM is awkward to use. The problem is getting more production data to aid in design. A very big plus for HHI is that, unlike most American outfits, it does fabrication as well as design.

Foreign engineers in other subdivisions also maintain that the major stumbling block confronting HHI is a lack of experience. There haven't been enough mistakes or enough knowledge to make correct decisions. If computer programs for designs are commercially available, then there is no problem. But if know-how is company specific, it is hard to get. HHI has had to develop the same know-how itself, with its own computer, for power plants, desalination plants, petrochemical equipment, etc.

Power Generating Equipment

In the case of most models of boilers, it was relatively easy for KHIC to catch up in manufacturing engineering with international practices in two or three years of extensive training – either at its licensors' plants or in Korea under its licensors' direction (GE and Combustion Engineering). The improvement of a design capability has been more difficult. There are various ways KHIC has attempted to improve boiler design. It has sent some 60–70 people to its licensor. Whether in the classroom, shop floor, or in a sample design case (KHIC's engineers join the licensor's team), learning covers design standards and the use of computer programs. This, however, is cookbook know-how. While such know-how may cover 90 per cent of the design of a boiler, the competitive edge is in the non-standardized remaining 10 per cent.

The second stage of design is attempting to uncover the (10 per cent) hidden know-whys. To do this requires comparing the characteristics of each design. The more experience, the greater the capability. In this second phase, the greatest help comes when the foreign licensor sends engineers to work at KHIC.

In the third phase, KHIC tries to design as much as possible itself; the licensor only does a review.

KHIC's progress, of course, has depended on the complexity of the boiler (or pressure vessel, heat exchanger, etc.). Complexity depends on many variables including size. The smaller the size, the greater the ability to build a pilot. Design capability depends on production. There is a feed-back from production to design, as taught by the Japanese.

KHIC is still lacking a capability in turnkeys. It can only design the components or hardware of most power plants (or any other plants, for that matter). It lacks manpower with knowledge of plant engineering: for supervision of architectural engineering, proposal engineering, conceptual engineering, etc. There is a vicious circle: KHIC need experience but can only get it with sufficient capability. This circle is only broken under fast growth conditions worldwide, when companies in advanced countries, typically licensors, pass on smaller orders to Korea.

Earthmoving Equipment

KHIC fabricates two models of excavators: one of its own design (medium hydraulic pressure) and one under foreign license (high pressure) which it is prohibited from exporting. Its own model is a conventional system more suitable for the Korean market. KHIC acquired a design capability while learning through the assembly of parts (for five years). It got additional technical information from anywhere it could: journals, the Korean Institute of Metals and Machinery (KIMM), etc. It made two sample machines and then evaluated them. Then it started the pilot production of 3–5 machines, which it leased to customers. Some parts were CAD, others not. The problem has been insufficient experience.

From narratives such as these, we infer the following about performance in the general machinery subsector of Korea. Despite the difficulties of technology transfer, technological capability has come to include design, at least for a limited subset of products. There are also many signs of progressive improvements in performance.

Conclusions

From narratives such as these, we infer the following about performance those which are renewed tend to be for more-complex models or to satisfy dubious customers. HHI will renew its license with Delattre-Levivier, but omit most items which it now can do on its own. HHI deems such a license necessary both for technological reasons and to secure overseas orders. Each year SHI also renews its license with its partner, IHI, but year by year the breadth of items declines while their depth increases.

Second, one notices progress on individual projects. Take, for example, 100 ton boilers ordered by POSCO, Korea's integrated steel works: in the first project *IHI* did 80 per cent of the design, in the second project *SHI* did 80 per cent, and in the third project SHI did 90 per cent. This mirrors an increase in local content in all of POSCO's projects. In Phase I of the construction of POSCO, 12.5 per cent of capital goods was supplied locally. By Phase IV, this percentage had increased to 35 per cent. This was in spite of the fact that total investment in capital goods was 442 in Phase IV compared with 7.52 in Phase I (billion won) (Amsden and Kim, forthcoming).

Third, word of mouth may not be the most reliable indicator of performance, but it is often one important criterion in the sales of machinery firms. This being the case, we simply record the fact that of all the foreign engineers we encountered who were connected in one way or another with the three companies we studied (licensors, employees, capital goods suppliers, inspectors, etc.), all had nothing but admiration bordering on amazement for both product and process.

Finally, orders for general machinery are sharply on the rise again. Whereas general machinery production amounted to $1 762 million in 1981 and $1 946 million in 1982, it leaped to an estimated $3 033 million in 1983 (KOSAMI, 1984).

We were surprised not to find performance constrained by a lack of familiarity with computer systems, either for manufacture, design, or incorporation in final product. 'Mechatronics' did not appear to constitute a major stumbling-block in the limited subset of machinery we examined. What remained a problem for design was collecting sufficient production data, whether to be stored in the mind of a craftsman or in the memory of a computer. We turn, therefore, to an examination of how fast rates of growth of production influence performance.

III THE TECHNOLOGICAL ADVANTAGES OF FAST INCREASES IN DEMAND

We think it fair to say that almost all economic historians recognize a phenomenon of cumulative causality in the process of economic development and decline. Economies which begin to grow rapidly tend to grow even more rapidly, but once decline sets in, there ensues a self-reinforcing downward spiral. We think it also fair to say that most economists recognize only one segment of this circular process: in the upward case, the loop that runs from technological progress (typically taken as exogenous) to increases in productivity to increases in output. What is ignored is the loop running from increases in output to increases in productivity, with technological change, broadly defined, sandwiched in between.

When the rate of growth of demand/output is very rapid, as it has been throughout Korean industry including the general machinery subsector, then the rate of growth of productivity tends to be very rapid as well. There are three reasons for this (Amsden, forthcoming), and each will be discussed in turn. First, faster growth gives rise to more investment which embodies new technologies. Second, faster growth gives rise to greater learning about manufacturing operations, which in turn sends signals up to Engineering about how to improve design and manufacturability. Thus, the whole process of innovation advances. Third, faster growth gives rise to greater economies of scale, specialization, and the division of labour.

The connection between increases in output, and improvements in productivity and firms' performance, is not automatic. It depends on the political economy of the country and the culture of the firm. The discussion of the general machinery subsector which follows incorporates these factors where appropriate.

Investment

The rapid rate of investment in the general machinery subsector can be fathomed by looking at the rate of growth of its tangible fixed assets and gross capital stock. According to calculations by the Bank of Korea, the average annual rate of growth of tangible fixed assets in the general machinery subsector was 54 per cent between 1975 and 1982 (Seung Jin Kim, 1983). Gross capital stock rose at an average annual rate of almost 60 per cent between 1973 and 1981 (KDI, 1982). Little wonder that during the same time period output and labour productivity in general machinery were growing at average annual rates of approximately 54 per cent respectively (EPB, various years).

Rapid increases in productivity presumably followed rapid increases in investment because the latter incorporated new innovations (the domestic content of such investments is unknown although most of the capital stock of the three machine shops we study is foreign made). Installations of new capacity also presumably prompted the high imports of technical assistance discussed in Section II. That is, Korea acquired foreign technology so rapidly, in part simply because it was growing so rapidly.

The investments of the general machinery branch have been financed by both foreign and domestic loans. The debt–equity ratio of the general machinery subsector, while slightly higher than that of the Japanese general machinery subsector in the late 1970s (MCI, 1979), has consistently fallen below the ratio for all of Korean manufacturing. Whereas the debt–equity ratio for all of manufacturing averaged 237 per cent in 1965–73, 350 per cent in 1973–9, and 470 per cent in 1980–81, the comparable percentages for the general machinery subsector were 177 per cent, 338 per cent, and 301 per cent respectively (BOK, various years). Nevertheless, these ratios are high by almost any other country's standards.

High debt–equity ratios tend to reinforce a fast growth syndrome: not only do they raise the level of investment above what it might otherwise be but they also push the break-even point on investment to a higher output level; which possibly pressures firms to produce still more, regardless of the degree of competitiveness of their environment (Piper and Weinhold, 1982).

New investments in general machinery have also been financed by direct foreign investments (DFI); although these have not been overly important in this subsector. DFI accounted for less than one-fifth of value added in general machinery in 1980 (up, however, from 4 per cent in 1971). The general machinery subsector accounts for approximately 6 per cent of cumulative total direct foreign investment in South Korea (Dong Se Cha, 1983).

Learning

The faster the rate of growth of output, the faster the accumulation of experience, which is central to learning and innovation. Learning in the industrial context, and the higher productivity with which it has come to be associated, once tended to be identified with the experience accumulated by individual workers through the repetition of tasks. Now it is more generally recognized to encompass firm-wide efforts to acquire greater control over products and processes. Organization-wide learning may be attributed to two overlapping yet distinct sources: 'science based' learning, furthered in the classroom or laboratory; and what might be termed 'art-based' learning, enhanced largely through on-the-job experience. The greater the cumulative number of jobs, the greater the potential for the enhancement of craftsmanship.

This may be illustrated with a simple graph (see Figure 3.2). On the horizontal axis is time and on the vertical axis is the gestation period

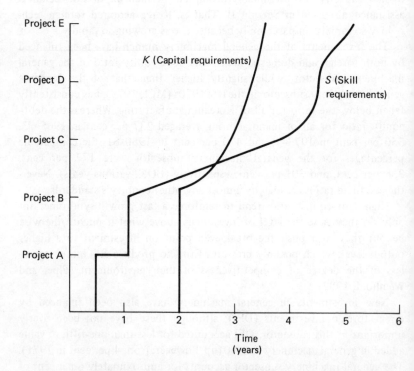

FIGURE 3.2 Gestation period for capital (K) and skills (S) necessary to execute progressively more difficult projects

necessary to accumulate the labour and capital needed for projects A, B, C, etc., whose technological complexity rises as one moves up the vertical scale. Thus, in the case of, say, Project C, it would take three years to ready the fixed capital necessary for production but it would take more than three years for labour, at some critical rank, to reach the required level of skill. To lower capital per unit of output and raise capacity utilization and profits, the 'S' curve must move towards the left.

How and to what extent the level of skills is raised may be expected to vary by industry, type of skill, and the length of the purse allocated by firms to learning. In, say, the petrochemical industry, the ability to increase yields of a semi-automatic process may necessitate extensive laboratory experimentation and in-class training of computer specialists. In the general machinery industry, by contrast, increased productivity may arise from superior designs which are informed partly from science-based learning but more especially from additional data gathered through additional production experience.

Samsung Heavy Industries suggests that if all the time of its designers had been spent in the office it would have taken as long as indicated in Figure 3.2 before an in-house capability to undertake, say, Project C was attained. But the acquisition of a design capability sufficient to execute Project C was moved forward in time by the extensive field experience gained in a fast-growth setting. Stated otherwise, although SHI, unlike its two closest Korean competitors, KHIC and HHI, has unlimited access to the drawings of its Japanese collaborator, its design capability is seemingly no greater than theirs because its manufacturing experience is no greater.

As noted earlier, despite the difficulties of technology transfer, manufacturers of certain subsets of general machinery have managed to acquire a design capability. This appears due to the fact that such a capability leans more towards the 'art' rather than the 'science' end of the learning spectrum, assuming that it is harder for firms in LDCs to reach the world technological frontier in R & D-intensive sectors versus sectors which lean more on the accumulation of experience. We can now add that movement down the 'art' end of the learning spectrum has tended to be rapid in Korea because the rate of growth of demand had tended to be rapid. In fast-growth, newly industrializing settings, therefore, industries such as general machinery may be hypothesized to advance further in the acquisition of a technological capability than industries which are science-based but easier to transfer, as measured by numbers of foreign licenses, multitude of sources, and diversity of processes involved.

Three factors operative in Korea but operative only to a lesser extent in other LDCs have facilitated the innovativeness of Korean industry. First, if learning is a function of experience, then the accumulation of experience by the Korean working population has been accelerated by exceptionally long hours of work. Official statistics are believed to understate average hours worked per year per worker (especially administrative and higher technical personnel). Even so, such statistics reveal a work-year in general machinery of 2800 hours (in 1977, a peak year) (Ministry of Labour, various years). For rough estimates, most studies in the United States assume a working year of 2000 hours (which is high by European standards). By contrast, a study of the Korean heavy machinery industry assumes for its capacity calculations an eleven-hour working day, 300 days a year, or a 3300-hour working year (KIET, 1982, p.476). The length of the Korean working-day appears to be longer than that of almost any other LDC (Amsden, 1981).

Second, the absorption of foreign technology has undoubtedly been facilitated by Korea's relatively highly educated population. Even by 1960, Korea enjoyed a level of human resource development far above what one would have expected by international standards from its GNP per capita (Harbison and Myers, 1965). The percentage of tertiary students in engineering in Korea is presently at least double the figure for Argentina, Brazil, India, and Mexico. Scientists and engineers per million population are also far greater in Korea than in these other NICs (Dahlman, 1982).

Third, innovativeness in Korea has been aided by what, to generalize, appears to be Korean corporate strategy to grow competitive by making use of sequentially more sophisticated foreign technologies but internalizing knowledge each step of the way as quickly and thoroughly as possible. This policy is complemented by a highly effective nationalism on the part of the government (as discussed shortly) with respect to the localization of both know-how and the production of capital goods (as in the case of POSCO, referred to earlier).

Finally, 'science-based' learning has begun to advance in Korea's general machinery industry, as measured by expenditures on R & D. These almost doubled between 1976 and 1978, then nose-dived during the depression of 1979–81, but then began to rise again in 1982. The subsector's expenditures on R & D as a percentage of sales has consistently exceeded the average for all of manufacturing; often by a factor of two. In 1976, 1980, and 1982, the percentage was 1.2 per cent (MOST, various years). Bearing in mind the difficulties of making international comparisons, this measures up somewhat favourably with the percentage (but not absolute value) for the general machinery subsector of Japan (1.9 per cent in 1979) but unfavourably even with the percentage for the USA (5.0 per cent in 1977) and West Germany (2.7 per cent in 1977) (Seung Jin Kim, 1983).

Economies of Scale

Faster growth may be expected to enhance firm and industry performance because of the greater opportunities it creates for specialization and a division of labour. None the less, neither greater specialization nor a finer division of labour between or within firms appears yet to have accompanied faster growth in either the general machinery industry as a whole or the three large job shops under consideration. Subcontracting or specialization among firms has advanced but little, as discussed in Section V. A lack of specialization by product also appears to characterize the three large job shops we study. What, then, are the advantages, if any, of the grandiose scale of such enterprises?

First, they allow a greater integration of horizontal managerial functions: Engineering and Manufacturing can be lodged under the same roof, allowing for better communications and co-ordination of activities. Ironically, in the US heavy machinery sector, where the division of labour is greater, these two functions tend to be the specialty of independent firms. Bechtel, say, does design engineering but little manufacturing. Yet assuming economies of scale in either manufacturing or engineering, then the three Korean firms we study may be representative of the firm size which must be attained to accommodate both operations.

Second, the structure of the general machinery subsector differs from that of the USA in so far as large machinery manufacturers in the USA tend to be more specialized by product. Generalizing somewhat, one American firm will make equipment for the steel industry while another will cater to the capital requirements of the petrochemical sector, etc. By contrast, large shops in Korea are multi-product. This appears to be a consequence of market rather than manufacturing considerations. The domestic market is too small for special-purpose industrial equipment manufacturers and a heavy reliance on foreign sales is presumably too risky, especially when firms are at the top of their learning curves. A supply-side virtue of combining the manufacture of multi-products in one firm may be a cross-fertilization of know-how and greater flexibility. A demand-side necessity is a reduction of reliance on a single product. Hence, the creation of integrated machine shops to reach international competitiveness in price and quality may be inescapable in Korea.

If all the above assumptions about scale are realistic, then there are important implications for the level and structure of tariffs necessary to protect the infant general machinery industry. If competitiveness requires integrated, multi-product machinery works with large capital outlays, then protection may have to be greater, less selective, and hence of longer duration than otherwise.

Large scale in the three machinery works we examine and in the general machinery subsector seems to have gone hand-in-hand with acute excess capacity. Capacity utilization throughout the general machinery subsector averaged only 51 per between 1973 and 1982 (KDB, 1982). This, however, was higher than the utilization rate (29 per cent) of the Korean ship-building industry, part of the transport machinery subsector and one of Korea's star exporters. Capacity utilization in general machinery, moreover, while low, tended to rise between 1973 (when it stood at 50.1 per cent) and 1979 (when it reached 74.9 per cent), although it tumbled during the depression of 1980–82.

One possible explanation for excess capacity is an insufficiency of skills both to produce higher value machinery and to make fuller use of existing facilities (as illustrated by Figure 3.2). One could also argue that either too much or too little state intervention is to blame. Capacity in the machinery subsector may be redundant due to the government's poor demand fore-casts for individual products (which appears to be the curse of KHIC in the case of power generating equipment – KIET, 1982) and to prodigal incentives which drew too many producers. Alternatively, one could argue that the failure of the government to limit entry through licensing (i.e., to arbitrate politically amongst the *chaebul*) has been at fault.

Before turning to a more focused discussion of tariffs and government incentives to the general machinery subsector, we mention one positive consequence of excess capacity for performance: it has allowed firms the luxury of moving down their learning curves without the additional worry of tight scheduling and production control. This may be another reason why a very rapid rate of growth of output has provoked increases in productivity rather than industrial disasters.

IV GOVERNMENT SUPPORT FOR THE GENERAL MACHINERY SUBSECTOR

The Korean government has come in for heavy criticism for excessively subsidizing the general machinery subsector.[7] Subsidization is said to be excessive in two senses. One is distributional: large machinery firms have been disproportionately nurtured relative to small ones, as discussed in the next section. The other is absolute: it is argued that the overall magnitude of subsidization has been superfluous. In what follows we attempt to convey to LDCs that wish to emulate the experience of Korea that sub-sidization of its general machinery subsector began early, has differed from the form it has taken in the consumer-oriented segments of the machinery industry as a whole, and has been 'substantial'. Unfortunately we offer no quantitative standard for comparison but merely list as briefly as possible, with some editorializing, the devices to which the government has resorted.

The build-up of a capability in general machinery as well as the manpower to complement it were conceived of fairly early on by the government. In 1968, when import-substitution of light manufactures was at its height during the second five-year plan, the government published the Machinery Industry Promotion Act, which sketched the elements of an industrial policy for capital goods production (MCI, 1979). An institution now called the Korea Advanced Institute for Science and Technology (KAIST), formerly organized into separate branches for R & D and university-level training, was planned as early as 1965.

It was only in 1973, however, with the proclamation of the government's turn to heavy and chemical industries, that plans to manufacture machinery began to be implemented and the importance of technology in industrialization began to be taken more seriously. We have already referred to the successes of the general machinery subsector in terms of rates of growth of output, exports, localization, and the creation of technological capability. The machinery sector as a whole also grew at a spectacular average annual rate of 33 per cent in the decade from 1973 to 1983 (figures for 1983 are estimates) (52 per cent between 1973 and 1978 and 10 per cent thereafter) (EPB, 1983). We turn now to the means used by the government to achieve these ends. We first look at the industrial protection and subsidization systems now in effect for machinery. Then we turn momentarily to the incentive schemes for manpower and technological development.

Current Industrial Protection System

Tariffs do not play an important role in the protection of the machinery sector, which constantly results in higher nominal than actual tariff rates.[8] Rather, protection has come in the form of quantitative import restrictions. With the implementation of promotion policies for the machinery industry in 1972, the import liberalization rate[9] in the machinery industry declined to around 40 per cent. During the second half of 1978, the government came under pressure to liberalize but its efforts were halted with the coming of recession in 1979. By the second half of 1983, the rate stood at 60.7 per cent, about 20 per cent lower than the rate for all of industry (see Table 3.1). Significantly, the liberalization rate was far higher in general machinery (53 per cent) than in electronics or automobiles (10 per cent and 0.0 per cent respectively).

TABLE 3.1 Trends on import liberalization rate[1] in machinery industry (by CCCN 4 digit) (in %)

	2nd half of 1967 & 1st half of 1968	2nd half of 1975 & 1st half of 1976	2nd half of 1977 & 1st half of 1978	2nd half of 1981 & 1st half of 1982	2nd half of 1982 & 1st half of 1983	2nd half of 1983 & 1st half of 1984
1 Industry	61.7	50.5	53.9	71.3	70.9	75.2
Machinery industry	55.9	35.4	44.5	55.0	55.9	60.7
Fabricated metal products	44.4	39.7	54.0	79.4	81.0	87.3
General machinery	66.7	28.8	41.0	47.0	48.5	53.0
Electrical machinery	40.0	14.3	22.9	31.4	31.4	34.3
(Electronics)	(40.0)	(10.0)	(10.0)	(10.0)	(10.0)	(10.0)
Transport equipment	70.4	59.3	59.3	59.3	59.3	59.3
(Automobiles)	(33.3)	(0.0)	(0.0)	(0.0)	(0.0)	(0.0)
(Shipbuilding)	(80.0)	(80.0)	(80.0)	(60.0)	(60.0)	(60.0)
Precision machinery	60.5	42.1	44.7	50.0	50.0	55.3

NOTE 1 The import liberalization rate is defined as follows:

$$ILR = \frac{T - R}{T}$$

where *ILR*: import liberalization rate.
   T: number of total items by CCCn 4 digit,
   R: number of restricted import items by CCCN 4 digit according to MCI's *Annual Export & Import Notice*.

Because the *ILR* here is calculated based on CCCN 4 digit level, the values here are underestimated compared with the values of ILR calculated based on CCCN 8-digit level.

SOURCE As cited in Seung Jin Kim (1983).

In addition to the quantitative import restrictions just described, the government monitors the flow of imports indirectly through its control of credit, import licensing, and domestic content requirements. An importer who intends to import machinery exceeding $1 million must announce this in advance to KOSAMI,[10] which may decide that if a comparable machine can be produced locally, the import ought not to occur. Escalating local content requirements for certain industrial products further discourage imports (the industries affected so far have largely been cement, paper, hydro, atomic, and electric power generation; chemicals and petrochemicals; steel; and most recently textiles).

Current Industrial Subsidization Systems

A certain portion of the investment costs of the machinery industry is subsidized either by being exempted an equivalent amount from corporate and personal income taxes or by being favoured with special depreciation scheduling (Tax Exemption and Reduction Act). The tax exemption ratio is lower for the machinery industry as a whole than for all manufacturing (see Table 3.2). The tax exemption ratio is also higher for general machinery than for other machinery subsectors.

TABLE 3.2   Domestic tax exemption for manufacturing (1979) (in billion won and %)

	Amount of tax computed (A)	Amount of tax exempted (B)	Tax exemption ratio (B/A) (%)
Manufacturing	269.3	57.1	21.2
Primary metal products	28.5	17.0	59.6
Machinery industry	59.1	18.5	31.3
Fabricated metal products	6.7	1.1	16.4
General machinery	7.9	3.2	40.5
Electrical machinery	26.2	9.1	34.7
Transport equipment	16.2	4.7	29.0
Precision machinery	2.1	0.5	23.8

NOTE   The amount of tax exempted is a function of the allowances made for key industries in Article 12, Tax Exemption & Reduction Act.
SOURCE   Tax Administration Agency, as cited by Seung Jin Kim (1983).

The differential treatment of general machinery and consumer-oriented machinery thus involves both import restrictions and tax exemptions; and seems quite sensible in principle. Because efficiency throughout industry depends on the quality of general machinery, importations of general machinery, on the one hand, are made *relatively* easy, should locally made equipment be judged to be of exceptionally poor quality; on the other, tax exemptions are relatively low, in order to stimulate higher-quality domestic manufacture. In the contrasting case of luxuries (mainly motor cars and consumer electronics), imports are effectively barred and domestic tax breaks are relatively small.

The majority of capital supplied to the machinery industry consists of preferential loans. To increase domestic demand for machinery, preferential loans have also been extended to the consumers of machinery. Finally, to push along design, preferential loans have been earmarked for firms which have 'Newly Developed Innovative Machines' (Linsu Kim, 1982). KDI sees such subsidies as excessive because the proportion of credit which the machinery sector has received has exceeded the proportion of value added which it has contributed. Yet, the machinery sector may best be able to absorb such funds because its debt–equity ratio has consistently been lower than the average for all of manufacturing (see Section III). Some of the production facilities for light manufactures which KDI wishes to promote further may be too loaned up to soak up much more credit.

The industrial protection and subsidization systems of the government are also called into question by KDI because they rest on the 'arbitrary evaluation' by KOSAMI of foreign and locally made machinery (Seung Jin Kim, 1983: 13). The preferred alternative is greater reliance on markets whose 'perfect knowledge' will presumably do a better job. To us, this seems an idealization of how markets work and an especially naive view in the case of the general machinery subsector where competition depends not only on price and quality but also on reputation. It is the reputation of the Korean-made machines which KOSAMI has tried to further in order to increase Korean market share and thus reap the benefits of scale and fast growth. KOSAMI does so by tagging the technological trajectories of local firms and *actively* seeking outlets for Korean equipment throughout the world; in conjunction with the general trading arms of the *chaebul*. Korean machinery manufacturers function seemingly well within the web of laws and regulations spun by the state because the two are mediated by this bureaucracy – an effective 'knowledge-broker' in a highly differentiated market.

Government Expenditures

There appear to be as many government schemes to build up manpower and technology in Korea as there are parts in a typical machine. Expenditures on education broadly defined as a percentage of the government's budget – which is notably parsimonious when it comes to social outlays – jumped from 4 per cent in 1954 to 18 per cent in 1980. This understates the share of resources which goes to education because most educational expenditures are financed privately (Mason *et al.*, 1980).

V SMALL FIRMS AND SUBCONTRACTING

A second line of attack against government policy towards heavy machinery manufacture is its alleged failure to give small and medium size firms a fair share of support, thereby frustrating specialization and subcontracting. South Korea's subcontracting system is primitive by comparison with that of Japan (Jae Won Kim, 1983). In the general machinery subsector in 1977, its subcontracting ratio was calculated to be only 31.3.[11] Consequently, its specialization ratio was also low (15.9).[12] There thus appears to be a vicious circle: if subcontracting is minimal, firms dare not specialize, and if they don't, the emergence of subcontracting is retarded (KIET, 1980).

The costs of an underdeveloped subcontracting system to large machinery works may be considerable in terms of low efficiency, quality, and long lead times, especially at the fabrication stage of the production process, whether fabricated parts are bought or made. The economy-wide costs also appear to be high. The largest group of imports within the general machinery classification is knocked-down parts or components which are elements of machinery to be finished locally (see Section I). 'This is due to the small base of small- and medium-size supplier industries' (Jae Hak Kim, 1982: 7).

Certainly some of the blame for the stunted growth of subcontracting both in the past and at present lies with the government. The incentive system of the Park regime was oriented towards exporting, which probably pointed small and medium size firms away from serving the local market in the capacity of dependent supplier. Whatever the industry, subsidies today also appear to be biased against firms which are small or medium in scale.[13] 'Bias' is typically charged when an industry's contribution to value added exceeds its share of government support.

In the late 1970s, small and medium size firms throughout the manufacturing sector accounted for roughly 50 per cent of employment and 35 per cent of value added. Yet fragmented data suggest that they accounted for only about 26 per cent of bank loans, net of foreign commercial and public credit (SMIPC, 1981). Throughout the 1960s and 1970s, except for two short periods interrupted by the oil crisis, foreign savings accounted for 30–40 per cent of gross domestic investment, and these foreign inflows were deliberately allocated to larger firms to realize economies of scale. Thus, the credit bias against small and medium size firms is probably worse when both local and foreign sources are counted. To add insult to injury, large firms tend to defer payment to small ones, so it could be said that small firms actually subsidize large ones.[14]

The vicious circle that arrests subcontracting is strikingly apparent in the machinery sector. Disaggregated data for the general machinery subsector are unavailable but those for the sector as a whole (ISIC 38) suggest that whereas small and medium size machinery firms accounted for 42 per cent of employment and 43 per cent of value added, their investments for new plant and equipment in the sector circa the late 1970s accounted very approximately for only 11.4 per cent (SMIPC, 1981; MCI, 1979a). Their share of expenditures on R & D very roughly was only 7.5 per cent (MOST, 1979).

Blame for the retardation of subcontracting in manufacturing in general or in general machinery in particular cannot be placed on the government's shoulders alone. If Japan and some of the more advanced countries are any guide, then the subcontracting system thrives on a set of conditions not yet ripe in South Korea. First, while contracting arrangements may engage a large number of firms of equal size, typically they involve a small cluster of large, prime contractors in a galaxy of small, satellite subcontractors; and large production units are just coming on stream in the general machinery subsector in South Korea. Second, subcontracting flourishes when large firms face excess demand. Yet most integrated general machinery firms in South Korea have been plagued by excess supply. Finally, subcontracting is stimulated by sharp differences between contractor and contractee in wages and employment practices: for example, work rules and overtime. While it is generally believed that wages and conditions of employment in the *chaebul* are somewhat superior to those in other firms, the differences are believed not to be as pronounced as in the advanced countries. *The chaebul*, being non-unionized, are free in matters of work assignments and length of the working day. One motive for subcontracting is thereby weakened.

We may end our discussion of the Korean general machinery industry with a word of caution. Government support for the industry could easily fail if it has the build-up of military preparedness as a dual objective. Defence-related support for the industry would in all probability end in excess capacity if, in the interests of security, several firms were licensed to produce the same product. Excess capacity, in turn, could be expected to slow down the accumulation of experience at the level of the operating unit, discourage specialization and subcontracting, and lead to high turn-over, as workers sought employment with firms in a better position to pay volume-related bonuses. The South Korean government allocates 6 per cent of GNP to defence, which is the highest figure among the non-socialist countries (Jan H. Yoo, 1983). While machinery builders in total might benefit from government defence spending, the effects on each firm of multiple sourcing and excess capacity might outweigh the gains and prove disastrous.

NOTES

1. I would like to thank the following people: J.C., J.E., J.G., H.H., M.S., and H.Z.
2. Our study was financed by The World Bank as part of a project under the direction of Carl Dahlman. The project examines the acquisition of a technological capability in South Korea, Brazil, Mexico, and India.
3. Newly industrializing countries.
4. The information in this paragraph is largely from KEB (1983).
5. The Ministry of Finance refers to non-electrical machinery which we take to mean mainly general machinery.
6. Which is not to ignore other types of technology transfer problems. Some local producers find it difficult to persuade foreign firms to sell their proprietary know-how.
7. One assault has been led by the Korea Development Institute (KDI) in a paper authored by Seung Jin Kim (1983). Much of the facts of government policy and the excesses of its critics presented below are drawn from this paper.
8. Actual tariff rates = (Tariff revenue collected)/Import value.
9. Import liberalization rate = $(IVT-IVR)/IVT$ where IVT = import value of total items, and IVR = import value of restricted import items for the first half of each year.
10. KOSAMI = Korean Society for the Advancement of the Machinery Industry.

11. The subcontracting ratio is defined as equal to the number of sub-contractors divided by the total number of small and medium size firms (times 100).
12. Specialization ratio = (number of specialized firms/total number of small and medium size firms) × 100.
13. According to the Small and Medium Industry Promotion Act (as amended in 1982), small firms in the industrial sector are those with less than 20 full-time workers and medium firms are those with less than 300 – but there are exceptions: for example, a firm with 700 workers in a highly labour-intensive branch may be defined as medium size.
14. Subsidization in the form of technological know-how may also flow from small, specialized, suppliers to larger prime contractors (Jae Won Kim, 1983).

REFERENCES

Amsden, Alice H. (1981) 'An International Comparison of the Rate of Surplus Value in Manufacturing Industry', *Cambridge Journal of Economics*, 5, 229–49.
——————(1983) '"De-Skilling", Skilled Commodities, and the NIC's Emerging Competitive Advantage', *American Economic Review Proceedings* (May) 73,2; 333–7.
——————(forthcoming) 'The Rate of Growth of Demand and Technological Change', *Cambridge Journal of Economics*.
—————— and Linsu Kim (1982) 'Korea's Technology Exports and Acquisition of a Technological Capability' (Washington, D.C. Productivity Division, Development Research Department, World Bank).
——————(forthcoming) *The Acquisition of a Technological Capability in the Republic of Korea*.
BOK (Bank of Korea) *Financial Statements Analysis*, various years.
Cha, Dong Se (1983) *The Effects of Foreign Capital* (Seoul: KIET Press) (in Korean).
Dahlman, Carl F. (1982) 'Analytical Framework for Acquisition of Technological Capability Research Project' (World Bank, Development Research Department, Productivity Division, mimeo).
EPB (Economic Planning Board) *Report on Mining and Manufacturing Survey*, various years.
——————(1983) *Major Indicators of the Korean Economy*.
FKI (Federation of Korean Industries) (1980) *Plant Exports of Korea*.
Harbison, Frederick and Charles Myers (eds) (1965) *Manpower and Education; Country Studies in Economic Development* (New York: McGraw-Hill).

KDB (Korea Development Bank) (1982) 'Current Trend and Issues in Korean Investment' (December).

KDI (Korea Development Institute) (1982) 'Korean Industry Capital Stock Calculations, 1960–77', Research Report 82–06.

KEB (Korea Exchange Bank) (1983) *The Korean Economy: Review and Prospects*, 5th edn.

KIET (Korea Institute for Industrial Economics and Technology) (1980) *Current State and Issues in the Machinery Industry*.

———————— (1982) *The Heavy Machinery Industries of Korea: Problems and Prospects, Final Report* (December)

KOSAMI (Korea Society for the Advancement of the Machinery Industry) (1980, 1982, 1984) *Machinery Industry Manual*.

KTA (Korea Traders' Association) (1966) *Trade Annals*.

Kim, Jae Hak (1982) 'Promotion of the Machinery Industry' (mimeo). Presented at the International Forum on Industrial Planning and Trade Policies, Seoul, Korea, June 1–12.

Kim, Jae Won (1983) 'Subcontracting, Market Expansion, and Subcontracting Activities Promotion: The Case of Korea's Machinery Industry', Korea Development Institute Working Paper 8305.

Kim, Linsu (1982) 'Technological Innovations in Korea's Capital Goods Industry: A Micro Analysis', International Labour Organization, Working Paper WEP 2-22/WP92.

Kim, Seung Jin (1983) 'Evolution of and Reform Proposals for Promotion Policies in the Korean Machinery Industry', Korea Development Institute, Working Paper 83–06.

Lee, Kyu Uck (Forthcoming) 'Conglomeration and Economic Power', Korea Development Institute, working paper.

Lewis, W. Arthur (1965) 'A Review of Economic Development', *American Economic Review Proceedings* (May) 55, 1–16.

Mason, Edward S. *et al.* (1980) *The Economic and Social Modernization of the Republic of Korea* (Cambridge, Mass.: Harvard).

MCI (Ministry of Commerce and Industry) (1979) 'Master Plan for the Development of the Machinery Industry' (mimeo).

———————— (1979a) *Annual Report of Small and Medium Industry*.

Ministry of Labour, *Yearbook of Labour Statistics*, various years.

MOST (Ministry of Science and Technology) *Annal of Science and Technology*, various years.

Piper, Thomas R. and Wolf A. Weinhold (1982) 'How Much Debt is Right for Your Company?', *Harvard Business Review* (July/August) 60,4.

SMIPC (Small and Medium Industry Promotion Corporation) (1981) *A Survey Report of Small and Medium Industry in Mining and Manufacturing*.

Westphal, Larry E. (1981) 'Empirical Justification for Infant Industry Protection', World Bank Staff Working Paper No. 445.

Yoo, Jan H. (1983) 'Economic Growth and National Security: Korea's Experience and Prospects', in Richard F. Kosobud (ed.), *Northeast Asia and the United States* (Chicago, Council on Foreign Relations).

4 A History of the Machine Tool Industry In Japan

TOSHIAKI CHOKKI

INTRODUCTION

The first part of this chapter deals with the history of the machine tool industry up to the end of the Second World War. The second and third parts consider major events in the post-war period up to the 1980s.

I HISTORY UNTIL 1945

The User and Maker of Machine Tools

Machine tools were originally introduced into Japan from abroad. They were imported from European countries such as Holland, England and France when the Tokugawa Government and other feudal rulers began to establish arsenals in Nagasaki, Kagoshima and Yokosuka. In the 1860s Japan was compelled to abandon its traditional isolation, which had been the national policy since 1639, and open diplomatic relations with Western countries. The number of machine tools imported is not known, but a document ('History of Mitsubishi Nagasaki Ship-building Corporation') describes that there were lathes, threading machines, boring machines, drilling machines, planing machines and punching machines using at Tokugawa Shogunate Nagasaki Iron and Steel Works.

In 1868 the Tokugawa Regime ended and a new government was established. This was the Meiji Restoration with which the modernisation of Japan began.

The majority of early machine-tool users were the arsenals. The Meiji Government took over the Tokugawa and other feudal rulers' industrial facilities and reconstructed several military and naval arsenals in Tokyo, Osaka and Yokosuka. At this time the formation of a Western style army and the production of modern weaponry was a priority for the government, since Japan was in danger of losing her political independence. The Osaka Arsenal was for the production of cannons and guns, the Tokyo Arsenal for rifles, and the Yokosuka was the first modern naval shipyard.

All these arsenals were equipped with machine tools, but there are few documents left concerning the equipment of the Tokyo Military Arsenal Rifle Division. There they began to increase the facility for production from 1872 onwards following government policy to strengthen armaments. Table 4.1 shows the machine tools installed from 1872 to 1877. Many machine tools were being imported from aborad but it is notable that some were manufactured in-house, and in addition there was a domestic supplier, the Nakajima Works. There were other factors producing machine tools and the figures show that the users of machine tools were also producers.

The second source of machine tool production in Japan was from craftsmen. Before the Meiji Restoration iron work was undertaken on a very small scale with craftsmen working in their own shops. After the Restoration some of them were employed at modern machine factories. But some craftsmen still wanted to be independent producers so when they had saved enough money they set up their own factories making miscellaneous machinery or parts. These small producers were potential producers of machine tools at this early stage of industrialisation.

These producers had two reasons to start producing machine tools, one technological and the other economic. The craftsmen had all the skills necessary to build their own machine tools and at the same time they found that imported machine tools were too expensive for them to buy. They copied imported machines spending several months making replicas. Outside orders were subsequently received for some of these machines and the craftsmen became professional machine tool producers. This type of machine tool builder came into being around the turn of the century while Japan was going through its industrial revolution and the demand for machine tools was gradually increasing.

During the Russo-Japanese War machine tools for military use were ordered by the government in large quantities from domestic producers. Some manufacturers became producers of machine tools around this period, such as the Ikegai Iron Works and the Wakayama Iron Works.

The third source of producers came from the repair shops. During the industrial revolution in Japan the mining industry was also modernised and modern mining machinery was imported and installed. Repair shops were established on a neighbouring site for the repair and rebuilding of these

TABLE 4.1 Yearly addition of machine tools in the Tokyo Military Arsenal Rifle Division (from 1872 to 1877)

Year	Machine	Qty	Maker
1872	Milling machine	2	Self-made
	Lathe	2	Richard Huntsman
	Grinding machine	2	Greenwood and Batley
	Two head bench drilling machine	1	Self-made
1873 (49)	Milling machine	1	Self-made
	Milling machine	5	Greenwood and Batley
	Bench milling machine	3	Nakajima Works
	Bench milling machine	3	Greenwood and Batley
	Bench milling machine	11	Self-made
	Lathe	6	Richard Huntsman
	Bench drilling machine	3	Self-made
	Multi-spindle drilling machine	2	Nakajima Works
1875 (7)	Lathe	2	Richard Huntsman
1876 (13)	Milling machine	1	Self-made
	Milling machine	1	Greenwood and Batley
	Bench milling machine	1	Greenwood and Batley
	Lathe	7	Richard Huntsman
1877 (45)	Two head bench drilling machine	2	Self-made
	Bench drilling machine	1	Self-made
	Milling machine	3	Self-made
	Milling machine	2	Greenwood and Batley
	Bench milling machine	21	Self-made

Lathe	2	Richard Huntsman
Horizontal type bench drilling machine	4	Self-made
Two head bench drilling machine	1	French-made
Grinding machine	1	Greenwood and Batley
Lathe for making barrel	5	Greenwood and Batley
Reaming machine	3	French-made
Two spindle reaming machine for barrel	3	Greenwood and Batley
Horizontal type drilling machine	6	Self-made
Horizontal type multi-spindle drilling machine	1	Greenwood and Batley
Grinding machine	3	Greenwood and Batley
Reaming machine	1	Becharin
Reaming machine	3	Self-made
Turret lathe	1	Whitworth
	22	

1874

Milling machine	1	Self-made
Milling machine	1	Greenwood and Batley
Grinding machine	1	Greenwood and Batley

NOTE The spelling of 'Richard Huntsman' and 'Becharin' is not assured. And strictly speaking, this is not the list of real yearly addition of machine tools in the division. This is based on the investigation of the machine tools existing in 1923. The machine tools abolished before then are not counted in the list.

SOURCE Toshiaki Chokki, *Analysis of the Process of Development of Japanese Machine Tool Industry* (Dissertation, in Japanese) (1963) p. 63.

machines. These repair shops could also be used for shop production and some occasionally made machine tools. Some repair shops found that they received orders from outside and found it profitable to become machine tool producers. The Karatsu Iron Works and the Niigata Engineering Company are examples of producers that originated from this source.

The Machine Tool Industry and the First World War

The machine tool industry has always been linked with military uses. In order to produce the weaponry required during wartime, a large quantity of machine tools were demanded. The Sino-Japanese and especially the Russo-Japanese wars created a large demand for machine tools and encouraged the development of several machine tool producers.

The First World War stimulated the development of the Japanese machine tool industry in a different way. Japan joined the war, but the demand for machine tools from the national market was not only for military use but also for use within a wide range of ordinary companies. Following the start of the war in 1914 neither private companies nor government arsenals could import foreign machines, upon which they had been dependent, because the foreign suppliers (mostly English, German and American) could not afford to export machine tools to Japan. As there was such a great demand from their own domestic market Japanese producers took the place of machine tool suppliers instead of foreign manufacturers. Table 4.2 shows this process clearly.

TABLE 4.2   Increase and decrease of production after 1914 (value in million yen)

Year	Production (A)	Export (B)	Imports (C)	Domestic demand (A − B + C)	Dependence on Imports $\dfrac{C}{(A - B + C)}$
1914	0.003	0.3	2	2.0	100
1915	1	1	0.9	1.6	56
1916	8	1	2	9.0	22
1917	12	0.8	3	14.2	21
1918	18	1	7	24.0	29
1919	6	0.9	11	16.1	68
1920	11	...	14	25.0	56
1921	9	0.4	11	19.6	56
1922	7	0.4	7	13.6	52

SOURCE   Same as Table 4.4, p.47.

After the First World War the Japanese machine tool producers lost most of the domestic customers they had acquired to the English and American manufacturers who re-started exporting machine tools to Japan. Up to 1922, some manufacturers supplied machine tools to shipbuilders who were building warships for the Japanese Navy under the warship enforcement plan. But the Washington Treaty was concluded in 1922 and this regulated the number of warships in Japan, England and America. This Treaty compelled the Japanese Navy to abandon their enforcement plan and to stop building new ships, which also meant that the orders for machine tools had to be cancelled. This is a well-known episode in the history.

After this the national market for machine tools was depressed. A limited amount of work came from the Japanese Railroad Bureau which ordered some special-purpose machine tools to be built for the repair of locomotives and other rolling stock to be undertaken by them (JRB).

During the 1920s and the first half of the 1930s the Japanese machine tool industry went through a difficult period. Five major manufacturers (Ikegai Iron Works, Okuma Machinery Works, Karatsu Iron Works, Niigata Engineering Company, and Tokyo Gas and Electric Company) continued to produce machine tools. In this period the Japanese economy as a whole was very depressed. The rate of economic growth was low. In the early part of the century many producers had entered the machine tool industry, but after the First World War the numbers declined. The major five remaining producers have already been mentioned but there were still a few small-scale producers.

The Machine Tool Industry During the Second World War

In 1931 the Japanese army invaded Manchuria and Japan remained at war until 1945. Military demand stimulated industrial activity in Japan and revived the machine tool industry. Around 1937 the war expanded into China and the demand for munitions increased rapidly. Many firms began to produce machine tools again. Both domestic production and the importation of machine tools increased to cope with the increased demand for the production of weaponry and miscellaneous machinery for private companies' use. As the demand for machine tools increased, the government decided to expand the machine tool production capacity of the domestic producers to meet the increased demand. The government regarded the industry as a strategic industry and made a plan to develop the industry by selecting producers. They introduced 'Kosakukikai Seizo Jigyo-ho' (The Machine Tool Industry Law) in 1938. The most important provision was that the government authorised the production of machine tools by 'patended companies' ('Kyoka Gaisha') and promoted the production of high-quality machine tools for military use during the way. The 'patented companies' were guaranteed material supplies, tax-reductions, low-cost financing of funds and other concessions. The 'patented companies' in 1938 are shown in Table 4.3. Products of these companies were distributed to the munitions producers.

The noteworthy achievement of this period was that the Japanese Zaibatsu established the machine tool companies or created the division. Up to this time they had imported machine tools – mostly large-sized and high precision – from abroad, especially from America. In 1940 the American Government decided to forbid the export of machine tools to Japan as a result of the Japanese invasion in China. It thus became impossible for manufacturers to depend on American-made machine tools to enlarge their production capacity. As munitions-related facilities were

TABLE 4.3   'Patented Companies' approved in 1938

Name of company	Month of approval	Name of plant
Okuma Machinery Works	July	Nagoya
Hitachi Machine Tool Co.	July	Omori and Kawasaki
Ikegai Iron Works	July	Mita and Kanagawa
Niigata Engineering Co.	July	Niigata
Toyo Seiki Co.	July	Nakamaruko
Tsugami-Ataka Seisakusho	July	Nagaoka
Kokusan Seiki Co.	October	Adachi and Abiko
Toyo Kikai Co.	October	Hiroshima
Shibaura Machine Tool Co.	October	Tsurumi
Osaka Wakayama Iron Works	October	Shinodayama
Dai Nihon Heiki Co.	December	Shonan Machine Tool Plant

SOURCE   Toshiaki Chokki, *Analysis of the Process of Development of Japanese Machine Tool Industry* (Dissertation, in Japanese) (1963) p. 137.

expanded, 'Kosakukikai Seizo Jigyo-ho' gave inducements to firms to enter the machine tool industry. Mitsubishi, Mitsui, Hitachi and Toshiba were among the *zaibatsu* who began to produce machine tools. During the Second World War the machine tool industry expanded, domestic production in 1944 amounting to 723 million yen, three times greater than 1938.

II DEVELOPMENT SINCE 1945 AND STRUCTURE OF THE INDUSTRY

Overview

After Japan's defeat in 1945 a large part of manufacturing industry was out of work. Military demand suddenly disappeared, many were unemployed, industrial equipment had been damaged by American bombing, and a militant labour movement emerged. The first thing Japan had to do was restore economic order, and increase industrial production and employment. Moreover, because of Japan's lack of material resources, exports were needed to earn foreign exchange.

After the war Japan adopted a democratic system of government with free enterprise as a basic principle of economic activity. The Government and the Ministry of International Trade and Industry (MITI) guided industrial activity in order to strengthen Japan's competitiveness and keep industrial peace.

Government Legislation

The 'Machine Tool Industry Law' was repealed after the war and there has been no subsequent legislation that has been specific to the machine tool industry. But legislation and policies for industrial development in general were put forward by MITI. One of these was the 'Gaishi-ho' (Foreign Capital Law) in 1950. This provided for the regulation of foreign investment. Through this legislation MITI guided the introduction of foreign technology and improved the technological level of Japanese enterprises.

Another law, the 'Kikaikogyo Rinji Sochi-ho' (Temporary Measures for the Development of the Machinery Industry Law) was introduced in 1956. This law selected twenty-one industries (most of them involved in the production of basic equipment and parts) and MITI assisted the modernization of their equipment. The machine tool industry was included. This law was not company-related, but MITI provided long-term and low-cost government loans, through the Japan Development Bank, for investment in new equipment by the producers. In 1971 the law was repealed, by which time machine tool producers had renewed their equipment. The renewal of equipment by other producers in different industries created a large domestic demand for machine tools. This also gave foreign producers the opportunity to export machines to Japan but it gave an impetus to the development of the domestic machine tool production at the same time.

The introduction of foreign technology by machine tool producers began in 1952 under the 'Gaishi-ho'. The first licence agreement was between Tsugami and Cri-Dan, a French company, for the production of a thread cutting lathe. Many further foreign licensing agreements were signed. Some examples are shown in Table. 4.4.

In most cases commercial Japanese firms or third parties acted as intermediaries. The Japanese producers paid an initial lump-sum and a royalty. The royalty was around 6–8 per cent of the selling price of the product. Usually the Japanese producer also had the exclusive right to sell in Japan and neighbouring countries.

Up to March 1981 Japanese producers concluded 161 foreign technology agreements. The agreements came from the following countries, USA (67), West Germany (33), France (32) Switzerland (18), England (5), Italy (5), and Belgium (1). 'Gaishi-ho' was repealed in 1980 and after March 1981 MITI approval was no longer required for foreign technology agreements.

Post-War Machine Tool Production

After the war the Japanese economy was depressed, there was little demand, and production of machine tools declined. In 1946 the total value of machine tool production was a seventh of that in 1944. Some manufacturers stopped producing machine tools, and in some companies the management was changed. For example, after the war the Ikegai Iron Works which had been founded and run by the Ikegai Family since 1889 was taken over by the Industrial Bank of Japan, a private long-term credit bank, since the firm was in a state of financial crisis. One of the causes of this crisis was labour opposition within the firm.

After 1957 the demand for machine tools increased rapidly, as a result of rapid economic growth in 1955 and 1956. Machine tool production in 1957 was double that of 1956. Large industries such as iron and steel, automobiles and electrical machinery began to renew their production facilities, and invested in high-quality machinery and tools, and consequently greatly improved their technological capacities.

As a result of post-war demands new maker–user relationships developed. Subsidiary machine tool companies contributed to the technological innovations of their parent companies. For example, Toyoda Machine Words has manufactured various kinds of transfer-machines for Toyota Motor Co. since 1956. Similarly, Hitachi Seiki co-operated with Nissan Motor Co. to develop transfer-machines for automobile production; both Hitachi Seiki and Nissan Motor were member companies in the Nissan

TABLE 4.4 Examples of Technology Introduction (1953 to 1961)

Date of approval	Japanese firm	Foreign firm (country)	Type of machine tool introduced
20 Oct 1953	Shoun Machine Tool	Cazeneuve (France)	Copying Lathe
19 Jan 1954	Mitsubishi Heavy Industries	Oerlikon (Switzerland)	Copying lathe
20 July 1954	Niigata Engineering Co.	Sundstrand (U.S.A.)	Bed type milling machine
6 Sep 1955	Toshiba Machine Co.	Berthiez (France)	Vertical boring and turning mill
1 Nov 1955	Toyoda Machine Works	Gendron (France)	Grinding machine
2 April 1957	Mitsui Seiki Kogyo Co.	Renault (France)	Special-purpose machine
4 Nov 1959	Mitsubishi Heavy Industries	Innocenti (Italy)	Boring and milling combined machine tool
6 June 1961	Mitsubishi Heavy Industries	Lorenz (West Germany)	Gear hobbing machine
18 July 1961	Osaka Kiko Co.	Ramo (France)	Engine lathe
1 Aug 1961	Toyoda Machine Works	Somua (France)	Bed type milling machine
3 Oct 1961	Tsugumi	Progres (Belgium)	Autocycle lathe

SOURCE   Japan Machine Tool Builders' Association, *Thirty Years' Progress of 'Mother Machine'* (in Japanese) (1982) p. 88.

Group during the war. Mazda Motor Co., the third auto-manufacturer, had its own machine tool division which made transfer-machines to increase the productivity of machining processes within the company. During the latter half of the 1950s and in the 1960s a large number of transfer-machines were installed in many industries. Almost all of these were manufactured by domestic machine tool producers or by the user company's own machine tool division.

Machine tool producers, as capital goods suppliers, made various types of machine tools for domestic users. They produced high-quality general-purpose machines for ordinary machining processes as well as special-purpose machines such as transfer-machines. The value of general-purpose machine tools sold was much larger than that of special-purpose machines. Each producer had his own field of production, so users had to buy different types of machine tools from different manufacturers. There was a strong relationship between the user and the specific manufacturer (including their own machine tool divisions), although the user also looked for new manufacturers who could supply high-quality and low-priced machine tools. The intense competition in the post-war machine tool industry provided the foundation for the rapid development of the capital goods sector in Japan.

Several joint ventures using Japanese and foreign capital were introduced in the post-war machine tool industry. The first joint venture was Koyo-Van Norman, a manufacturer of centre-less grinding machines established in 1963. Kearney & Trecker-Toshiba Machine, Japan-Cazeneuve, Murata-Warner Swasy, Enshu-Cross and Sansei-Bryant followed in the 1960s and 1970s. These are joint ventures between Japanese and American enterprises, with the exception of Japan-Cezeneuve, which is a Japanese–French venture. While joint ventures had some impact on the post-war machine tool industry, their production and sales capacity was not large enough to exert a great influence. Foreign investment in large-sized Japanese machine tool producing companies remained rare. Litton Industries, an American conglomerate, with a 13.4 per cent share of stocks of Nippei Industrial Co. is one of the few examples.

Another new phase of post-war machine tool production is emergence of new producers. Makino, Yamazaki and Mori are among these. They originated from small business and succeeded in developing new products such as NC machine tools and machining centres.

In the 1970s there was a rapid increase in the use of numerical control systems. See Table 4.5 for an indication of the importance of numerical control devices in a number of leading firms.

TABLE 4.5 Production of numerical control devices (percentage of total in brackets)

Year	Fanuc	Hitachi	Mitsubishi	NEC	Oki	Toshiba	'Self-made'	Other domestic maker	Foreign maker	Total
1972	1013	17	43	20	19	32	143	36	37	1.360
	(74.5)	(1.2)	(3.2)	(1.5)	(1.4)	(2.4)	(10.5)	(2.6)	(2.7)	(100)
1973	1738	25	64	62	82	64	347	74	22	2.478
	(70.1)	(1.0)	(2.6)	(2.5)	(3.3)	(2.6)	(14.0)	(3.0)	(0.9)	(100)
1974	1739	1	97	78	91	59	241	19	31	2.356
	(73.9)	(—)	(4.1)	(3.3)	(3.9)	(2.5)	(10.2)	(0.8)	(1.3)	(100)
1975	1226	5	112	41	83	54	346	5	24	1.896
	(64.6)	(0.3)	(5.9)	(2.2)	(4.4)	(2.8)	(18.2)	(0.3)	(1.3)	(100)
1976	1791	0	213	52	119	34	853	13	56	3.131
	(57.2)	(0)	(6.8)	(1.7)	(3.8)	(1.1)	(27.2)	(0.4)	(1.8)	(100)

NOTE 'Self-made' means production by the machine tool manufacturers. Enshu, Hitachi Seiko, Japax, Okuma, O-M, Tayoda and Washino make the devices.

SOURCE JMTBA, *Machine Tool News* (in Japanese) July 1978, p. 23.

R & D Activity

As mentioned, the government enacted 'Gaishi-ho' in 1950 and encouraged the introduction of foreign technology with the approval of MITI. Machine tool producers have continued to introduce foreign technology since 1952.

Before, and during, the Second World War Japanese machine tool producers copied foreign machine tools. Domestic users, especially the arsenals, thought highly of foreign machine tools and asked domestic producers to produce the same models. R & D activity during this time was directed towards copying foreign machine tools. After the war Japanese producers continued to import high-quality machine tools and dismantle them to study their construction and the materials used. MITI subsidised the costs of importing these high-quality and high-priced foreign machine tools. This was a joint activity through a special committee of the Japan Machine Tool Builders' Association (JMTBA) from 1956 to 1961.

The government also gave loans for the development of new products. These loans were conditional and the money borrowed had to be repaid to the government on a long-term basis. This policy lasted for three years between 1953 and 1955. Under 'Kikaikogyo Rinji Sochi-ho' the government also subsidised R & D activities. Between 1965 and 1978, 455 million yen was loaned to finance twelve projects.

As technology advanced, competition among producers became more severe, and machine tool manufacturers began to organise R & D departments to carry out research and development on machine tool production. Hitachi Seiki Co. established a technical laboratory and Toyoda Machine Works organised a research institute as a subsidiary company in 1960. These laboratories carried out basic research as well as product development. In the 1960s new Japanese-developed products became available.

Marketing

Historically Japanese machine tool producers did not pay much attention to marketing. Many manufacturers started producing machine tools during the war when there was a shortage. Furthermore, little machine tools could be imported, with the result that manufacturers easily found customers.

After the war, marketing became a very important part of industrial activity in the machine tools business, because of increased competition among the producers. From 1962 the Japan International Machine Tool Fair has been held every other year, in Tokyo and Osaka alternately. This

Fair is the arena of marketing by Japanese machine tool producers. In addition to that, some machine tool companies have established sales agencies both for the domestic market and abroad, while several have set up links with the large trading companies. In a few cases these trading companies ('Sogo-Shosha') entered the machine tool industry. Mitsui & Co., Mitsubishi Corporation and C. Itoh & Co., were among these.

Small-sized machine shops have been the main consumers of domestic machine tools since the 1960s. As the Japanese economy grew, wage rates increased, with the result that small machine shops were compelled to renew their equipment and automate to survive in the severe competition. They were the first users of home-made NC machine tools in the domestic market.

The value of exported machine tools has increased since 1966. In 1962 the machine tool producers founded the Japan Machine Tool Trade Association which began to publicise Japanese machine tools.

The government introduced the 'Kigyo Gorika Sokushin-ho' (Enterprise Rationalisation Promotion Law) in 1952, to encourage the importation of foreign high-quality machine tools. Tariff-free importation of these machines was allowed. On the other hand, the importation of standard machine tools, which the domestic producers could supply was restricted. However, in 1961, liberalisation of trade in machine tools began. In 1970 importation of all kinds of machine tools was liberalised, but tariffs of 10 per cent to 20 per cent were imposed on imported machine tools according to whether they competed with domestic producers. In 1983 all tariffs were removed.

Financing

Before the Second World War several leading machine tool companies were family businesses, including Ikegai, Okuma and Karatsu, the major stock-holders of these companies being members of a specific family. After the war the banks and big industrial corporations became the biggest stock-holders in the large machine tool companies. The Ikegai family gave up the ownership and management of their company, while the members of Okuma continued to manage their company even though their percentage of the stock-holding decreased as more stocks were issued. The Karatsu Iron Works can still be regarded as a family business, belonging to the Takeo family, but they did not expand their business as other leading companies did after the war. The largest stock-holder in Ikegai is the Industrial Bank of Japan with 10 per cent of the issued stocks. In the case of Okuma the largest stock-holder is Nihon Seimei, a life-insurance company with 8.8 per cent of issued stock, and the second largest is the Tokai Bank with a holding of 6.3 per cent. (The data are from *Japan Company Handbook*, 1983 Fall, Toyo Keizai Shimpo-sha. The same is as below.)

The other type of post-war machine tool companies are those whose major stock-holders are big industrial corporations. For example, Toyota Motor Co. is the largest stock-holder of Toyoda Machine Works with 24.9 per cent of the issued stocks, and in the case of the Toshiba Machine Co. the largest stock-holder is Toshiba Corporation with 50.1 per cent. These companies started as subsidiaries of their parent company during the war and remain as member companies of the interest group.

In addition some machine tool production is carried out as a divisional activity of big industrial enterprises. Mitsubishi Heavy Industries produces machine tools at their Hiroshima and Kyoto plants, and Mazda Motor, an automobile corporation, is also a fairly large producer of machine tools. These companies undertake machine tool production as a branch of their diversified industrial activities.

For the financing of post-war industrial companies (including the machine tool industry) large sums of money have been borrowed from the banks and insurance companies. Industries depended on loans from these financial groups when they enlarged their production facilities. They have also issued additional shares in order to fund expansion but this has not decreased the sum of borrowed money. Each machine tool company has one bank (or in some cases a few) with whom they have special relations, referred to as the 'main bank'. For example, the 'main bank' of Ikegai is the Industrial Bank of Japan, that of Okuma the Tokai Bank, and that of Mazda the Sumitomo Bank. 'Main banks' are usually major stock-holders of the machine tool producer and take considerable interest in the financing of the company.

During the latter half of the 1950s and the first half of the 1960s, the Japan Development Bank (a governmental bank) financed a fairly large sum for the modernisation of equipment by machine tool producers. This was the 'Kikaikogyo Rinji Sochi-ho' in 1956, and was not specific to the machine tool industry. During this period the financing provided by private banks was limited, so the government bank made additional funds available. After the latter half of the 1960s the 'main bank' of each producer became a main supplier of funds to each machine tool producer. Two examples are shown in Table 4.6.

TABLE 4.6 Change of Weights of long-term borrowing from the standpoint of suppliers (in the cases of Okuma and Ikegai) (value in thousand yen, ( ) %)

Fiscal year	Okuma Machinery Works				Ikegai Corporation			
	Total	from JDB	from 'Main Bank'	from others	Total	from JDB	from 'Main Bank'	from others
1960	227500 (100.0)	163000 (71.6)	14500 (6.4)	50000 (22.0)	255500 (100.0)	149500 (58.5)	106000 (41.5)	0 (0)
1961	276227 (100.0)	163300 (59.1)	63779 (23.1)	49148 (17.8)	312921 (100.0)	201450 (64.4)	111491 (38.8)	0 (0)
1962	247021 (100.0)	116500 (47.2)	52279 (21.2)	78242 (31.6)	451237 (100.0)	183450 (49.7)	142914 (31.7)	124873 (27.6)
1963	189441 (100.0)	61700 (32.6)	47009 (24.8)	80732 (42.6)	1038762 (100.0)	327000 (31.5)	321492 (31.0)	390280 (37.5)
1964	85343 (100.0)	0 (0)	36481 (42.7)	48862 (57.3)	1951273 (100.0)	305800 (15.7)	558053 (28.6)	1087420 (55.7)
1965	251095 (100.0)	0 (0)	25949 (10.3)	225146 (89.7)	1739491 (100.0)	314300 (18.1)	1001244 (57.5)	423947 (24.4)
1966	159383 (100.0)	0 (0)	15407 (9.7)	143976 (90.3)	1331080 (100.0)	209800 (15.8)	788885 (58.3)	332395 (24.9)
1967	139601 (100.0)	0 (0)	4875 (3.5)	134726 (96.5)	1512819 (110.0)	121400 (8.0)	660538 (43.7)	730881 (48.3)
1968	209394 (100.0)	0 (0)	100000 (47.8)	109394 (52.2)	1745123 (100.0)	66000 (3.8)	513651 (29.4)	2165472 (66.8)
1969	931029 (100.0)	0 (0)	400000 (43.0)	531029 (57.0)	1958378 (100.0)	26000 (1.3)	593583 (30.5)	1333795 (68.1)

NOTE   Ikegai Corp. was formerly Ikegai Iron Works.

SOURCE   Financial Reports (each company).

Local Structure

The local structure of the post-war machine tool industry is very different from that existing before the war. Keihin (Tokyo and Yokohama), Chukyo (Aichi), Hanshin (Osaka and Kobe) and North Kyushu were the major industrial areas of Japan before the Second World War. Pioneering machine tool producers appeared in these areas. Examples from each area are the Ikegai Iron Works established in Tokyo in 1889, Okuma Machinery Works in Aichi in 1918, Wakayama Iron Works in Osaka in 1896, and the Karatsu Iron Works in North Kyushu in 1916. After this many firms began to produce machine tools in Keihin, Chukyo and Hanshin and to a lesser extent in North Kyushu.

There were also some other machine tool producers in other areas. For example, Niigata Engineering Co. was established in Niigata (a prefecture facing the Japan Sea) in 1910, and Toyo Kogyo Co. (now the Mazda Motor Corp.) began to produce machine tools in 1929 in the Hiroshima Prefecture, while a few producers were found near other industrial areas in Japan.

During the Second World War some machine tool producers moved to the rural districts or established plants in more remote areas away from the industrial centres. For instance, Tsugami moved from Tokyo to Nagaoka in the Niigata Prefecture in 1937 seeking low-cost premises and a diligent labour force. Toshiba Machine Co. was established as a plant of Shibaura Machine Tool Co. at Numazu in Shizuoka Prefecture in 1942, as the ground is firm enough to produce high-precision machine tools.

After the war the above four areas were still the centres of industrial activity and many machine tool producers were operating in Keihin, Chukyo and Hanshin. But some producers moved to the outskirts of these areas seeking larger premises. The improvement of transportation facilities reduced the disadvantages of locations remote to the industrial centres. For instance, Okuma Machinery Works built a new factory at Oguchi, a small town in North Aichi in 1969. New producers could not acquire large premises at a moderate price in the central areas of industrial districts. As a result the number of machine tool producers operating in the neighbouring areas of these districts have increased.

In 1982 the number of member companies of JMTBA was 113 with 133 plants. [According to the Census of Manufacturers 1981, the total number of firms making metal-working machinery (including machine tools) was 1,343.] The largest number of members in any prefecture is 20 in the prefecture of Aichi, followed by Kanagawa (a prefecture to the West of Tokyo) having 12, Niigata having 11, and Saitama (a prefecture to the

North of Tokyo) having 9. Tokyo has 8 plants and Osaka 6. The centre of the machine tool industry is now in Chukyo, the 'middle urban area' of Japan, and sub-centres are scattered around other industrial districts.

III MAJOR CHANGES AFTER THE SECOND WORLD WAR

Relations with the Government

The biggest change the Japanese machine tool industry underwent after the war was the abolition of all military and naval arsenals by the government. After the war, JNR (Japan National Railways) was formed, and they ordered machine tools for the production and repair of rolling stock from domestic producers. This was the only governmental purchase of machine tools, so state influence over the industry as a user and a buyer was considerably weakened.

This applies to other industries as well as the machine tool industry. Before and during the war the government was a large buyer of goods and services and the Japanese economy was strongly dependent on this demand. After the war the government sector of the economy shrank drastically and almost all economic activity had to be carried out in the private sector. To supply goods and services to these sectors, producers had to produce and sell under severe competition. In order to restore the war-damaged economy, the government played a positive role as a policy-maker. Major industries, including the machine tool industry, were influenced by government policies, one of which, 'Kikaikogyo Rinji Sochi-ho', played a great part in the development of the post-war machine tool industry in Japan.

Content of Government Policy

The most important feature of post-war government policy is that it was mainly based upon administrative guidance and some financial support. After the war the government was no longer an important buyer of machine tools, except for JNR, which could exert some influence on domestic machine tool producers by ordering specific products. However, the government constructed several 'economic restoration and development plans' during the 1950s and 1960s.

There were two types of administrative guidance given by MITI. One involved gathering data and giving information to the sector, in order to strengthen the competitive power of Japanese industry. For example, MITI demanded that JMTBA present a 'basic plan of rationalisation of machine tool production' of member companies during the period of 'Kikaikogyo Rinji Sochi-ho'. The other type of guidance by MITI was the suggestion of a desirable structure for the industry. MITI thought that in the machine tool industry there were too many producers and that the number should be reduced. This reduction would expel 'excess competition' among domestic producers, promote the rationalisation of production, and bring about the strengthening of the basic competitive power of the industry. In 1965, during the biggest recession since the war. MITI suggested that domestic machine tool producers should co-operate in groups. This suggestion or administrative guidance was followed and several groups headed by a few leading firms emerged, but these groups functioned only for a short time. When demand recovered, the groups' activities were substantially reduced and 'excess competition' again emerged.

Administrative guidance by MITI was actually not as influential as they thought it would be, but this did not apply only to the machine tool industry. In the automobile industry MITI also suggested that the number of manufacturers should be cut, but this did not happen and the number of auto-makers (including truck manufacturers) has remained at eleven. Japanese manufacturers have always resisted any suggestions that might be harmful to their own managerial autonomy. Even MITI was unable to invade the autonomy of management of private companies.

The financial power of the government was influential during the period of economic growth. The government established the Japan Development Bank (JDB) in 1951. This was a reorganisation of 'Fukko Kinyu Kinko' (Reconstruction Finance Bank), a government financial body that had been set up for the restoration of the economy after the war. JDB was set up for the same purpose, but the emphasis was put on development rather than restoration. Article One of the JDB Law states, 'In order to promote the economic restoration and industrial development through supplying long-term credit, JDB has the duty of supplementing the financial activity of the private banks and/or encouraging their activity of financing' (author's translation).

JDB was a specially incorporated body with managerial autonomy but almost all of its funds came from the government. The finances were allocated on the recommendations of each ministry. In the case of the machine tool industry this was MITI. JDB had the same function as the private banks in the financing of loans to private companies. But it supplied only long-term credit and its rate of interest was determined according to political criteria. The 'standard rate' was about the same as that of the private banks, but the 'special rate' was lower than the market rate. In 1961 the special rate was 6.5 per cent to finance 'Kikaikogyo Rinji Sochi-ho', while the standard rate was 9 per cent.

According to the *History of 10 Years of the Japan Development Bank*, the money lent for machine tool production by the JDB was 715 million yen in 1957, 424 million yen in 1958, 987 million yen in 1959, 504 million yen in 1960, and 1,130 million yen in 1961.[1] The ratios of the sum lent for machine tool production to the total sum lent under 'Kikaikogyo Rinji Sochi-ho' in each year are 22.1 per cent, 21.3 per cent, 35.8 per cent, 19.6 per cent, and 21.1 per cent respectively. This shows that the rationalisation of machine tool production was one of the priorities. This financing supplemented the financial activity of the private banks. If a firm was financed by JDB then it was thought to be financially creditable by the private banks who would provide the rest of the funds.

The role of the JDB as a financier has changed since it was originally set up. The proportion of long-term financing by JDB was fairly high during the latter half of the 1950s and the first half of the 1960s but it was subsequently reduced. When there was little demand for funds, the managers of the private banks would oppose the lending of large sums at low interest rates by the JDB. JDB was not intended to compete with the private banks (Article 22, JDB Law). Accordingly, government regulated JDB to maintain good relations with the private banks.

Business Philosophy and Management Innovation

Before 1945 when the Japanese machine tool industry was heavily dependent on military demand, the leaders in this industry thought that their contribution to the interests of the nation should be through the production of machine tools. They accepted orders from the military and naval authorities and made machine tools for such use. By adopting this philosophy, machine tool producers enlarged their production capacity for military production.

Even after the war this business philosophy did not disappear as some managers still thought highly of the national interest. The nationalistic idea of business in Japan has its roots in the Meiji era when Japanese industrialisation began. After the war Japanese firms were obliged to live with severe competition both from inside and outside the country. As the competition among enterprises became stronger, the need for rationalization of businesses became more urgent and the attitude of managers to business administration gradually changed. Managers of all industries now think of the benefits to their own company first and have had to innovate in their method of management in order to survive severe competition and rationalization. This has been the driving force behind the high growth in the economy in post-war Japan.

The management of machine tool producers were not pioneers of innovation in management. The so-called Japanese style of management — for example, the labour-management consultation system and QCC (quality control circles) — originated from the consumer goods industry, such as the electrical appliance industry and the automobile industry, and spread to other sectors like the iron and steel industry and the machine tool industry.

Upgrading of Japanese Products

Historically, Japanese products were notorious for their low quality. They were cheap, their quality was poor and they often broke down. This remained somewhat as a major problem after the war.

The Japan Automobile Manufacturers' Association published a report, 'Japan's Machine Tool Industry, as Surveyed by the Auto Makers', in March 1954, based on the Association's study of fourteen machine tool builders in the latter part of 1953. Their assessment of the technological level of the machine tools at that time may be summarised as follows. (i) From the year the war ended up to 1953, the auto makers had ordered 326 units of machine tools from domestic builders. Though their precision was excellent to begin with, some of them rapidly lost their accuracy with the passage of time. (ii) Many of the machine tool builders seemed uncertain as to the kinds of machines that would meet the needs of the market. Some of them continued to produce machines they had produced during the war on speculation and encountered difficulties in selling them.[2]

Through the 1950s and until the 1970s Japanese products improved remarkably. Not only domestic users but also foreign users have come to accept that Japanese machine tools are of good quality, easy to use, and are reasonable in price. It would be impossible to explain in a single article how this radical change took place, but there are three major factors which were important in this change.

Firstly, there was renewal of equipment by machine tool producers as a result of 'Kikaikogyo Rinji Sochi-ho'. Through the renewal of equipment, the producers were able to make high-quality machine tools at a lower cost.

The second was the introduction of foreign technology realised through MITI's approval system 'Gaishi-ho'. Through the introduction of foreign technology Japanese producers established a formal relationship with

TABLE 4.7 Trends of expenses for R & D and advertisement (in the cases of Okuma and Hitachi) (value in thousand yen, ( ) %)

	Okuma Machinery Works			Hitachi Seiki Co.		
Fiscal year	Total sale	Expense for R & D	Expense for advertisement	Total sale	Expense for R & D	Expense for advertisement
1962	6407767 (100.0)	96787 (1.5)	61989 (1.0)	7301580 (100.0)	n.a. (–)	98227 (1.3)
1967	8709885 (100.0)	183182 (2.1)	57869 (0.9)	8291296 (100.0)	186467 (2.2)	69753 (0.8)
1972	16637439 (100.0)	416199 (2.5)	205788 (1.2)	12144715 (100.0)	285557 (2.4)	157937 (1.3)
1977	17068807 (100.0)	391280 (2.2)	97683 (0.6)	15586090 (100.0)	245925 (1.6)	164621 (1.1)
1982	47161668 (100.0)	1234813 (2.6)	388763 (0.8)	30648577 (100.0)	799640 (2.6)	697791 (2.3)

SOURCE Financial Reports (each company).

foreign producers and learnt about new technology after the war and this stimulated the development of their own new products.

Third, there was more investment in R & D. Initially Japanese producers did not undertake R & D and copied foreign products. Since the 1960s they began to enlarge R & D facilities and employ many college-graduate engineers (including industrial designers) and researchers. The cost of R & D activity increased more rapidly than that of advertising. Two cases are shown in Table 4.7. At present the ratio of R & D costs to total sales for the sector as a whole is more than 2 per cent, while in the 1960s this ratio was about 1 per cent.

Japanese machine tool producers have registered many patents and are applying for more than a thousand new patents every year, some of which are registered in other countries including the USA and European countries.

The upgrading of Japanese products may seem to have been very fast but it was the result of more than two decades of effort by Japanese producers. The management of the leading Japanese machine tool producers visited American and European firms to learn of their new techniques. Through the 1950s to the 1970s almost all Japanese industry was interested in innovations in technology and in management. The absorption of new techniques and knowledge also took place in the iron and steel, automobile, electrical and other industries which modernized and upgraded their products during this period. This created big demand for machine tools.

Growth in Exports

The machine tool industry is now one of the major exporting industries in Japan. The ratio of exported value of machine tools to total production has been over 30 per cent since 1976 (see Table 4.8). Major destinations for exports are the USA, West Germany, Australia, England, the Soviet Union, South Korea and Taiwan. The USA has been the largest importer of Japanese machine tools since 1972 and in 1981 they imported nearly half of all the machines exported from Japan. The Japanese Machine Tool Trade Association established its first overseas branch offices in Chicago and Dusseldorf in 1962. The machine tool import ratio has declined considerably. The ratio of exports of NC machine tools and machining centres to that of the total exports of machine tools is now around 60–70 per cent (see Table 4.9).

TABLE 4.8 Production exports and imports of machine tools in recent years (value in million yen)

Year	Production (A)	Exports (B)	Ratio of Exports (B)/(A) %	Imports (C)	Domestic Demand (A)−(B)+(C)=(D)	Dependence on Imports (C)/(D) %
1975	230 739	61 611	26.7	21 575	190 703	11.3
1976	228 604	76 073	33.3	13 867	166 398	8.3
1977	312 844	115 493	36.9	15 720	213 071	7.4
1978	365 525	162 138	44.4	19 638	223 025	8.8
1979	484 132	206 643	42.7	26 214	303 703	8.6
1980	682 102	269 577	39.5	38 221	450 746	8.5
1981	851 561	310 763	36.5	38 623	579 421	6.7
1982	782 776	247 576	31.6	43 585	578 785	7.5
1983	701 541	237 445	29.6	32 517	496 613	6.5

SOURCES Japan Machine Tool Builders' Association, *Thirty Years' Progress of 'Mother Machine'* (in Japanese) (1982); JMTBA, *Machine Tool News* (in Japanese)

TABLE 4.9   Exports of NC machine tools and machining centers and its ratio to the total exports (value in million yen)

Year	Exports of NC machine tools and matching centres (A)	Total exports (B)	Ratio (A)/(B) %
1975	8055	61 611	13.1
1976	18 108	76 073	23.8
1977	36 407	115 493	31.5
1978	62 807	162 138	38.7
1979	99 587	206 643	48.2
1980	172 756	269 577	64.1
1981	218 970	310 763	70.5
1982	163 302	247 576	66.0
1983	155 438	237 445	65.5

NOTE   The ratios of production of NC machine tools and machining centres to the total machine tool production in value were 53.9% and 60.1% in 1982 and 1983 respectively.

SOURCES   Japan Machine Tool Builders' Association, *Thirty Years' Progress of 'Mother Machine'* (1982); JMTBA, *Machine Tool News*.

Agreements with Foreign Manufacturers on Production and Distribution

There were no licensing agreements before the Second World War. Okuma Machinery Works gave licenses for the production of their engine lathe and shaping machine to an Indian machine tool producer in 1962. This was one of the first cases of technology being exported by a Japanese producer. In the 1970s a few manufacturers exported the technology for the production of conventional machine tools, such as lathes and drilling and milling machines, to Korea and Taiwan.

More recently several Japanese machine tool companies have signed contracts with American and European manufacturers for the production and distribution of their products. For instance, Toyoda Machine Works gave the marketing rights of their machining centre to the Bendix Corporation, Okuma Machinery Works sold the marketing and manufacturing rights of a machining centre to Alfred H. Schuette, a West German machine tool company, and Mitsubishi Heavy Industries decided to develop jointly with the Acme-Cleveland Corporation of the USA an NC two-spindle automatic lathe. All these agreements were reached in 1982.[3]

The background for these agreements has been the increasing demand for high-quality, labour-saving machine tools.

CONCLUDING REMARKS

The import ratio is now low, approximately 7–8 per cent since 1976 (see Table 4.8). This means that the majority of required machine tools are sourced in Japan. However, Japan still imports high-precision machine tools from the USA and Europe, especially West Germany and Switzerland. Furthermore, conventional machine tools such as engine lathes, milling machines and drilling machines are now being imported from Korea, Taiwan and China.

The constituents of the Japanese machine tool industry may be classified into five elements: government, domestic producers, domestic users, foreign producers and foreign users. The process of development of the machine tool industry can be understood in terms of changes in the pattern of the relationship among these five elements. As Figure 4.1 shows, there are four stages in the development of the machine tool industry in Japan.

Stage I: During this stage domestic users were dependent on foreign products and domestic producers satisfied only a small proportion of domestic demand. The government's only role was that of a machine tool user.

Stage II: During the Second World War, domestic users could not import the foreign products they required and were obliged to use home-made machine tools. The government played a positive role as a policy-maker as well as being a large user. Foreign producers withdrew from the Japanese market and the domestic producers took their place.

Stage III: After the war, the government's role as a policy-maker was strong and both domestic producers and users benefited from these policies. However, the government's role as a machine-tool user declined considerably. Foreign producers provided technological assistance to Japanese producers. During this period the Japanese machine tool industry developed to become a major branch of the capital goods sector in the economy.

Stage IV: The present stage of development. Domestic producers are supplying machine tools to both domestic and overseas users, but there are still some imports of foreign machines. Technological assistance is becoming bi-lateral between foreign and domestic producers. Domestic producers now have a widespread distribution network for their products. The government's role as policy-maker and consumer is limited. The

Stage I: Early times

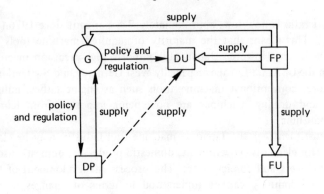

Stage II: Wartime

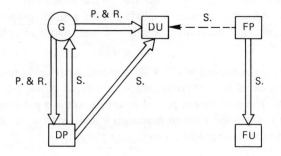

NOTE

Constituent	Indicator:
G stands for government acting as the policy-maker, regulator and the user of machine tools.	$\Longrightarrow$ indicates strong relationship. $\longrightarrow$ indicates moderate relationship $--\rightarrow$ indicates weak relationship
DP stands for domestic producer.	
DU stands for domestic user.	
FP stands for foreign producer.	
FU stands for foreign user.	

Stage III: Around the 1950s – '60s

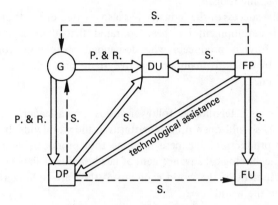

Stage IV: Present Time

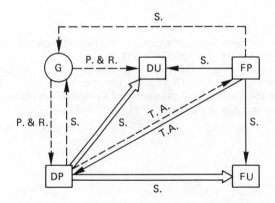

FIGURE 4.1 Relationship among constituents of Japanese machine tool industry at four stages of history

renewal of equipment by small domestic enterprises has created a large demand for machine tools.

However, the success of the industry has also created difficult problems. The speed of development has been so rapid that there is increasing conflict with foreign producers who demanded protection from their governments. In order to maintain the free trade principle this conflict must be overcome.

Japan began as a technology follower and is now a leader. The forthcoming Stage V should open up new patterns in the worldwide division of machine tool production. Japanese machine tool producers should contribute to the technological advancement of newly industrializing countries and the development of the world economy if they are to hold a respectable position in the world.

NOTES

1. Japan Development Bank, *History of 10 Years of Japan Development Bank* (in Japanese) (1963) pp. 297, 301.
2. 'Special Reports on JMTBA 30th Anniversary', *Metalworking: Engineering and Marketing* (November 1982) p. 156.
3. 'Japan is at the Forefront of International Co-operation', *Metalworking: Engineering and Marketing* (July 1983) pp. 32-3.

5 International Competitiveness, International Diffusion of Technology and the State: A Case Study from Taiwan and Japan[1]

MARTIN FRANSMAN

INTRODUCTION

The economic rise of Japan and the Asian newly industrialized countries – Hong Kong, Singapore, South Korea and Taiwan – has had a major impact on both analysis and policy. But while it is fairly easy to describe the economic success of these countries, problems of a different order arise in attempting to explain this economic performance.

The second section of this chapter begins with a summary of the most widely accepted explanation of the economic performance of the Asian newly industrialized countries, based on the concept of comparative advantage. It is argued, however, that this analysis has a number of serious shortcomings which render it unacceptable as a complete explanation. Three weaknesses are considered in more detail. First, the determinants of technical and productivity change are omitted in the conventional account. Second, a passive role for the state is implicitly assumed. Third, the conventional view based on the theory of comparative advantage does not explain economic growth. It is accordingly concluded that a richer account is needed to explain the economic performance of these countries, one that takes account of the determinants of technical and productivity change, including the international diffusion of technology, and the role of the state.

In Sections III and IV it is argued that a detailed microstudy of the machine tool industry in Taiwan and Japan will throw light on the important questions of international competitiveness and economic growth raised in a more theoretical way in Section II. Introductory details are presented of the Taiwanese and Japanese sample firms included in the study. In Section V the 'technological trajectory' of the machine tool industry is examined for the post-war period in order to understand the technological changes that were required of firms in Taiwan and Japan. Indicators of the international competitiveness of the machine tool industries in Japan and Taiwan are then considered in Section VI.

The task of explaining this international competitiveness is tackled in Section VII. In sub-sections a number of different elements are examined which enter into the explanation of the international competitiveness of the Taiwanese and Japanese industries. These include the following: relative labour costs; the international diffusion of technology and indigenously generated technical change; the intensity of competition; the role of the state; social relations within the factory; and supply-side determinants.

Finally, in Section VIII, the strategy of making use of technology developed elsewhere, that is the 'frontier-following strategy', is examined in the case of Taiwan. The section begins with a quantification of the price and performance differential between Taiwanese and best-practice machine tool producers. A discussion of the future of the Taiwanese machine tool industry follows, examining the debates currently taking place in Taiwan about the degree and form of state intervention necessary to maintain international competitiveness in the industry. Some conclusions are drawn in the last section.

II INTERNATIONAL COMPETITIVENESS AND COMPARATIVE ADVANTAGE

In Hong Kong, the epitomy of the open economy, the economists' injunction to 'get prices right' was automatically obeyed. As a result investment inevitably was in activities and methods that used a great deal of the cheap factor – labour – and conserved scarce capital, in manufacturing for export to the world market. (Chow and Papanek, 1981)

[The present study] points to a number of weaknesses in the conventional 'international-trade-theory' approach. This theory is apt to assume too readily that, once we have removed the trade distortions and biases, the latent comparative advantage of a country will automatically exert itself. What Taiwan's experience has suggested is that there may be 'many a slip twixt cup and lip' in acquiring a comparative advantage in labour-intensive exports theoretically supposed to be 'given' by an abundant labour supply on the basis of the 'given' technology. (Myint, 1981)

The major economic question in the case of Japan and the Asian newly industrialized countries (NICs) – Hong Kong, Singapore, South Korea and Taiwan – relates to their actual and potential long-term economic growth. While the recent rapid growth of these countries can be readily described, a far more complex problem arises in attempting to *explain* this growth performance.

The most widely accepted explanation of the growth of the Asian NICs has been couched in terms of the theory of comparative advantage. According to this explanation government policy in these countries ensured that factor prices were 'right', in the sense that they more or less accurately reflected social opportunity costs, and that there was no bias against exports in terms of incentives. In particular, wage rates reflected the relatively low opportunity cost of labour that existed in these labour surplus economies in the 1960s. Given these relative factor prices, profit maximization led to the choice of relatively labour-intensive techniques of production. With the removal of trade distortions and biases, government facilitated the realization of the country's comparative advantage in labour-intensive goods which in turn resulted in a rapid increase in the exports of these goods. These exports had beneficial second-round effects, among which was the increase in imports that was made possible. When, in a later stage in the process, labour surpluses were used up as a result of the increased demand for labour that accompanied the rise in exports and growth, real wages began to rise, leading to an improved distribution of income, a reduced rate of profit, an increase in capital-intensity and the establishment of new areas of comparative advantage guided by the changing factor endowments and scarcities. Thus Little (1979) concluded:

The major lesson [emerging from the study of South Korea, Taiwan, Hong Kong and Singapore] is that labour-intensive export-oriented policies, which amounted to almost free trade conditions for exporters, were the prime cause of an extremely rapid and labour-intensive industrialization which revolutionized in a decade the lives of more than fifty million people. (p. 34)

While this view has been extremely influential,[2] it has a number of important shortcomings which limit its ability to satisfactorily explain the economic performance of the Asian NICs. The limitations which will be discussed here include the following: technology and productivity are assumed to be exogenously determined; a 'passive' role for the state is implicitly assumed; the theory of comparative advantage does not provide an explanation of growth.

The Exogeneity of Technology and Productivity

The explanation of the economic performance of the Asian NICs in terms of the theory of comparative advantage (referred to here as the 'conventional view') assigns a very limited role to technology issues. In general, technology is assumed to be exogenously determined and the acquisition of technological knowledge (including new technology) is assumed to be unproblematical. Within the exogenously given technology, the choice of a particular technique is automatically 'given' by relative factor prices and the assumption of profit maximization. Accordingly, the problem of achieving international competitiveness and long-term economic growth is reduced to one of 'getting prices and incentives right', as is made clear in the quotation from Chow and Papanek given above.

However, the implicit suppression of questions relating to the 'technology dimension' leads to difficulties. The reason is that technology is never 'given' in the sense that it is known to all producers and can be used with equal efficiency by them. Even in the case of non-proprietary technology the process whereby the technology is acquired and used at international levels of efficiency is costly in terms of the firm's resources and is fraught with uncertainty. Yet the attainment of international competitiveness is largely dependent on this process of technology acquisition, generation and use. Accordingly, a theory which ignores these issues relating to technology by assuming the technology itself to be given leaves out a central determinant of international competitiveness. As Nelson (1978) puts it:

> There doesn't exist a well defined set of 'technological options' out there that a firm can scan and assess easily and reliably. This is not to deny that there isn't a wide range of choice, and that finding out about the options and thinking about the choices isn't important. However, it is likely to be a far more difficult matter than generally assumed for a firm to be able to judge how a particular technique employed by

another firm would operate for it. Its own version of the technique invariably would involve a variety of idiosyncracies, some intended and some not. Invariably, there would be teething problems, and a need to learn-by-doing, and perhaps by researching. (p. 18)

Endogenizing the 'technology dimension', however, raises further problems. Once it is accepted that the activities involved in seeking technology from external sources, assimilating and adapting the technology to the firm's circumstances, and over time improving upon it are costly activities requiring a complex range of skills, then some important alterations have to be made to the way in which the conventional view sees the process of attaining international competitiveness. The steps in the conventional argument from resource endowment (usually capital, labour and natural resources, but sometimes including human capital) via exogenously determined productivity levels to costs and international competitiveness[3] begin to appear too mechanistic and automatic. The conventional view fails to capture the complex process whereby firms and countries become, or fail to become, internationally competitive. One essential part of this process relates to the acquisition, generation and use of technology and it is misleading to think of this as being 'given' by the country's resource endowments. Many other determinations and processes must be taken into account if we are to grasp the importance of technical change in the attainment of international competitiveness and this requires that we move beyond the conventional view.[4]

A related problem with the conventional view follows from the treatment of productivity. The theory of comparative advantage (of either the Ricardian or the Heckscher/Ohlin variety) deals with the price of inputs relative to their productivity. While input prices are variable, productivity is exogenously determined. The result in the conventional view is a one-sided emphasis on factor input prices, particularly the wage rate. To some extent this emphasis is understandable, and indeed correct, in view of the relatively low wage rates that prevailed in the Asian NICs compared with the industrialized countries which constituted their major trading partners. However, it is inadequate to base a theory of international competitiveness entirely on the prices at which factor inputs are purchased on the market. The reason is that these factors must still be 'brought into the factory gates' and a large number of circumstances will determine whether they are ultimately able to produce and sell internationally competitive goods and services. The emphasis on factor prices and the assumption that productivity is exogenously determined suppresses questions about the determinants of productivity, and hence international competitiveness.

Yet in explaining the economic performance of the Asian NICs it is surely necessary to ask why productivity levels are what they are. Otherwise there is the danger that the 'explanation' of international competitiveness will become circular: country A is internationally competitive in the production of good X because, given its wage rates and productivity levels, its units costs in producing X are at least as low as any competing country. In other words, country A is cost-competitive because it is cost-competitive.

In order to provide a more satisfactory explanation of the economic performance of the Asian NICs we will want to know more, not only about the determinants of the wage rate, but also about the determinants of productivity. But this leads us into further difficulties since at present we lack an adequate theory of productivity change.[5] Nevertheless, since the point of this discussion is to indicate some of the problems that follow from the assumption that productivity is exogenously determined, we shall confine ourselves to two separate comments.

The first is that once productivity and related technical change are endogenized, it is possible that the conclusions which emerge will be quite different from those conventionally accepted. One possible causal mechanism is spelled out by Liebenstein (1981):

> A standard conclusion of conventional theory is the desirability of expanding international trade in accordance with the comparative advantage in production of each country ... However, according to X-efficiency theory a more important gain from trade may also result from the importation of products *similar* to those produced reasonably well in the country in question. Such imports put pressure on local producers to produce at lower costs than would otherwise be the case. (p. 106)

This example points to the importance of dropping the assumption that productivity, a central determinant of international competitiveness, is exogenously determined.

The second comment, pursuing the point made above about the importance of 'following factors into the factory gates', is that there is a large and growing body of evidence to suggest that relationships within the factory have an important bearing on productivity and technical change. Most recently this view has received support from the studies that have been done in Japanese factories.[6] As Nelson (1981) points out, while the standard theory of the firm emphasizes 'management "choice" among clearly defined options' it fails to understand that the firm is in fact 'a social system which may be resistant or unresponsive to management commands'. He suggests that 'in general, the employees of firms do not automatically share the same objectives as managers. So there is a requirement for motivation and monitoring' (pp. 1037-8). While in the Japanese case this point is now unexceptional, it has not yet entered seriously into the explanation of the economic performance of the Asian NICs. This serves as a further example of the need to go beyond the discussion of factor prices and effective government incentives stressed in the conventional view.[7]

The Passive State

A further shortcoming in the conventional view is the implication of a relatively passive role played by the state. According to this view, and apart from the provision of 'infrastructural' preconditions such as a suitable legal and monetary system etc., the state's role in industrialization is limited to (a) establishing 'correct' factor prices and (b) ensuring that the system of effective incentives, usually measured by the effective rates of protection and subsidy, does not discriminate against exports.

A major objection to this implicit view of the state's role arises on empirical, rather than analytical, grounds. The point, quite simply, is that in three of the four Asian NICs state intervention has gone substantially further than implied in the conventional view. In Singapore, Taiwan and South Korea the state has done more than influence factor prices and ensure non-discrimination against exports, with the degree of intervention greatest in South Korea and least in Singapore. Measures taken have included the granting of selective, and therefore discriminatory, incentives to priority industries and firms in the form of credit subsidies and tax reductions; interference with international trade flows through measures ranging from tariffs to total prohibition of imports (in Taiwan and South Korea); and a variety of steps taken to enhance firms' technological capabilities including state scrutiny of licensing and other technology transfer agreements and direct intervention through public industrial technology research institutes.[8]

While the conventional view offers an essentially similar explanation for the economic performance of all the Asian NICs, it is clear that there are radical differences in the extent and forms of government intervention undertaken by each of the four states. This ranges from Hong Kong at the 'minimal intervention' end of the spectrum through Singapore and Taiwan (in that order) to South Korea where the state has been most vigorous in its use of 'carrots and sticks', including highly subsidized credit and the outright prohibition of imports coupled with an insistence on export performance. In the present case-study a section will be devoted to the examination of state intervention in the machine tool sector in Japan, Taiwan and South Korea. However, since Hong Kong appears to come closest to the conventional view of the role of the state, it is worth making a few brief comments here about this country.

The first point to note is that, while it is important to attempt to explain the lesser degree of state intervention in Hong Kong, something that will not be attempted here, it must be kept in mind that this country is the great exception, not only among developing but also among developed countries. The rule, therefore, is a significantly greater amount of intervention. Second, it is worth bearing in mind that although Hong Kong, unlike the other three Asian NICs, has never had a period of infant industry and learning protection, the managers and personnel of many of its largest enterprises have. Thus, for example, many of the textile producers who came to Hong Kong around the time of the communist victory in 1949 on the mainland built up their businesses in the more sheltered environments of Shanghai and Canton. From this point of view, therefore, Hong Kong is less of an exception than might at first appear. Third, it is worth noting that the Hong Kong government has more recently acknowledged that government intervention is in some cases necessary in order to facilitate technological advance. The official *Report of the Advisory Committee on Diversification* published in 1979 acknowledged the need for assisting firms in the acquisition of new technology and the improvement of products and processes, particularly in the case of metal working and finishing. The Committee accordingly recommended the provision by government of 'industrial support facilities' and steps have since been taken to put this into effect. Significantly, the Committee felt that the greater degree of government intervention in Taiwan and South Korea was 'of relevance to Hong Kong's circumstances'. Finally, it should be kept in mind that the Hong Kong government has intervened in important ways in order to influence the price of labour. Here special mention should be made of immigration policy which has been tightened or relaxed partly in order to suit labour requirements, and government housing policy which has made subsidized housing available to workers, taking commercial land prices into account, thus helping to keep down real wages.[9]

Since Hong Kong, however, is exceptional, attempts must be made to understand better the role that government has played in influencing the economic performance of the Asian NICs.

Comparative Advantage and the Explanation of Economic Growth

A further problem with the conventional view is that the causal link between comparative advantage and economic growth remains unspecified. According to this view a combination of the 'right' factor prices and a removal of trade distortions and biases will lead to a country achieving a comparative advantage in particular areas, which in turn will lead to the growth of exports in these areas. But why will the growth in exports lead to a faster growth in output than would have occurred had the 'distortions and biases' in favour of the domestic market remained in force? One possible argument is that growth rates will be higher under free trade. In considering the relationship between exports and economic growth Krueger (1981) notes that 'At first glance the superiority of the export-promotion strategy appeared to vindicate the view of trade theorists, who had advocated free trade and who saw export promotion as coming closer to a free trade regime than did import substitution' (p. 3). However,

the simple 2 × 2 comparative advantage model would seem to suggest that growth rates would be the same under autarky and under free trade, once the once-and-for-all losses associated with accepting a non-optimal trade policy are absorbed. Thus, there are no theorems from standard trade theory with regard to the effect on the growth rate of departures from optimal trade policy. (p. 6)

Therefore, free trade, as theorised in the standard trade model, does not provide an explanation of the faster growth rates observed in the export-oriented economies.

In pursuing the question of the relationship between exporting and economic growth Krueger (1981) suggests a number of causal mechanisms, such as that incentives to increase total factor productivity are greater under export-oriented regimes and that the greater degree of competitive pressure forces firms to increase efficiency. In doing so she implicitly agrees with Findlay (1981) who, in discussing the same question, concludes that 'it is clear that an answer must be sought outside the conventional bounds of the standard model, in the murky but relevant waters of such concepts as X-efficiency and "learning-by-doing"' (p. 31). However, to tread into these waters is to confront questions about the determinants of productivity and technical changes, and, as we saw, it is precisely these issues that are held at arm's length in the conventional view.

Conclusion

We may conclude, therefore, that the conventional view as it stands is inadequate in order to explain the economic growth of the Asian NICs. While aspects of this view are undoubtedly relevant, the need remains to provide a more robust explanation of the growth of these countries. In such an explanation a central place must be occupied by an analysis of the determinants of productivity and technical change and the role of the state.

III THE RELEVANCE OF A STUDY OF MACHINE TOOLS IN TAIWAN AND JAPAN

In the light of the shortcomings of the conventional view and since at present we lack satisfactory theories of the determinants of productivity and technical change as well as state intervention, it is suggested that microstudies have a particularly important role to play. It is suggested further that a study of machine tools is potentially illuminating for the following reasons:

(a) The machine tool industry in Taiwan and Japan has become highly competitive internationally as witnessed by the rapid growth of exports, particularly from the 1970s.

(b) The machine tool industry has been selected as a priority industry in these countries as well as in all the Asian NICs.

(c) An examination of the 'technology dimension' in the case of machine tools reveals how important technical change has been in the attainment, and maintenance, of international competitiveness.

(d) The state has been important in the establishment of international competitiveness.

(e) In these respects (points a to d) the machine tool sector has a good deal in common with other sectors in these countries, particularly the engineering sector, even though some of its production and market characteristics distinguish it from these other sectors. Accordingly, a study of the machine tool sector is also relevant for other sectors.

IV THE PRESENT STUDY

The main primary source of information for the present chapter came from interviews held with machine tool producing firms in Taiwan and

Japan and from government officials in these countries. Ten firms were interviewed in Taiwan, out of twenty-two firms that exhibited numerically controlled machine tools at the 1983 Taiwan Machinery Show, and four firms in Japan, including two of the largest firms, one of the oldest, and a medium-sized firm (the sudsidiary of which had earlier been interviewed in Singapore). In addition detailed interviews were held with numerous officials in government agencies and trade associations including the Industrial Technology Research Institute (ITRI), the Mechanical Industry Research Laboratories (MIRL), the Council for Economic Planning and Development, the Science and Technology Advisory Group, and the Taiwan Association of Machinery Industries in Taiwan, and the Japan Machine Tool Builders Association and the Machinery Division of the Ministry of International Trade and Industry in Japan.

The major constraint in the study arose from the realistic assumption that firms would be unwilling to allocate more than a few hours of the time of senior management in answering questions. This placed a serious constraint on the collection of data, particularly time series data, and meant that in places recourse was necessary to more indirect evidence.[10]

In Tables 5.1a and 5.1b further information is given on the Japanese and Taiwanese firms. (The tenth Taiwanese firm produced CNC controls, and information on this firm is presented below in the text of this paper.)

Two factors stand out in comparing the firms. The first is the longer history of the Japanese firms. (The history of the Japanese machine tool industry will be considered in more detail below in the section on the role of the state). The second is the larger size of the Japanese firms.[11]

TABLE 5.1a   Japan: General data on firms

Firm (A)	Gross value of sales (B)	Year in which production began (C)	Number of employees (D)	Most important product (E)
1	94.5 billion yen	1938	3641	CNC machine centre
2	38 billion yen	1936	1500	CNC turning centre
3	30 billion yen	1889	1000	CNC turning lathe
4	20 billion yen	1926	520	Surface grinding machine

TABLE 5.1b Taiwan: General data on firms

Firm (A)	Gross value of sales (B)	Value of fixed capital assets (C)	Year in which production began (D)	Number of employees (E)	Most important CNC product (F)
1	$600 million NT	$1000 million NT	1943	700	CNC machining centre
2	$ 14 million US	$ 600 million NT	1969	500	CNC vertical machining centre
3	$500 million NT	–	1951	450	CNC lathe
4	$850 million NT	–	1978	420	CNC machining centre
5	$ 6 million US	–	1949	250	CNC slant lathe
6	$ 12 million US	$ 200 million NT	1973	200	CNC lathe
7	$ 6 million US	–	1965	200	CNC milling machine
8	$150 million NT	$ 70 million NT	1968	180	CNC milling machine
9	$ 3 million US	$ 2.5 million US	1966	140	CNC machining centre

V THE TECHNOLOGICAL TRAJECTORY IN THE CASE OF MACHINE TOOLS

Since the present study is concerned broadly with the competitiveness of the Japanese and Taiwanese machine tool industries in the post-Second World War period, it will be useful to trace the development of machine tool technology during this period. This will give some idea of the changes that Japanese and Taiwanese machine tool producers have had to make in order to keep up with the shifting technology frontier and become, and remain, internationally competitive. In examining the development of machine tool technology the notion of a 'technological trajectory' is helpful.

The concept of a 'technological trajectory' has been introduced into the technology literature by Rosenberg and Nelson and Winter. In writing about technological trajectories, Nelson and Winter (1977) state that 'there is a sense that innovation has a certain inner logic of its own. . . advances seem to follow advances in a way that appears somewhat "inevitable" and certainly not fine tuned to the changing demand and cost conditions' (pp. 56-7). They go on to identify two technological trajectories that have been particularly common: 'the progressive exploitation of latent scale economies and increasing mechanization of operations that have been done by hand'. Regarding the latter they comment that 'Mechanization seems to be viewed by designers of equipment as a natural way to reduce costs, increase reliability and precision of production, gain more reliable control over operations etc.' (p. 59). There is a strong similarity between this argument and that of Rosenberg (1976) who, in an article on Marx's analysis of the role of machinery, suggests that an underlying theme in the design of machinery has been the attempt to reduce human, subjective control of the production process and replace it with more constant, predictable control by the machine itself, thus facilitating a greater application of the natural sciences to production. While the extent to which the processes of mechanization and automation are indeed relatively immune to changes in demand and cost conditions is an important, and contentious issue, a history of the development of different kinds of machinery could no doubt be written on the basis of this theme. In the case of machine tools such a study would include an analysis of the introduction of devices such as cams, automatic feeds, stops and throw-out-dogs which reduced the number of manual tasks that the operator had to undertake, and jigs and fixtures which made it possible for less-skilled workers to operate a machine once a skilled operator had set it up.

The notion of a technological trajectory has more recently been incorporated into the broader concept of a 'technological paradigm' by Constant (1980) and Dosi (1982). Drawn from Kuhn's idea of a scientific paradigm, a technological paradigm refers to a particular technological approach to solving problems of specific kinds. In the case of machine tools a fundamental watershed was reached with the merging of a newer with an older technological paradigm. The older paradigm was that of mechanical engineering while the newer paradigm was based on electrical and later electronic processes and formed the basis for increasingly sophisticated machine control systems. It was the automation trajectory, the search for more accurate and cheaper methods of machine control, that brought these two paradigms together and, in the process, fundamentally altered the technological basis and capabilities of sophisticated machine tools.

The watershed came with the introduction of numerical control which Mansfield (1977) has called 'one of the twentieth century's most important innovations' (p. 126). Numerical control involves translating the specifications of the work-piece into a mathematical representation of the required path of the cutting tool and then, in turn, translating this into a stream of co-ordinates represented in a numerical code recorded on tape. The idea for numerical control came originally from John Parsons, a United States air force subcontractor, who was attempting to cut the contours of helicopter rotor-blade templates.[12] Parsons contracted a good deal of the research work to the Servomechanisms Laboratory at MIT and in 1952 the first numerically controlled machine tool, a vertical milling machine, was demonstrated. With the passage of time a number of important advances in the technology were made, particularly in the area of programming. The next big breakthrough occurred in the early 1970s with the development of CNC (computer numerical control). CNC involves direct input of co-ordinate data into a microprocessor. Present-day versions of CNC control spindle drive speed, tool selection as well as cutting specifications. Advances, largely in microelectronics and motor technology, have enabled the cost of CNC control units to be substantially reduced and as a result, since the CNC unit is a significant proportion of total price, the relative selling price of CNC machine tools has fallen sharply. Jacobsson (1984a) calculates that the unit price ratio between CNC and conventional lathes, the most common kind of machine tool, fell from 4.85 in 1975 to 2.89 in 1981. However, it is important to bear in mind, particularly with the potential of the machine tool industry in developing countries in view, that the new CNC technology has not entirely replaced standard semi-automatic and automatic machine tools. In 1981 in Japan 51 per cent of the total value of machine tool production comprised NC and CNC machine tools, although it must be said that the ratio has increased rapidly, with strong encouragement from the Ministry of International Trade and Industry (MITI), and was only 26 per cent in 1978. The cost-minimizing choice between NC/CNC and conventional machine tools depends on a number of considerations including batch size, component specifications, and precision.[13] The co-existence of the new with the older technology raises a number of interesting questions regarding the competition between technologies, as opposed to firms, although it is clear that in an increasing number of areas NC/CNC is establishing itself as the superior technology. This has a number of important implications for the projection of national and world demand and therefore for the planning of the machine tool industry.

Most recent developments have seen CNC machine tools being incorporated into larger manufacturing systems. Direct Numerical Control (DNC) involves central computer control of a set of machine tools. In flexible manufacturing systems (FMS) a series of CNC machine tools work in sequence with the work-piece moved automatically from one machine to the other. Such systems have been aided by the development of transfer mechanisms, particularly robots, the capability of which is being continually improved with advances in robot vision and artificial intelligence. Computer integrated manufacturing (CIM) integrates computer aided design (CAD) and computer aided manufacturing (CAM).

The significance of the insertion of machine tools into broader manufacturing systems from the point of view of developing countries lies in the fact that increasingly the mastery of progressively more complex technology will become necessary in the bid to remain internationally competitive. While the demand for stand-alone machine tools will continue to be substantial, increasing use will inevitably be made, particularly by larger users, of manufacturing systems beginning with simpler systems such as flexible manufacturing cells (FMC) and FMS. In Taiwan, progress along the systems road is being made. In the July 1983 issue of the major Japanese machine tool trade journal, *Metalworking*, it was reported that at the Ninth Taiwan Machinery Show held in April 1983 two full-scale FMSs were exhibited developed by the government-run Mechanical Industries Research Laboratory (MIRL) of the Industrial Technology Research Institute (ITRI) and the country's largest machine tool producer, Yang Iron. Significant progress was also reported on the development of Taiwanese CNC control systems. The journal reported that of the 62 CNC units exhibited at the show, 61 per cent used Fanuc systems (Fanuc, a Japanese subsidiary of Fujitsu, is the world's largest producer of CNC systems) while 27 per cent used Taiwan-made systems. However, the journal went on to report that since the Taiwanese CNC units had only recently been developed and in small numbers, 'data on actual results such as reliability were insufficient. For this reason it has been regarded as ahead of its time until such a time [as] Taiwanese-made CNC units would be available on a large scale' (p. 82). More information will be given below about the development of Taiwanese CNC units. However, a senior engineer at MIRL expressed the view that if Taiwan was one year behind Japan in the development of CNC machine tools, the lag in the case of more sophisticated machining systems was ten years, and acknowledged some concern about the ability of Taiwan to catch up given its weakness in the fundamental enabling technologies. The policy implications of this concern are discussed in more detail in Section VIII below.

VI THE INTERNATIONAL COMPETITIVENESS OF THE MACHINE TOOL INDUSTRY IN JAPAN AND TAIWAN

Under conditions of free trade the best indicators of international competitiveness are probably change in market share and export growth. In the presence of trade restrictions of one form or another other indicators may also have to be used, such as total factor productivity growth, changes in unit cost and product quality, etc. Since trade is relatively free at present in Japan and Taiwan (see below for further details), most attention shall be paid to market share and exports.

In examining market share it makes sense to look at the US market since this is the largest, most sophisticated, and most competitive. In Table 5.2 the share of major exporters in total value of United States machine tool imports is given for the years 1976 and 1981.

Table 5.2 shows that while the share of Japan and Taiwan increased dramatically, that of all the other exporters of machine tools to the USA decreased. Japan's share increased from 21 per cent in 1976 to 49 per cent in 1981, while that of Taiwan increased from 4 to 7. More detailed information is available on Japanese exports of machining centres (CNC) to the USA as a proportion of apparent US consumption. In 1976, in value terms, Japanese exports were 2.1 per cent of apparent US consumption, rising to 38.2 per cent in 1981. In terms of units, the figures were 3.7 per cent and 50.1 per cent respectively, reflecting the fact that the Japanese tend to specialize in the medium price and performance range building standardized machine tools. In Table 5.3 information is presented for Japan on the share of exports in gross output, and annual growth rates of apparent consumption and exports.

TABLE 5.2 Major exporters' shares in total value of United States machine-tool imports, 1976 and 1981 (percentage)

Country or area	1976	1981
China (Taiwan Province)	4	7
Germany, Federal Republic of	29	14
Italy	5	4
Japan	21	49
Switzerland	9	6
United Kingdom	10	11

SOURCE   UNIDO (1984).

From 1910 until the early 1960s the export ratio for the Japanese machine tool sector was fairly low, ranging in most years from about 2 to 7 per cent.[14] From then, however, the export ratio increased steadily to reach around 40 per cent in the late 1970s and early 1980s. In part this reflected the targets of the Ministry of International Trade and Industry (MITI), coupled with incentives and perhaps even some pressures. The export ratio for numerically controlled machine tools and machining centres was far higher, rising from 13 per cent in 1975 to 66 per cent in 1983 (see Chokki, present volume). By the early 1960s, Japan (both firms and research institutions) had mastered numerical control technology diffused from the United States (in ways that will be considered later), and the export drive to the United States began. This is reflected in the figures in Table 5.3 showing the annual growth rate of exports.

The domination of the world machine tool industry by Japanese firms is now practically indisputable. According to *American Machinist*, in 1982 Japan for the first time became the largest producer of machine tools in value terms, followed by the United States and West Germany.[15] In terms of value of exports, however, West Germany was first, followed by Japan and Italy with the United States in sixth position.[16] In terms of production, Taiwan was in twenty-second position, but fifteenth according to exports. Other relatively large developing-country producers in 1982 were the People's Republic of China (eleventh), India (eighteenth), Brazil (twentieth, and South Korea (twenty-first). However, the exports of all these latter countries were relatively insignificant compared with that of Taiwan. In 1982 the value of Taiwan's machine tool exports was 149 million US dollars compared with South Korea (65 million), India (26 million), Singapore (22 million), and Brazil (21 million). In Table 5.4 the increase in Taiwanese unit output of machine tools from 1961 to 1982 is shown.

TABLE 5.3 Machine tools in Japan: share of exports in gross output, and annual growth rates of apparent consumptions and exports, 1966–1980a (*percentage*)

Year	Share of exports in gross output	Annual growth rate of consumption	Annual growth rate of exports
1966	19.2	−10.2	47.3
1967	12.7	76.3	10.3
1968	9.9	60.2	9.1
1969	9.1	27.3	23.4
1970	8.2	28.7	16.4
1971	12.0	−17.8	23.2
1972	16.3	−13.8	25.6
1973	14.6	64.9	51.9
1974	18.7	3.7	43.5
1975	33.9	−42.3	0.7
1976	35.4	−2.5	17.6
1977	38.5	33.6	68.2
1978	48.7	21.8	66.5
1979	42.7	39.2	33.0
1980	39.8	39.1	12.6

aBased on current dollars.

SOURCE   UNIDO (1984).

In Taiwan the machinery sector as a whole contributed only 0.4 per cent to total exports in 1961 but this rose to 3.5 per cent by 1979.[17] However, the machinery sector has been selected as a strategic industry and it has been projected to contribute 22 per cent to GDP by the year 1994. While the machine tool sub-sector contributed only 6 per cent to the total value of machine production in 1976, its contribution to machinery exports was far more significant. In 1979/80 machine tools comprised 26 per cent of total machinery exports making them the most important single category, followed closely by sewing-machines. As in Japan, the export ratio in the machinery sector as a whole increased rapidly from the early 1960s. While in 1961 only 5 per cent of the total value of machine production was exported, by 1979 this figure had reached 37 per cent.

There is an important similarity in the location of Japanese and Taiwanese export markets. From 1951 to 1960 the bulk of Japanese machine tool exports went to South East Asian countries, while from the early mid-1960s exports were increasingly destined for the United States. In Taiwan the change in destination occurred in an even shorter period of time. In 1972, 89 per cent of Taiwanese machine tool exports went to developing countries, mainly in South East Asia. However, by 1979, 77 per cent of such exports went to developed countries (of which 53 per cent went to the United States, 12 per cent to Europe and only 2 per cent to Japan, indicating a relatively high degree of substitutability between Japanese and Taiwanese machine tools in the lower price and performance range where Taiwanese exports are concentrated). However, this switch was not typical for all Taiwanese machinery, and in 1979 88 per cent of all machinery exports went to developing countries, 70 per cent to South East Asia. These figures indicate the early acceptability of Japanese and Taiwanese machine tools in the highly price elastic market of South East Asia, where in the price–quality trade-off quality tends to be sacrificed. The figures also suggest the importance of accumulating export experience in relatively 'easy' markets, before going on to utilize, and extend, this experience in more demanding markets. However, the potential substitutability between machine tools from countries like Taiwan and those from Japan was a source of concern, as well as a stimulus for improvement, to the Japanese. In 1979 the Japan Machine Tool Builders Association's committee appointed to study the industry's 'vision' for the 1980s concluded that 'We must clearly recognize that newly industrializing countries are bent on improving their technological competence in the field of machine tools. Hence, in order to enhance our international competitive stand, each firm must endeavour to firmly establish its identity in the marketplace with superior products.'[18] We shall later examine quantitatively the price/quality difference between Taiwanese and best-practice machine tools. Furthermore, we shall provide some indication of the importance of product competition as a source of price and product quality improvement.

Information on the export ratios of the sample firms is given in Tables 5.5a and 5.5b. The Japanese firms interviewed, shown in Table 5.5a, exported between 20 per cent and 40 per cent of their output. This is more or less in line with the figures for the Japanese machine tool industry as a whole. From Table 5.5b it can be seen that the export ratio for the Taiwanese firms interviewed tended to be higher than the Japanese firms.[19]

In this section we have examined a number of indicators establishing the international competitiveness of the machine tools industries in Taiwan and Japan in the 1970s and 1980s. In the following section we shall examine some of the major factors that must be taken into account in explaining this international competitiveness.

TABLE 5.4 Output of principal industrial products –Taiwan

Date	Pig iron	Steel bars	Aluminium ingots	Machine tools	Sewing machines	Electric fans	Television sets	Motor vehicles	Ship-building
	m.t.	m.t.	m.t.	unit	set	set	1000 units	set	g.t.
1952	9 927	17 842	3856	...	25 050	9852	—		565
1955	16 389	63 062	7001	...	48 398	53 183	—		1045
1956	16 638	78 827	8759	...	38 018	81 544	—		1435
1957	19 738	89 032	8259	...	64 517	102 775	—		1582
1958	17 122	106 933	8577	...	60 899	104 546	—		23 178
1959	33 106	158 880	7455	...	66 748	169 024	—		36 074
1960	24 444	200 528	8260	...	61 817	203 843	—		27 051
1961	52 844	148 464	9017	2319	37 115	188 135	—		8753
1962	63 381	174 436	11 009	3143	38 781	206 950	—		12 683
1963	63 610	196 026	11 929	4784	48 181	185 299	—		19 503
1964	61 837	211 158	19 372	6803	91 281	198 461	31		14 216
1965	72 038	266 144	18 911	8735	79 473	226 817	50		16 063
1966	75 340	323 594	17 216	11 822	124 591	363 704	66		25 866
1967	84 811	127 610	15 440	13 466	212 092	374 198	112		67 472
1968	86 052	418 311	20 020	17 426	361 450	349 168	650		79 183
1969	88 634	512 116	22 108	19 617	519 277	413 654	948		117 329
1970	95 905	607 016	26 991	23 296	629 096	478 205	1254		217 421
1971	108 453	722 215	26 546	13 134	787 870	562 756	1892	19 591	279 711
1972	128 104	862 161	32 104	18 777	916 458	666 499	3591	22 102	305 405
1973	149 954	1 072 498	35 111	30 057	1 255 889	714 914	4542	23 759	341 249
1974	111 143	1 029 022	31 320	30 166	1 227 952	500 922	4036	28 915	355 743
1975	93 382	1 173 540	28 111	41 780	1 047 065	477 219	2999	31 278	315 089

1976	190 938	1 733 622	25 512	124 139	1 378 595	623 868	3847	31 013	456 284
1977	275 027	1 976 696	29 740	181 702	1 546 572	1 048 377	4926	44 272	703 550
1978	293 735	2 901 398	50 512	342 859	2 007 786	1 898 395	7095	77 177	431 130
1979	301 676	2 449 539	56 218	436 508	2 076 175	2 741 668	6699	116 103	382 051
1980	235 951	3 651 486	63 549	436 233	2 193 092	3 743 498	7041	132 580	572 224
1981	185 578	3 395 024	30 532	556 571	2 997 425	5 917 869	6924	137 901	776 195
1982	148 110	4 127 610	10 120	597 274	2 443 990	6 780 883	4752	134 192	925 353

Annual Increase (%)

	1.5	17.0	−10.9	41.3	10.3	26.1	2.8	19.8	11.7
	−20.0	21.6	−66.9	7.3	−18.5	14.6	−31.4	− 2.7	19.2

TABLE 5.5a   Japan: Production of output to domestic and export markets

Firm	Domestic market (%)	Export market (%)
1	75	25
2	62	38
3	60	40
4	80	20

TABLE 5.5b   Taiwan: Domestic and export markets for most important CNC product

Firm (A)	Proportion of sales to export markets (B)	Two most important export markets and proportion of export sales (C)
1	60%	US – 65%; Germany – 10%
2	34%	US – 80%; Asia and Australia – 20%
3	–	–
4	20%	US – 70%; Australia – 10%
5	60%	US – 50%; South East Asia – 30%
6	All exports to licensor	
7	60%	US – 65%; South East Asia – 20%
8	20%	US – 50%; South Africa – 13%
9	0%	–

VII   EXPLAINING INTERNATIONAL COMPETITIVENESS

Relative Labour Costs

In examining the role of labour costs in international competitiveness, the crucial magnitude is not wage rates *per se*, but labour costs per unit of output. In other words, we are concerned not only with the cost of labour, but also with the quantity and quality which that labour produces. The greater the quantity and quality produced by a given amount of labour, *ceteris paribus*, the cheaper and better the firm's output, and therefore the greater its international competitiveness.

Information, however, does not exist which would enable a comparison of labour costs per standardized unit of output between countries. Accordingly, attention is restricted to wages and salaries. In Table 5.6 information

TABLE 5.6 Comparative wages and salaries (mid-year 1978) (mean monthly salary[a] in US $)

Professional group	Taiwan	Korea	Hong Kong	Singapore	Philippines	Thailand	Indonesia	Malaysia	Japan	Federal Republic of Germany
Industrial engineer	358	639	618	821	190	437	752	652	1587	2884
Mechanical engineer	407	587	627	710	191	460	786	677	1244	2884
Electrical engineer	322	509	590	803	203	492	299	762	1025	2884
Accountant	482	930	904	923	189	498	733	949	1521	1923
General manager	1051	1192	2389	2097	809	1784	1513	2672	3413	5495
Prod. manager	729	1049	1203	1215	498	669	851	1050	2488	3745
Section chief	461	889	1015	518	219	392	439	786	1587	3222
Executive secretary	435	590	729	503	175	425	496	404	1360	1465
Typist	184	318	245	211	73	153	214	133	756	1099
Junior clerk	150	344	258	198	114	135	173	180	785	1190
Foreman	369	493	425	413	198	203	241	390	1500	1328
Skilled worker	167	318	255	206	81	86	137	181	1161	1282
Semi-skilled worker	115	311	189	133	70	76	96	129	982	1145
Unskilled worker	93	146	158	102	52	51	65	84	698	915
Tool maker	245	330	303	210	64	135	482	304	665	1465
Cleaning worker	120	208	170	108	59	77	53	82	550	824

[a]In addition to the monthly base salary, most companies also pay regular bonuses ranging from 1 to 12 months of the salary, varying by company and by country. In order to make the monthly base salary information meaningful in terms of actual cost, this survey has increased the monthly base salary to include any bonuses paid, i.e. annual wage – 12 months plus bonus – monthly base salary – however, extra-ordinary bonuses, commission payments, etc. have not been included.

SOURCE Amsden (1984).

is given on comparative wages and salaries in 1978 for a number of countries. From this table it is clear that wages and salaries are substantially lower in Taiwan than in the other competing countries. In the case of mechanical engineers, for example, Taiwanese salaries were 69 per cent of that in South Korea, 57 per cent in Singapore, 60 per cent in Malaysia, 33 per cent in Japan, and 14 per cent in West Germany. The salaries of mechanical engineers were substantially lower in Japan than in West Germany, amounting to only 42 per cent of the latter. In the case of skilled workers the Taiwanese salaries were 53 per cent of that prevailing in South Korea, 81 per cent in Singapore, 92 per cent in Malaysia, 14 per cent in Japan, and 13 per cent in West Germany. The salaries of Japanese skilled workers were 91 per cent of those in West Germany. Further information is presented below on the importance of labour costs in international competitiveness from the point of view of the sample firms.

In assessing the significance of these wage and salary figures, account must be taken of the proportional importance of direct labour costs in total costs. Here it must be recognized that important changes occur with the production of CNC machine tools. While direct labour costs are important in the case of conventional machine tools, thus giving Taiwanese producers a significant advantage in these products, this is not so with CNC machine tools. The main reason is the increased importance of bought-in components, particularly the CNC control system. In the case of lathes, for example, Jacobsson estimates that the CNC control system can account for 20 to 50 per cent of total production costs. (Jacobsson, 1984a). Figures below for CNC lathes produced by one of the largest Taiwanese firms suggest that the imported servo motor, controller, and spindle motor, all part of the electronic control system, accounted for about 60 per cent of total production cost. Furthermore, it has been pointed out that with the improvement in CNC technology, CNC products have accounted for a growing proportion of total machine tool sales. This is seen, for example, in the share of CNC machine tools in total Japanese exports of machine tools. These rose from 24 per cent in 1976, 32 per cent in 1977, 48 per cent in 1979, 64 per cent in 1980 to 71 per cent in 1981. There has also been a significant increase in the proportion of CNC machine tools in Taiwan.

As mentioned earlier, a start has been made in producing CNC control systems in Taiwan. To the extent that relatively lower professional and skilled labour costs facilitate a comparative reduction in the cost of control systems produced in Taiwan, this may enhance the industry's competitiveness. However, as will be seen later, Taiwanese producers of controls still have some way to go before reaching international standards.

Accordingly, we may conclude that while labour costs have been a significant factor enabling Taiwanese producers to establish an international competitiveness in the area of conventional machine tools, this factor has become less important with the increasing production of CNC machine tools. The same conclusion is reached by UNIDO (1984) where it is stated that 'wage costs lose a lot of their significance in determining overall production costs when a producer changes over to the design and production of CNC machines... Thus, for CNC machines as for other advanced machine tools, labour costs are not significant as a determinant of comparative advantage' (p. 92). Later in this section we shall examine briefly some of the factors relating to the productivity of labour.

The International Diffusion of Technology and Indigenously Generated Technical Change

Introduction

The importance of the international diffusion of technology for international competitiveness has long been recognized and has at times been the subject of intense debate. One such time was between 1824 and 1841, when laws were passed in Britain restricting the export of machinery and the emigration of artisans in the attempt to prevent the international diffusion of machinery technology to competing countries. Although support for these laws had by and large crumbled by 1841 for a variety of reasons, it is worth noting the argument of John Kennedy, of the Manchester Chamber of Commerce, a vigorous proponent of the restrictions on the export of machinery:

> The exportation of machinery absolutely compels the foreign manufacturer to possess the means of becoming his own machine maker; and the more machines you send abroad, the greater the number of mechanics become necessary to keep their parts in order. Hence again arises a demand for those tools which are necessary to mechanics, the mechanics with their tools are sure to be ultimately employed, not merely in repairing the existing machines, but in the making of new ones.[20]

In the case of machine tools, however, British producers were unable to prevent the international diffusion of their technology. In a historical study of the British machine tool industry, Floud (1976) concludes that 'The evidence of the reports on the major exhibitions of the period from 1850 to 1914 thus suggests a chronology of British competitiveness in the international market in machine tools in which the British lead is eroded between 1850 and, approximately, 1870 to 1880. From that time commentators... [treat] Britain as one among equal competitors' (p. 71). From the middle 1890s American machine tools swept successfully into Europe, in much the same way as Japanese machine tools now flood into the US market.

In examining the achievement of international competitiveness by American producers by the 1890s, or by Japanese and Taiwanese producers by the 1970s, account must be taken of the role played by the international diffusion of technology. A few examples are considered in the following subsections.

The Development of Numerical Control in Japan

The increase in Japanese exports in the mid-1970s was largely the result of the introduction of cheap and reliable CNC controls and the production of standardized CNC machine tools (see Jacobsson, 1984a; UNIDO, 1984; and Sciberras and Payne, forthcoming). Accordingly, it is illuminating to examine how the Japanese acquired a mastery of numerical control technology.

There is no comprehensive account available of the mastery of numerical control technology in Japan. However, although important questions remain, part of the story can be pieced together from the available evidence.[21]

As mentioned earlier, a good deal of the early research on numerical control was done in the Servomechanisms Laboratory of MIT in the United States and in 1952 the first numerically controlled machine tool was demonstrated. The following year the first commercial NC milling machine was introduced by the American firm Giddings and Lewis. Early work on numerical control in Japan was done by university and government research institutions as well as by private firms, notably Fujitsu and its subsequently formed subsidiary, Fanuc.

According to Vogel (forthcoming), research on numerical control, stimulated by the news forthcoming from MIT, began in Japan in 1953 at the AIST Mechanical Engineering Laboratory, at the Tokyo Institute of Technology, and at the Engineering Faculty of Tokyo University. However, the nature of the research and the amount of progress made in this and subsequent years, as well as the degree of reliance on information coming from MIT and American firms, is not known. Further details, however, are available from Dr Seiuemon Inaba, President of Fanuc, who recalled the origins of the work done on numerical control by him and his colleagues.[22] Inaba stated that in 1956 he 'heard for the first time a report on an NC milling machine developed at MIT, which was described by Mr Y Takahashi, then professor at the University of California'. This report was clearly an important source of initial information. 'The fifty-page microfilmed report was excellent. In fact for us it was a sort of Bible on NC.' From the date mentioned by Inaba it may be inferred that at this stage little communication took place between the research institutions referred to above and those working in the private sector. Nevertheless, it is clear that Japanese users played an important early role in stimulating the development of NC technology through their requests. The firms of Makino, whose president was also head of the Japan Machine Tool Builders' Association, Mitsubishi, and Hitachi Seiki were particularly active in this regard.

However, many important questions remain. For example, to what extent in the 1950s were Japanese researchers 'replicating' American technology as opposed to making modifications, adaptations and improvements? What information channels did they use to acquire knowledge about the emerging American systems – such as academic papers, trade journals, and reverse engineering – and what was the relative importance of each of these channels? From Inaba's account it would appear that from the start Japanese researchers actively searched for improvements rather than reproducing entirely what had been done in the United States. Thus, for example, parametrons which were developed at Tokyo University were substituted for vacuum tubes, since the latter were unreliable, although eventually the firm reverted to the use of vacuum tubes. It is also clear that licensing in some instances played an important role. In 1952 the first foreign machine tool license was signed between Tsugami and the French firm Cri-Dan, and in the succeeding few years further licenses were obtained from other French firms. Shortly after this, occurred what the Japan Machine Tool Builders Association has called the 'first technological licensing boom' when from 1961 to 1964 29 licenses were concluded some of which applied to NC technology. From 1952 to 1964 a total of 34 licenses were signed, 14 with French companies and 12 with American firms. The first licensing boom was followed by an increased interest in the United States market and by a sharp increase in the machine tool sector's export ratio which levelled off from 1964 to 1970, as is shown in Figure 5.1.

From 1970 to 1973, the time of the 'second technological licensing boom', 12 licenses were signed relating to NC technology of which 9 were

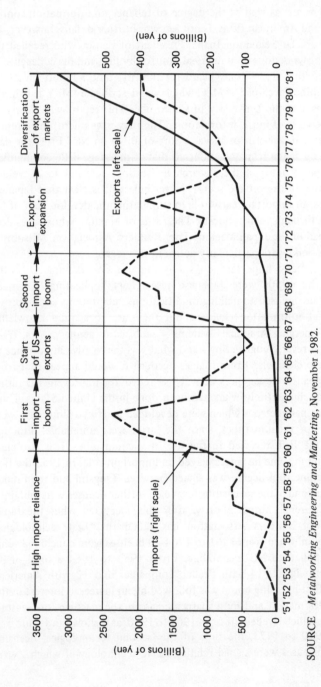

SOURCE *Metalworking Engineering and Marketing*, November 1982.

FIGURE 5.1 Changes in imports and exports in past 30 years (calendar year basis)

with American firms. From 1965 to 1974 a total of 78 licenses had been concluded, 34 with American and 19 with West German companies. By 1975 Japanese machine tool firms had sold 10 licenses, five to South Korea, three to Taiwan, and one to Britain and Spain.

Although exports increased rapidly after the second licensing boom – see Figure 5.1 – it is not clear how much of the export performance is due to improved technology transferred through licensing, and how much is due to the complementary technological efforts of Japanese firms. Furthermore, very little is known about the restrictive clauses in the licenses and the effectiveness of these clauses. As will be discussed later, from 1950 with the passage of the Foreign Capital Law (Gaishi Hó) the Japanese government exercised a substantial degree of control over foreign licensing, although no information exists about the effects in the machine tool industry of such control.

Many questions also remain to be answered about the introduction of microprocessor technology in CNC controls in the early to middle 1970s. It is frequently suggested in the literature on the world machine tool industry, for example, that (a) United States and European suppliers of control systems were far less responsive to user needs than their Japanese counterparts, and (b) were far slower than the Japanese to move over from hard-wired to solid-state microelectronic systems. In a descriptive sense there is probably a good deal of truth in this. Indirect evidence of this comes from the rapid rise of Fanuc to become the world leading supplier of CNC controls. By the early 1980s Fanuc supplied more than 50 per cent of total world output of CNC controls. Far more difficult, however, is the task of explanation. While it is clear that by the end of the 1970s few of the fundamental innovations in CNC technology had been produced in Japan, and that Japanese success was based rather on a process of incremental improvement, no clear picture is yet available of the causal factors behind this improvement. How important were flows of information to Japanese producers from United States and German and firm and research institutes? What role was played by Japanese R & D efforts going beyond existing knowledge? How significant in the process of incremental improvement were the efforts of non-research employees, such as production engineers and workers institutionally organized through quality circles etc.? To what extent is Japanese success the result of broader industrial structural features of the Japanese economy, such as the sub-contracting system which facilitates 'just-in-time' deliveries etc.? How important is the intense degree of competition between Japanese producers in their domestic market? (It is often forgotten here that not all Japanese machine tool producers have succeeded. Among the firms that have failed to keep up and have declined relatively and absolutely are some of the oldest.) What role has been played by information flows generated by distributors and users in the highly competitive export markets? Finally, how important has government intervention over the years been in accounting for the ultimate Japanese success?

Equally important are the large number of questions that arise in attempting to explain the failure of United States and European producers to keep up with Japanese incremental improvement.

An adequate answer to all these questions would require a far more detailed explanatory account than we yet possess of the factors shaping the process of technical change in the machine tool industry. However, and that is the major point in this subsection, it is clear that the international diffusion of knowledge played an extremely important role in facilitating ultimate Japanese success. None the less, it is probably correct to conclude that international diffusion was a necessary, but not a sufficient, condition for the attainment of Japanese international competitiveness. Also crucial were many of the factors hinted at in the questions asked above about the Japanese machine tool industry even though their precise causal significance is not yet clear.

However, the end-result of Japanese incremental technical change is far clearer. In a report by the United States Academy of Science published in 1983, entitled 'The Competitive Status of the United States Machine Tool Industry', it was stated that 'The early development of numerically controlled machine tools gave the American industry a considerable jump on foreign competitors in international markets, but in recent years this advantage has eroded considerably, particularly in relationship to Japanese-manufactured CNC units that, in the opinion of the panel, are now more advanced than those produced by the United States builders' (p. 25).

The Development of CNC in Taiwan

Just as Japan, benefiting from the international diffusion of technology, introduced NC in the middle-1950s, so in the late 1970s and early 1980s Taiwanese firms, enjoying the fruits of similar international flows of knowledge, introduced CNC technology. The production of CNC products was a relatively new experience for all the Taiwanese sample firms. Furthermore, the production of CNC machine tools was a potentially difficult problem, involving as it did the integration of a new 'technological paradigm', that of microelectronics, into the previously exclusive domain of mechanical engineering. Before the introduction of CNC, Taiwanese firms had no reason to employ electronic engineers. Accordingly, it is of interest to enquire further into the factors facilitating, and the constraints on, the introduction of CNC products.

Significantly, none of the Taiwanese sample firms reported serious difficulties in the introduction of CNC products. Furthermore, none of them foresaw major difficulties in upgrading product quality over time in order to keep up with Japanese advances. Nevertheless, firms marshalled different resources in order to introduce CNC products. While all of them were required to buy in the services of electronic engineers, only the strongest firms were able to make the change in-house.

All of the Taiwanese firms used CNC controls supplied by Fanuc. Furthermore, one of the important findings of the study was that Fanuc also provided some of the Taiwanese firms with assistance in introducing CNC. This is reflected in Table 5.7. While information was not available for four of the nine firms, three of the firms received important assistance from Fanuc. This took the form of Fanuc sending engineers to help sort out interfacing problems and in one case the firm sent its technicians to Fanuc in Japan for further instruction and training. Thus, somewhat paradoxically, Fanuc, the major supplier of CNC controls to Japanese firms, was also helping to cultivate competition for these firms from Taiwanese machine tool producers.

Five of the nine firms turned to the government-owned Mechanical Industries Research Laboratory (MIRL) for assistance with the design of CNC machine tools. Further discussion of this, however, is postponed to the later section dealing with government intervention.

Table 5.7 also shows that three of the five firms reported making some use of Taiwanese-produced CNC controls. Earlier it was stated that at the

TABLE 5.7 Assistance from Fanuc and MIRL; use of Taiwanese CNC control units

Firm	Assistance from Fanuc	Assistance from MIRL	Some use of Taiwanese CNC control
1	n/a	No	No
2	No	Yes	No
3	Yes	No	n/a
4	Yes	Yes	Yes
5	n/a	No	n/a
6	No	n/a	n/a
7	n/a	Yes	Yes
8	Yes	Yes	Yes
9	n/a	Yes	No

Ninth Taiwan Machinery Show held in 1983, 27 per cent of the CNC units exhibited used Taiwanese-produced controls although it was pointed out that these controls had not yet been produced in sufficient number for their reliability to be assessed. In 1983 there were five CNC-controls producers. Four of these firms only produced CNC units for machine tools, while the remaining firm also produced calculators, cash-registers and microcomputers. Research on CNC controls was also undertaken by MIRL. In general, however, the quality of Taiwanese-produced CNC controls was far below that of Fanuc. This is reflected in the fact that all the Taiwanese firms used Fanuc rather than locally produced controls in the export machine tools, although this decision was also influenced by the highly efficient after-sales service provided by Fanuc in the major export markets. Nevertheless, a start has been made and time will tell whether the Taiwanese control producers are able to narrow the gap.

As in the Japanese case, therefore, the international flow of knowledge has been an important factor facilitating the introduction by Taiwanese producers of CNC machine tools. In part this flow has been market-mediated, as for example in the sale of licenses to the Japanese firms or the supply of technical assistance by Fanuc to the Taiwanese firms, but in part the flow of knowledge has been non-market-mediated. A major example of the latter is the use of foreign models in the design of machine tools. This will be considered in the next sub-section.

Source of Design and Price and Quality Improvement in Sample Firms

Although several licenses were sold to Taiwanese firms and government research institutes, the majority from the United States and Japan, licensing has been less important in Taiwan than in Japan, with a correspondingly greater emphasis on reverse engineering. In Tables 5.8a and 5.8b the source of original design and date of original production is shown for the sample firms.

From these tables it is apparent that for all the Japanese and Taiwanese firms the products of other firms provided an important design input (with one exception where the design came from a local government research institute, MIRL in Taiwan). As has already been pointed out, substantial modifications and improvements took place in the Japanese firms although it was not possible to collect more precise information on the changes that were brought about. In the case of the Taiwanese firms all but one of the designs came originally from Japanese models. This is unsurprising in view of the technical competence that Japanese firms had achieved by the late

TABLE 5.8a Japan: Source of original design and date of original production of major product

Firm	Country of original design	Production date
1	USA (Kearney and Trecker) and in-house	1974
2	Multiple	1968
3	USA	1963
4	Germany	1930

TABLE 5.8b Taiwan: Source of original design and date of original production of major product

Firm (A)	Country of original design (B)	Production date (C)
1	Japan	1979
2	Japan (Makino)	1980
3	Japan (Hitachi, Yamazaki, Okuma)	1980
4	Japan (Toyoda, Okuma)	1983
5	Japan (Mori-Seki, Ikegai)	1981
6	Japan (Okuma)	1981
7	Japan	1982
8	–	1978
9	Taiwan (MIRL)	1982

1970s and early 1980s and also the fact that these firms also tended to specialize in the more standardized, medium-price range. While CNC was first introduced on the world market in 1973, it is apparent from Table 5.8b that some five or six years later the first CNC machine tools began to be produced commercially in Taiwan.

However, as stressed earlier, incremental changes were subsequently made by Japanese and Taiwanese producers. These improvements were of great cumulative significance and largely account for the international competitiveness of Japanese and Taiwanese firms. But what were the *sources* of the improvements made in both quality and price? An answer to this question would give us an idea of the factors shaping the technical change process in the machine tool industry. However, the question is extremely difficult to answer because of the complex interaction between the large number of factors which simultaneously determine price and quality improvements. Nevertheless, despite the difficulties, it seemed helpful to ascertain the views of senior management on the question of the sources of improvements in quality and price.[23] Accordingly, an attempt was made to get respondents to weight the importance of various sources on a four-point scale, ranging from 1 (very important) to 4 (unimportant). The results are reproduced in Tables 5.9a and 5.9b. The procedure followed in these tables is to calculate the mean by aggregating across firms and then, on the basis of the mean, to rank the importance of the particular source. The result, however, should be treated as only indicative, as a consequence of the inherent methodological difficulty in making such inter-subjective comparisons.

However, as Tables 5.9a and 5.9b show, it is of considerable interest that in both Japanese and Taiwanese sample firms, customers in foreign and domestic markets and the products of competing firms appeared to be the most important sources of improvements. Not surprisingly, the order was to some extent reversed. With their superior in-house technological capabilities (to be documented in more detail later) Japanese firms attributed more significance to customers in both foreign and domestic markets (bear in mind here the significance and sophistication of the Japanese market) than to the products of competing firms. In the case of the Taiwanese firms, however, with their greater degree of dependence, as we have seen, on reverse engineering together with in-house adaptation, the

TABLE 5.9a   Japan: Sources of improvements in design and selling price

Source	1	2	3	4	Mean	Rank
1. Worker suggestions	3	3	3	2	2.75	4
2. Suppliers of components/ parts	2	2	2	3	2.25	3
3. Customers in foreign markets	1	1	1	1	1.00	1
4. Customers in domestic markets	1	1	1	1	1.00	1
5. Sub-contractors	4	4	4	3	3.75	6
6. Consultants	4	4	3	3	3.50	5
7. Professional or trade journals	1	4	2	2	2.25	3
8. Products of competing firms	1	2	2	2	1.75	2
9. Government incentives or pressures	4	4	4	4	4.00	7

1-4 explained at foot of Table 5.9b.

TABLE 5.9b Taiwan: Sources of improvements in design and selling price

Source	Firm									Mean	Rank
	1	*2*	*3*	*4*	*5*	*6*	*7*	*8*	*9*		
1. Worker suggestions	2	3	1	2	n/a	2	1	3	2	2.0	4
2. Suppliers of components/parts	3	4	1	1	n/a	4	3	4	4	3.0	6
3. Customers in foreign markets	1	2	n/a	2	n/a						
4. Customers in domestic markets	1	2	4	1	n/a	1	1	1	4	1.88	3
5. Sub-contractors	4	4	4	3	n/a	2	2	4	4	3.38	8
6. Consultants	4	3	4	3	n/a	4	2	4	2	3.25	7
7. Professional or trade journals	2	3	1	2	n/a	3	3	3	4	2.63	5
8. Products of competing firms	1	2	1	1	n/a	1	2	1	4	1.63	1
9. Government incentives or pressures	4	4	4	2	n/a	4	3	1	4	3.25	7

1 = Very important 2 = Important 3 = Fairly important 4 = Unimportant

products of competing firms were ranked as the most important source of improvement. With their more-sophisticated sub-contracting network, Japanese firms ranked the suppliers of components third in order of importance as a source of improvement, probably more so in the case of price than design. For Taiwanese firms this source was sixth, although the special role of Fanuc as the major supplier of the CNC units should be kept in mind here. Japanese firms also ranked professional and trade journals third, while this source was ranked fifth by the Taiwanese firms. Both sets of firms ranked worker suggestions fourth in importance. This is of interest since, as Rosenberg (1976) notes, a distinguishing feature of the machinery sector, and in particular machine tools, is that firms themselves use the machinery that they produce. As a result the 'learning-by-using' interaction between producer and user which, as Rosenberg (1983) has shown is an important source of improvement in some industries, is internalized within the same firm. In touring the factories of the sample firms the present writer was struck by the prominence of the firm's own machinery on its production lines, particularly in the case of the larger Japanese firms where the majority of machines used were produced in-house. Interestingly, in both sets of firms government incentives or pressures for improvements were ranked seventh, although it is significant that while the Japanese firms consistently ranked government measures as 'unimportant', two of the nine Taiwanese firms ranked such measures as 'very important' or 'important'. As will be shown later in a special section dealing with state intervention, some Taiwanese firms received substantial assistance from the government in a variety of forms. Similarly, the Japanese ranking of government measures considerably understates the historical significance of state intervention as will be discussed in more detail in the same section.

It is worth noting that, while Tables 5.9a and 5.9b include both market and non-market-mediated sources of technical change, it was the latter sources that in general were felt to be more significant. This is very important since hitherto most attention has focused on market-mediated forms of technical change such as licensing. The evidence here, however, suggests that the 'externalities'[24] referred to ought to form a part of the study of the sources of technical change.

Conclusion

Two points emerge clearly from the examination in this sub-section of the international diffusion of technology. The first is that international diffusion, through both market and non-market processes, played a central role in the achievement of international competitiveness by the Japanese and Taiwanese machine tool industry. The second point is that the firms themselves were not passive beneficiaries of the diffusion process, but actively took steps to take advantage of the international availability of relevant knowledge. However, the state has also played a central role in facilitating the international diffusion of technology. This is examined in more detail later.

The Intensity of Competition

It has long been realized that pressure exerted by other firms through competition is a powerful force for technical change and productivity (including product quality) improvement. In *Capitalism, Socialism and Democracy*, Schumpeter noted that

> new products and new methods compete with the old products and old methods not on equal terms but at a decisive advantage that may mean death to the latter. This is how 'progress' comes about in capitalist

society. In order to escape being undersold, *every* firm is in the end compelled to follow suit, to invest in its turn and, in order to be able to do so, to plough back part of its profits ie to accumulate. Thus, everyone else accumulates. (pp. 31–2)

In order to establish the degree of competition faced by the Taiwanese and Japanese sample firms, a 'competitive pressure index' was constructed. Firms were asked to rate on a four-point scale the degree of difficulty that their customers in domestic and export markets would have in finding alternative sources of supply if the firm ceased production. All the firms in the sample indicated that there would be no difficulty whatever. This therefore indicated that firms operated under a substantial degree of competitive pressure and accordingly were compelled to pay close attention to the products and production methods of competitors.

It is, however, important to distinguish between competitive pressure in domestic and export markets. In principle it is possible for the lack of domestic competitive pressure to be compensated for by competition in export markets, provided the latter markets are sufficiently important to the firm. Similarly, domestic competition might to some extent compensate for the lack of exports. In this connection it is worth recalling the information provided in Tables 5.5a and 5.5b which showed that Japanese sample firms exported between 20 and 40 per cent of their output while the export ratio for Taiwanese firms tended to be higher.

It is also conceivable that competitive pressure might, under some circumstances, be regarded as excessive and therefore counterproductive. Thus, for example, Peck and Tamura (1976) point out that the Japanese Ministry of International Trade and Industry (MITI) frequently intervened in order to prevent what they regarded as excessive competition. Similarly, at various points in time both the Japanese and Taiwanese governments have intervened in order to protect their local machinery industries from foreign competition. This will be examined below in the section dealing with the state. However, protection of the local market, and therefore a reduction of external competitive pressure, is not inconsistent with an increasing export ratio. An early example is provided by Floud (1976) when in the 1890s American machine tools swept into European markets at the same time as a nominal rate of protection of 40 per cent existed in America. A more recent example is South Korea where, as Jacobsson (1984b) notes, increasing exports of machine tools have gone together with severe forms of protection of locally produced 'similars', including complete prohibition of imports.

However, although the net effects of competitive pressure can be positive or negative, it is clearly important to take it into account in any examination of the sources of technical change and international competitiveness.

The State

Introduction

Any account of the attainment of international competitiveness in the machine tool industries of Japan and Taiwan must include an analysis of the role played by the state. In this section the major forms of intervention by the Japanese and Taiwanese states in their respective machine tool industries will be examined. Information is then presented on the importance of various kinds of state intervention as seen by the sample firms.

Japanese State Intervention in the Machine Tool Industry[25]

The close connection between Japanese machine tool firms and military users was a notable feature of the industry, from the time when machine tools were first produced in state arsenals during the Tokugawa period through the Japanese wars with China in 1895 and Russia in 1904.[26] Similarly, during the military build-up in the latter 1930s, state intervention profoundly affected the structure of the machine tool industry. In this connection one of the most important measures was the Machine Tool Manufacturing Industry Law of 1938 (Kósakukikai seizó jigyó-hó). This law established twenty-one 'authorized firms' in the machine tool sector. These firms, which included Okuma, Hitachi, Ikegai, Niigata, Toyo and Tsugami, were assured of material supplies and were given subsidized financing and tax reductions. However, the 1938 law also induced some of the *zaibatsu* to move into the machine tool industry, including Mitsubishi, Mitsui and Toshiba. This law was responsible for a significant increase in concentration in the Japanese machine tool industry. In 1939 the twenty-one 'authorized' machine tool firms accounted for 27 per cent of total output of machine tools. By 1941 this had increased to 47 per cent. After the war, however, the 1938 law was abolished.

After the war substantial intervention continued, despite the occupying American administration which opposed such measures. As Johnson

(1982) notes in his study of the Ministry of International Trade and Industry (MITI), one important intervention was the Foreign Exchange and Foreign Trade Control Law of 1949. This law concentrated all foreign exchange holdings in government hands and facilitated the control of imports by requiring that importers make special application for foreign exchange. Johnson notes that 'MITI made every effort to suppress imports of finished goods, particularly those that competed with domestic products, but it urgently sought imports of modern technology and machinery' (p. 217). Until 1962 importers had to apply for foreign exchange and this was used to provide protection for local machine tool producers. After this date tariffs and duties were used as protective devices.

The problem with foreign technology, however, was (a) that it was expensive and (b) that it frequently came together with foreign control. This problem was tackled by the Foreign Capital Law of 1950 (Gaishi hó). This law set up a Foreign Investment Committee which was empowered to license all agreements involving foreign acquisition of assets or transfer of technology. In this way the Japanese authorities attempted to reduce the price of technology by 'unpackaging' imported technology and 'restricting the import of foreign technology to those cases deemed necessary for the development of Japanese industries' (Johnson, 1982, p. 217). Similarly, Peck and Tamura (1976) suggest that while the official rationale for such controls lay in concern for the balance of payments situation and the possibility of disruption to the small-business sector, 'More important than any stated rationale for controls is their impact on the price of technology, the composition of the imported technology, and the industrial structure – all areas in which the evidence suggests that government control did make a difference' (p. 546).

The authorities in MITI were also of the view that foreign control could be undesirable and one of the aims of the Foreign Capital Law was to limit such control. In 1960 the Enterprise Bureau of MITI provided the rationale in a memorandum stating that where

the share holding ratio of the foreign company is high and the foreign company has substantial influence on the operations of the Japanese company... it is quite possible that such union hampers healthy development of the Japanese economy... [Accordingly] applications for acquisition of stock for the purpose of participation in management of [Japanese] operations have been handled in an extremely careful manner, and approval has been granted only in the case involving license of an important technology where a foreign investor denies the license unless acquisition of stock is approved in exchange, or in similar cases.[27]

While in 1970 capital inflows were liberalized so that foreigners could invest more easily in some industries, this excluded CNC machine tools and computers. The Foreign Capital Law was abolished in 1980 and after 1981 MITI approval was no longer required for foreign licenses. However, while inflows of foreign capital and technology into the machine tool industry were undoubtedly significantly influenced by this law, there is no detailed analysis available of the precise nature of the influence.

Government bodies also influenced the machine tool industry through their direct purchases. Perhaps the most important example is that of the Japan National Railways in the immediate post-war years when the machine tool industry had been considerably weakened by the effects of the war and the surge in imports. In 1948, for example, 54 per cent of the total Japanese output of machine tools went to the JNR, as a result of its policy of purchasing locally wherever possible. An official history of the Japanese machine tool industry by the Japan Machine Tool Builders Association later noted that under the 'severe circumstances' that existed after the war, the JNR's 'policy of supporting domestically made machines was of considerable reassurance to the machine tool industry'.[28] As a result of the pressures, and also possibly as a consequence of government purchase policies, the number of machine tool producers declined sharply from 1945 to the beginning of the 1950s. Some American machine tool producers allege that discriminatory purchase of locally made machine tools by the JNR has continued to the present time.

One of the most important government interventions took place from 1956 with the passage of the Law on Temporary Measures for the Development of the Machinery Industry (Kikaikógyó rinji sochi-hó). Under this law, twenty-one industries, mainly heavy industries, were selected, including the machine tool industry, in an attempt to modernize production facilities and equipment in Japanese industry.

The main purpose of the 1956 Law was the 'rationalization' of the selected industries. Under the law the Minister of International Trade and Industry was charged with drawing up a basic rationalization plan. The machine tool industry was designated as one of the specific machinery industries covered by the law under Cabinet Order No. 238 of 1956. The basic rationalization plan for the machine tool industry was announced on 15 March 1957 under MITI notification No. 112 of 1957. Three objectives were specified: first, to reap economies of specialization by concentrating the production of machine tools; second, to increase the standardization of parts; and third, to establish collaborative research on machine tool technology.

In August 1957 the Japan Machine Tool Builders' Association established a 'Manufacturing Shares Deliberation Committee' and one of its main aims was to encourage the degree of concentration of production in the industry. In November 1960 the Committee's proposals led to the conclusion of an 'Agreement Regarding Concentrated Manufacturing'. The major purpose of this agreement was to get members to concentrate on their existing products, thus preventing them from moving into new lines.

In April 1961 the effective period of the 1956 Law was extended for a further five years to June 1966. In September 1961, with MITI Notification No. 474, a new basic promotion plan for the machine tool industry was put forward. This plan also aimed at increasing specialization and the concentration of production. For the first time 'appropriate' batch sizes were stipulated for various types of machine tools.

After the passage of the 1956 Law, provision was made for subsidized credit to be made available by the Japan Development Bank to the designated industries. According to Chokki (present volume), in 1961 the rate of interest charged under this programme was 6.5 per cent, at a time when the going commercial rate was 9 per cent. From the years 1957 to 1961 just over 20 per cent of the total amount allocated under the 1956 Law went to the machine tool industry. This provides an indication of the importance accorded to this industry. Apart from private sources of funding, finance was also made available to the machine tool industry by other government bodies such as the Industrial Bank of Japan and the Long Term Credit Bank.[29]

In June 1966 the 1956 Law was again extended for five years to March 1971. One of the specific objectives was to promote the exportation of machine tools. In July 1968 MITI Notification No. 304 was issued which, in the light of current attempts to increasingly liberalize the Japanese economy, aimed at improving the international competitiveness of the industry, defined specifically in terms of product quality, performance, and cost. Again, explicit attempts were made to increase specialization and concentration, and reduce excessive competition. For the first time mention was made of firms discontinuing the production of machines which did not meet the required standards and which were produced in quantities that were too small. The Notification stated that 'manufacturers should discontinue producing those machine types whose share in the industry is less than 5 per cent and whose share in an enterprise is less than 20 per cent'. At the same time the Notification declared that 'Manufacturers should seek centralization of companies by mergers.' In order to give effect to the stipulations of the Notification, the Japan Machine Tool

Builders' Association passed an amended Agreement Regarding Concentrated Manufacturing which took force from April 1969. However, permission was given to any producer to enter into the production of machining centres on the grounds that increasing emphasis should be given to the production of this type of machine tool. Numerically controlled machine tools, though, were treated in the same way as other machine tools. Under a new agreement, entitled 'Standard Regarding Notification of New Products', approved by the Association in January 1971, it was stated that any member wishing to manufacture a new product must submit a notification of intent to the Association. No exception was made in this agreement for machining centres.

Corresponding to the 1956 Law to promote the machinery industries was a law passed in 1957, the Temporary Measures Law for the Promotion of Electronic Industries. In 1971 the 1956 Law expired and since it was recognized that electronic control systems were increasingly being used in the machinery industry, a unified law was passed. This was the Temporary Measures Law for the Promotion of Specific Electronic Industries and Specific Machinery Industries (Law No. 17 of 1971). According to this law MITI was required to produce 'elevation plans' to improve production techniques and increase rationalization in the industries covered. In August 1971 the Elevation Plan for the Metal Cutting Machine-Tool Manufacturing Industry was issued by MITI in Notification No. 346. The first goal of the plan was 'To try to increase the degree of specialization so that the production share of numerically controlled. . . and computer controlled. . .machine tools in each manufacturing enterprise is increased to approximately 50 per cent of the total production of the metal cutting machine tools manufactured.' The second goal was to 'further promote joint operation of enterprises concerning technology, production, materials, marketing, exportation, etc.'.

In March 1978 the 1971 Law expired and was replaced by a further law in July 1978, 'The Temporary Measures Law for the Promotion of Specific Machinery and Information Industries' (Law No. 84 of 1978). Again under this law MITI was instructed to prepare 'elevation plans' in order to promote production techniques and rationalization in the industry. In Notification No. 608 issued in December 1978 MITI published its elevation plan for numerically controlled (including CNC) machine tools. An exhibit to this Notification states that 'joint research [between machine tool manufacturers] and manufacturers of computers, controlling devices, measuring instruments, tools and work instrument[s] is to be promoted'.

Protection of the local market was one of the measures frequently used to promote the Japanese machine tool industry. Even after the widespread liberalization of all trade from 1970, protective measures continued to be extended to the industry. Chokki (present volume) notes that nominal rates of protection of 25 per cent and above were imposed after 1970 on specific machine tools. As mentioned above, when restrictions on foreign investment were relaxed in 1970 the area of CNC machine tools was specifically excluded together with other items such as computers.

The Japanese state also promoted the machine tool industry by providing technology inputs in various forms. These include the activities of MITI's Mechanical Engineering Laboratory and the Japan Research Development Corporation. In addition there is the Japan Society for the Promotion of Machine Industry which received the proceeds of taxes on racing and which, while officially private, consulted closely with MITI.

From this brief examination it is clear that the Japanese state has intervened in numerous ways with the intention of promoting the development of the machine tool industry. These included the imposition of protective measures, intervention in the negotiation of technology agreements, attempts to minimize the degree of foreign control, the provision of subsidized credit, planned intervention to increase economies of specialization through greater degrees of concentration of production and measures aimed at eliminating firms producing small quantities, and the provision of technology inputs. The Japanese state undoubtedly devoted a substantial amount of resources in attempting to promote the machine tool industry. However, although the measures undertaken can be fairly easily documented, research has not yet revealed the precise effects of these measures. Accordingly, a large number of important questions remain regarding the consequences for the Japanese machine tool industry of state intervention. For example, in the 'negotiations' that took place between MITI and the machine tool producers, represented by their association the Japan Machine Tool Builders' Association, it is not clear whether the 'balance of power' lay with the former or latter. To form a clearer picture, more information would be needed about the measures which MITI officials wanted to take, the extent to which the Association members accepted or disagreed with these measures, and, where there was conflict, which side ultimately prevailed in the specific case. This information would be crucial in order to understand better, for example, the consequences of the attempts to increase economies of specialization and increase concentration. Unfortunately, however, such information is not available.

Similarly, it is not possible to form an accurate picture of the precise effects of the other government policies undertaken to promote the machine tool industry. How widespread were protective measures and how high were the barriers? What effect did these measures have on machine

tool firms? What has been the effect of research and development undertaken by government institutions? At present questions such as these
cannot be answered adequately. However, despite this, it is clear that the
Japanese state has been unwilling to allow the machine tool industry to
evolve independently of its control. Rather, it has made numerous attempts
to shape and direct the evolutionary process in order to encourage improvements and eliminate negative influences. That the evolutionary process was
ultimately successful cannot be doubted. Less clear, however, are the
precise effects of the government intervention.

Taiwanese State Intervention in the Machine Tool Industry[30]

Like in Japan, the Taiwanese state has also intervened in numerous ways
to encourage the development of the machine tool industry. The need for
some intervention is widely acknowledged. Thus, for example, the President
of the Export–Import Bank of China stated in 1981 that 'in the early stage
of industrial development, based on the experience of industrialized
countries, the machinery industry of a nation usually needs. . .strong
support from the government'.[31] More controversial, however, is whether
enough support is being given. In the same year the Chairman of the
Taiwan Association of Machinery Industry's Machine Tool Committee,
and Director of the largest machine tool firm in the country, stated that
'Although the government does have a programme for the machine tool
industry, it is not considered to have enough initiative.'[32] We shall consider
in a later section the vigorous debate currently being undertaken about the
desirable forms and extent of state intervention in the Taiwanese machine
tool industry.

One of the most important forms of assistance given by the state to the
Taiwanese machine tool industry has been the provision of subsidized
technology inputs. As noted in Tables 5.1a and 5.1b, Taiwanese machine
tool firms, even the largest, tend to be significantly smaller than their
Japanese (and South Korean) competitors. This has provided a rationale
for the state provision of certain technology inputs. Apart from fiscal
incentives for in-house R & D, the main form of state intervention in this
area has been through the activities of the state-owned Industrial Technology
Research Institute (ITRI) and one of its divisions, the Mechanical Industrial
Research Laboratories (MIRL), including its Machine Tools Centre.

Having been established in 1969, the MIRL was reorganized as one of
the research laboratories in ITRI in 1973. In 1977 the Machine Tool
Centre was established in MIRL in order to conduct research on numerically

controlled machine tools. In 1980 MIRL was charged by the Ministry of Economic Affairs with carrying out the 'Automatic Machine Tools R & D Programme'. With the initiation of this programme, work began on designing CNC machine tools, including machining centres, building on research that had begun a few years earlier on the design of CNC control units. In 1983 MIRL employed about 120 mechanical and about 100 electronic design engineers and had an annual budget of around US$15 million.

Evidence of the success of MIRL comes from two sources. The first is its successful production, and exhibition at the Ninth Taiwan Machinery Show held in 1983, of a flexible manufacturing system (FMS) involving automatic transfer of workpieces between several CNC machine tools and machining centres. Second, and more important, is the evidence that Taiwanese machine tool firms have turned in increasing numbers to MIRL for assistance with the design of CNC machine tools and machining centres. By mid-1983 MIRL had 22 contracts with 18 firms, all involving the complete design of new CNC machine tools and machining centres. While the largest firms frequently possessed the in-house capabilities to design their own machines, and therefore tended to limit their co-operation with MIRL to joint research in several selected areas, all the firms interviewed by the author acknowledged the high quality of the technical expertise provided by MIRL. A few, however, expressed the opinion that while the quality of the machine tool designed by MIRL was very satisfactory, not enough attention had been paid to keeping costs down.

There is, however, a subsidy element in the technology inputs provided to firms by MIRL. Firms make a payment consisting of two components in return for the design assistance they receive. The first is a lump-sum amount, while the second is a royalty of 1.5 to 3 per cent of the selling price of the machine tool. However, it was estimated that firms only pay about one third of the manpower costs involved. For example, of the total development costs of US$600 000 for designing a machining centre, the firm would pay between 50 and 80 per cent including its royalty payment. Furthermore, the signing of a contract with MIRL usually guarantees a firm access to subsidized loans from the Bank of Communication. By mid-1983 fifteen machine tool firms had borrowed a total of US$10 million. In four cases the Bank of Communication provided loans in return for a holding of 25 per cent of the firm's total equity. (By mid-1983 the Bank of Communication had loaned a total of US$141 million to all the so-called strategic industries, including the machine tool industry.) By providing loans for the development of new products the Bank of Communication bears part of the risk and therefore encourages investments that might otherwise not be undertaken.[33]

Assistance given by MIRL and the Bank of Communication to the machine tool industry has been given not on an *ad hoc* basis but as part of a national policy to build up the so-called strategic industries, i.e. the machinery, electronics and information industries. These industries were first identified in the Ten Year Plan, 1980–1989. They were further examined by a conference of experts in 1981 where a number of criteria were used in order to make the selection of industries. These included: linkages with the rest of the economy, technology intensity, energy consumption, value added, domestic and export market potential, and degree of pollution. Further details for the machinery industry were put forward in the Four-Year Development Plan, 1982–1985. In the section on the machinery industry, the current situation is described: 'With respect to production, design depends entirely on the imitation of foreign patterns, technicians are in short supply, and development of spare parts and related industries is slow' (p. 50). Among the objectives for the machinery industry, reminiscent of the post-war Japanese measures, are the following:

1. Encourage machinery enterprises to renovate and modernize their equipment; gradually automate production; improve productivity, management, and the division of labour; and promote specialization and rationalization.
2. Strengthen development of numerical control machinery and automation.
3. Continue to guide and assist the export of whole plants and machinery design and manufacture, and to promote domestic production of important machinery. (p. 51)

One of the objectives stated in the section on the electronics industry is the 'strengthening of the development of computer numerical control in conjunction with the automation of the machinery industry' (p. 57).

Among the policy instruments that will be used to achieve the stated objectives are the following: 'Key mechanical products shall be given selective protection to lay a solid foundation for technical development; the investment tax credit shall be widened in scope. . .to stimulate investment by the private sector.' (p. 51).

Protection has not been as important in Taiwan as it has in South Korea where machine producers have been protected by tariffs and in some cases a total prohibition on imports.[34] Nevertheless, protection has played some role in encouraging machinery producers. As Westphal (1978) and Wade (1984) point out, the import licensing system has been used to prevent the import of machinery where products that are 'equivalent' in terms of price and quality are available locally. As Westphal notes, import controls would be unnecessary if the latter criterion were strictly adhered to, and there are cases where price competitiveness has not been insisted upon. At present an import duty of 20 per cent exists on imported machine tools, but the effect of this is to some extent negated by the duties imposed on many of the imported components for machine tools. The latter duties, imposed on items such as servo-motors, chucks, and hydraulic components, are intended to encourage the local production of such components.

As in Japan, therefore, the Taiwan state has intervened in numerous ways to promote the development of the machine tool industry. In the next sub-section we shall examine the importance of state promotional activities as seen by the sample firms.

The Importance of State Intervention according to Sample Firms

In Tables 5.10a and 5.10b sample firm assessment of the importance of various forms of state assistance is presented. For the Japanese firms, of the incentives given by the state in 1983, long-term technical assistance provided by MITI research laboratories was regarded as the most impor-

TABLE 5.10a Japan: Importance of government incentives

Incentive	Firm				Mean	Rank
	1	2	3	4		
Subsidised credit	4	4	4	1	3.25	4
Tax incentives	4	1	1	1	1.75	2
Export assistance	4	2	2	2	2.50	3
Technical assistance (long term)	1	1	1	2	1.25	1

TABLE 5.10b Taiwan: Importance of government incentives

Incentive	Firm									Mean	Rank
	1	2	3	4	5	6	7	8	9		
1. Protection of local market	4	2	1	3	3	n/a	2	3	4	2.75	3
2. Subsidised credit	1	4	1	4	2	n/a	2	1	3	2.25	1
3. Tax incentives	3	4	4	4	4	n/a	3	2	1	3.13	4
4. Export assistance	3	3	1	3	4	n/a	3	3	2	2.75	3
5. Technical assistance	3	2	3	2	4	n/a	3	1	1	2.38	2

tant. (Shorter-term R & D is generally undertaken in-house by Japanese firms.) Tax incentives were second in order of importance, followed by export assistance, and subsidized credit. In Taiwanese firms, by contrast, subsidized credit was the most important government incentive, followed by technical assistance provided by MIRL, protection of the local market and export assistance which both ranked third, and, lastly, tax incentives.

Social Relations Within The Factory

According to the conventional view of the firm underlying most micro-economic theory, firms are seen as decision-making entities which maximise profits on the basis of the existing technology and the array of product and factor prices. This view, however, fails to acknowledge the social complexity of firms. Quite apart from the fact that technology and prices are not known by the firm with certainty, decision-making and the imple-mentation of decisions are far more complex processes than allowed for in conventional theory. While by definition theory always involves abstraction and therefore is to some degree 'unrealistic', it must be asked whether a theory that omits an analysis of the social system within the firm leaves out a central determinant of the process of growth and change within the firm. If so, then theories have to be modified, or new theories created, to take account of these determinants.

'Social relations within the factory' refer to the sum total of the inter-actions between the individuals operating within the firm. These inter-actions are hierarchically structured. This is not the place for a more detailed discussion of the importance of social relations within the factory and no attempt was made in the present study to examine these relations. However, on the basis of the Japanese experience it is now unexceptional to observe that social relations within the factory can have a significant effect on the growth and international competitiveness of the firm, includ-ing its ability to improve processes and products. For example, in the present context it was shown in Tables 5.9a and 5.9b that worker suggestions were regarded by both Japanese and Taiwanese sample firms as the fourth most important source of improvement in design and selling price. Similarly, it would be inappropriate to leave entirely unmentioned related factors, such as the loss of only three to four days out of the last ten years due to strikes in two of the Japanese sample firms, and the regular meeting, after hours and without pay, of their quality circle members. The importance of factors such as these is underlined when it is realized, as noted above in the case of the machine tool industry, that the cumulative impact of incremental improvements in processes and products tends to be greater than that of more radical change. Such incremental improvements depend to a large extent on the social relations existing within the firm. This is clearly an area that calls for substantially more conceptual and empirical work if we are to understand better inter-firm and inter-country differences in productivity growth (including product improvement) and international competitiveness.

Some Supply-Side Determinants of International Competitiveness in Sample Firms

In order to gain some idea of the relative importance of 'supply-side' factors that have frequently been referred to as determinants of export market success, sample firms in Taiwan were asked to rank the importance of a number of these factors. The results are presented in Table 5.11. Respondents in firms felt that it was valid to distinguish experience from cost, and organizational and managerial experience was ranked first as a determinant of export success. This was followed by professional and managerial labour costs, second, and skilled labour costs, third. Access to cheaper locally manufactured components ranked fourth and the benefits of the protection of the local market fifth. Access to second-hand equipment was ranked last. All firms reported a fairly high degree of subcontracting of manufactured components, although it is not possible from the information collected to assess the significance of subcontracting in Taiwan compared with Japan.

TABLE 5.11 Taiwan: Supply-side determinants of export market success

| Determining factors | \multicolumn{9}{c}{Firm} | Mean | Rank |
	1	2	3	4	5	6	7	8	9		
1. Low skilled labour costs	2	3	3	1	2	2	1	3	n/a	2.13	3
2. Low professional/managerial labour costs	2	2	1	3	2	2	1	1	n/a	1.75	2
3. Access to cheaper locally manufactured components	4	3	2	2	2	1	3	3	n/a	2.5	4
4. Access to second-hand equipment	4	4	4	4	3	3	4	4	n/a	3.75	6
5. Organisational/managerial experience	1	2	1	1	2	1	2	1	n/a	1.38	1
6. Protection on the local market	3	2	1	3	3	3	3	3	n/a	2.63	5

Jacobsson (1984) has noted that the product design life of Japanese machine tools in the CNC range is on average about three years. This illustrates again the importance of design capabilities and the particular difficulties confronting firms such as those in Taiwan which are dependent on the products of other firms for design. Since design and the research that it embodies is central to international competitiveness, further data was collected on design and research inputs as well as patents as an indicator of technology output. This data is presented in Tables 5.12a and 5.12b.

While all the Taiwanese firms had specialized design departments, they tended to allocate R & D on a project-by-project basis unlike the Japanese firms which evidently followed an organizational rule allocating R & D expenditures as a given proportion of total sales. From Table 5.12a it can

TABLE 5.12a   Japan: R & D, Design engineers and patents

Firm	R & D as % of sales (A)	Design engineers (B)	Core design engineers (C)	Patents granted and pending (D)	Total employees (E)	'Research intensity' i.e. (B) ÷ (E) (F)
1	3.5	530	140	450	3641	14.6
2	2.5	190	90	800	1500	12.7
3	1.0	99	9	860	1000	9.9
4	1.0	50	5	20	520	9.6

TABLE 5.12b   Taiwan: Technology inputs and outputs

Firm	1	2	3	4	5	6	7	8	9
1. Employees in design/ development department	60	45	9	35	7	10	8	n/a	9
2. Total employees	700	500	450	420	250	200	200	180	140
3. 'Research intensity' i.e. (1) ÷ (2)	8.6	9.0	2.0	8.3	2.8	5.0	4.0	–	6.4
4. Employees with post-graduate degree in science or engineering	3	1	1	0	0	2	0	1	0
5. Employees with Bachelor's Degree in science or engineering	30	35	10	22	8	28	16	n/a	10
6. Patents held or applied for	10	1	0	1	0	1	0	0	2

be seen that the two largest firms allocated a large proportion to R & D, bearing in mind that the machine tools sector is not as R & D intensive as other sectors such as automobiles or consumer electronics. Two measures of 'research-intensity' are given in Tables 5.12a and 5.12b, although it should be kept in mind that these are not comparable since, while in the Taiwan case the figure refers to all employees in the design department, in the Japanese firms only design engineers and, a subset of this category, 'core' design engineers, are included. Nevertheless, the figures do give an idea of the design capabilities of the firm in each country. ('Core' design engineers, following Jacobsson (1984a), refers to those engineers who perform the most important design functions.) For the Taiwanese firms, employees with degrees in science or engineering provide some indication of the firms' technological capabilities. As is clear from these figures, the days when machine tool designers relied on their experience learned informally on the job are gone for at least the larger Taiwanese machine tool builders, and for these firms, science-based skills are becoming increasingly important. While patents have important shortcomings as an indicator of technological output, in particular since they do not reflect changes that are incremental although significant, they do provide a stark indication of the technological differences between the 'frontier' Japanese firms and their Taiwanese followers.

VIII THE FRONTIER-FOLLOWING STRATEGY: POLICY DILEMMAS IN TAIWAN

Introduction

In an interview with the author a senior member of one of the planning ministries in the Taiwan government argued that in sectors such as the machinery sector Taiwanese producers were able to make substantial improvements by using technology developed elsewhere without bearing its development costs. By following the technology frontier rather than attempting to reach it, Taiwanese firms are able to enhance their competitive strengths. However, there are numerous difficulties raised by this 'frontier-following strategy' arising from the fact that, as was seen in the discussion of the technological trajectory, the frontier is continually shifting outwards as improvements in machinery are made and costs are reduced. Accordingly, active attempts have to be made to 'keep up' but, as we shall see, it is not always clear what the necessary conditions are in order to do so.

Measuring the Disparity Between Follower and Leader

Taiwanese firms have never been able to compete on the basis of price *and* quality. In general, Taiwanese machines tend to be price, rather than quality, competitive. However, changes occurring at the technology frontier have forced Taiwanese firms to substantially upgrade the quality of their machine tools. As discussed earlier, the introduction by the Japanese of relatively cheap and reliable CNC controls has served to decrease the relative price of CNC compared with conventional machine tools. In view of the superior performance of CNC machine tools, this has meant that for many purposes users have switched to these machines. As a result, Taiwanese producers have been forced to begin producing CNC products. As we shall see below, this has presented further difficulties since the move to CNC machine tools has tended to undermine the cost competitiveness of Taiwanese producers.

As a first step, and prior to examining the policy dilemmas posed by the increasing move to CNC products, attempts were made to quantify the price and quality differential that existed between Taiwanese CNC machine tools and the best quality competing product in export markets. The resulting indices also serve as a measure of the distance of Taiwanese firms from the best-practice technology frontier.[35] The results are presented in Table 5.13.

In examining Table 5.13 it must be kept in mind that the source of information for this table was the producing firm itself, on the basis of the assumption that the firm would know best about its competitive position. The results, however, were confirmed by a senior (and critical) ITRI engineer who had an intimate knowledge of the performance of the firms concerned.

From column D of Table 5.13 it is apparent that the price differential ranged from 30 to 92 per cent of the price of the best competing product with a mean of 70 per cent. In six of the eight cases, however, the differential was above 75 per cent. It must be kept in mind that Table 5.13 relates to CNC products only and, as we shall see, a significant proportion of the value of these machine tools are imported. The price ratio in the case of conventional machine tools is accordingly far lower.

In order to measure quality, four indices were used: maximum spindle speed, motor power, durability, and precision. From column G it can be seen that in all cases the sample firm's maximum spindle speed was 81 per cent or above that of the best competing machine, with a mean of 93 per cent. The motor power, however, of three out of nine firms was between 67 and 73 per cent of the competing machine with a mean for all firms of

TABLE 5.13 Taiwan: Indices of product quality

Firm (A)	Export price of competing product ($) (B)	Firm's export price ($) (C)	(C) ÷ (B) (D)	Competing max spindle speed r.p.m. (E)	Firm's max spindle speed r.p.m. (F)	(F) ÷ (E) (G)	Competing motor power (H)	Firm's motor power (I)	(I) ÷ (H) (J)	Propnl. durability (K)	Propnl. precision (L)
1	US 180 000	US 150 000	83	4500	4500	100	15 hp	15 hp	100	75%	75%
2	–	US 62 500	–	4000	3500	88	7.5 kw	5.5 kw	73	–	–
3	US 80 000	US 60 000	75	3000	3000	100	20 hp	20 hp	100	80%	70%
4	US 40 000	US 35 000	88	3200	2600	81	3 hp	2 hp	67	–	100%
5	US 72 000	US 60 000	83	3150	2800	89	25 hp	20 hp	80	100%	90%
6	NT 2 000 000	NT 1 500 000	75	3500	3000	86	15 hp	15 hp	100	80%	100%
7	US 75 000	US 25 000	33	4200	4200	100	3 hp	3 hp	100	50%	50%
8	US 100 000	US 30 000	30	3150	3150	100	9 hp	6 hp	67	70%	70%
9	US 120 000	US 110 000	92	3150	2800	89	10 hp	10 hp	100	100%	100%
Unweighted mean:			70			93			87	79	82

87 per cent (column J). However, Taiwanese firms perform less well in terms of durability and precision, columns K and L, where the means are 79 and 82 per cent respectively. While it would not be meaningful to weight the four indices in order to construct a single index, since different characteristics will be important for different uses, they do give a quantitative idea of the overall performance of the Taiwanese sample machine tool firms and the 'distance' of firms from the best-practice technology frontier. (It must, however, be repeated that the sample firms were chosen on the basis of their technological sophistication – only firms producing CNC products were included – and therefore are unrepresentative of all machine tool producers.)

Having obtained a quantitative view of the difference in price and performance between Taiwanese and best-practice machine tool producers, we now turn to examine some of the analytical and policy debates that have taken place in Taiwan over the question of the future of the machine tool industry.

The Future of the Taiwanese Machine Tool Industry

Controversy surrounds the question of the necessary conditions for the future success of the Taiwanese machine tool industry. The antagonists, however, are agreed that firms will have to produce a larger proportion of CNC products in view of the increasing penetration of these products in domestic and export markets. They are also agreed that only the more sophisticated firms are likely to make the transition to CNC. The background to the controversy, however, comes from the 'fact' that in 1983 none of the Taiwanese firms producing CNC products made profits from these products. (There is, however, inconsistent evidence as to whether one of the largest firms was making profits on its CNC machine tools.)

There are two identifiable sides to the controversy. The one pole has its base in the Ministry of Economic Affairs (MOEA) and the relevant research institutes under it, ITRI and MIRL. The argument of the proponents of this view is that the larger, although perhaps not the largest, machine tool builders lack, with current resources, the in-house technological capabilities to make the improvements in product quality that will be required by competitive conditions on the international market. A major constraint here is the unwillingness of Taiwanese firms to merge, and therefore gain from the benefits of the economies of specialization and industrial concentration which, as we saw, was an important consideration influencing MITI intervention in Japan. As the Chinese proverb has it: 'Better the head of a chicken than the tail of a cow.' Accordingly, these firms will be at an increasing disadvantage *vis-à-vis* the far larger machine tool firms, including the subsidiaries of the Japanese *zaibatsu* and the South Korean *chaebol*. Accordingly, in view of the constraint on scale of production, it is argued that more assistance must be given to machine tool firms than is currently being given. Forms of assistance that are favoured include a greater degree of protection on the domestic market for both machine tool builders and makers of important components (such as is given in the South Korean machine tool industry), and a larger amount of design and research assistance, and at lower cost, through ITRI and MIRL. Only in this way, it is argued, will Taiwanese firms be able to withstand the increasing competitive pressure from the Japanese. Although Taiwanese firms tend to be relatively small, state-provided research facilities, assistance with design, and training of engineers will help compensate for the lack of size.

Apart from current profitability (it must be remembered that in 1983 when the present study was undertaken the world machine tool industry was in a depressed state and with vigorous competition, profit margins were abnormally low for all producers), another argument was also used to justify further state intervention. This argument was that a major determinant of longer-run profitability is the import ratio of CNC machine tools. In general, the higher this ratio, the lower the competitive edge of Taiwanese CNC producers. To illustrate the current situation, the figures below provide a breakdown of the imported and local cost components for a CNC lathe produced by one of the largest Taiwanese firms.[36]

Imported Components

1. Servo motor/controller/spindle motor	US$ 21 000
2. Hydraulic chuck	1000
3. Index tool magazine	1000
	23 000

Local Production

4. Major components (incl. ballscrew)	2000
5. Other (castings, gears, machined components, machining/assembly etc)	10 000
Total Cost	US$ 35 000
Selling Price (approx)	35 000

It is evident from these figures that some 66 per cent of the total cost of the CNC lathe was taken up by imported components. This compares with only 5 per cent for a conventional lathe. Accordingly it is argued that more needs to be done in order to increase the locally produced components and in this way, taking advantage of both local factor costs and local skills and experience, improve international competitiveness. It is argued, furthermore, that this will not occur automatically through the market process, as a result of the limited capabilities of many of the medium-sized and even larger firms, and therefore that state assistance must be given directly to firms and through an expansion of the activities of state technology institutes. It is acknowledged that progress is being made. Thus, for example, ballscrews have begun to be produced in Taiwan through a joint venture with a British firm. Similarly, there are three Taiwanese companies developing servomotors, two of which have Japanese licenses, and mention has already been made of the local firms beginning to manufacture CNC controls. However, the argument is that selectively targeted state assistance is a necessary condition in order to substantially increase local component production and reduce costs, although it is acknowledged that an important contribution will continue to be made by the in-house contributions of particularly the larger firms.

The other pole of the controversy is located in the Council for Economic Planning and Development (CEPD). Their argument is that market forces can and should be allowed to work. Far from size being a disadvantage, they suggest that smaller firms utilize what may be referred to as 'early Schumpeterian' entrepreneurial drives and talents which tend to be stifled in the more bureaucratic Japanese and South Korean conglomerates. Taiwanese machine tool producers, they argue, have already proved their ability in international markets and in time will be able to consolidate their gains and succeed in the CNC product range. In the case of these products Taiwanese firms are going through a period of infancy when new technologies need to be learned. However, it is a period when short-run losses can be internally financed from the profitability of conventional machine tools and with the help of adequately functioning capital markets. An important role for state technology institutes is acknowledged but it is argued that subsidies and forms of protection should be progressively eliminated. This will produce a more competitive machine tool industry.

This controversy has by no means been resolved and the debate continues. The price–quality dilemma, referred to at many points in the present chapter, has become a contentious issue in the debate. Those favouring a greater degree of state intervention have argued that, under competitive pressure from the Japanese, quality will have to be substantially improved, with the result that the 'low-price/low-quality' option, which has traditionally formed the basis of Taiwanese international competitiveness in the machinery industry, will be progressively undermined. On the other hand, their opponents have suggested that Taiwanese machine tool producers can continue to compete at the low-price end of the market, where full advantage is taken of relatively low labour costs and existing experience, and quality can be gradually improved as firms' in-house capabilities are expanded. However, those supporting more state intervention have also argued that there is a quantum jump in the technology frontier with the increasing importance of manufacturing systems referred to earlier and, in the longer run, with the probable introduction of radical new technology such as the use of lasers in metal cutting, currently a research priority in Japan. Most firms, it is argued, will be unable to make the necessary leap without significant state assistance.

IX CONCLUSIONS

One of the major conclusions to emerge from the present study is that a far richer account is needed in order to explain the economic success of the Asian NICs than is provided in the conventional view. This view is based almost entirely on relative factor prices and on the automatic substitution of factors in response to changing relative prices. Accordingly, the policy prescription that follows is to 'get the prices right'. On the other hand, one of the conclusions emerging from this paper is that, while relative factor prices certainly have played an important role at particular points in time in facilitating the achievement of international competitiveness, numerous other factors must also be taken into account in explaining this competitiveness. To put the matter metaphorically, factors of production must not only be purchased on the market at the going rate. They must also be 'brought into the factory gates' so that inputs may be transformed into outputs. This brings the transformation process itself to the focus of attention. It is here that factors such as technical change and the social relations within the factory become central, factors which determine the ultimate gains or losses in productivity which, via costs, in turn determine international competitiveness. Furthermore, it has been argued, on the basis of the Japanese and Taiwanese case study, that the state's role can also be an important determinant of international competitiveness.

It is, however, important to stress that the conclusion of this chapter does not amount to a plea for a greater degree of 'realism' in attempting to explain the economic performance of the Asian NICs and Japan. Any explanation by definition involves the identification of causes. However, in view of the complexity of social phenomena, it is inevitable that explanation must involve abstraction and theory. Rather it is suggested that the theorising that is necessary in order to produce a better explanation of the economic performance of the Asian NICs and Japan, and therefore form the basis for an account of inter-firm and inter-country differences in technical and productivity change, must include an analysis of the transformation process of inputs into outputs and the role of the state.

This chapter has also implicitly raised a central problem in the explanation of international competitiveness, namely the difficulty of attributing causal significance to the various factors which have influenced competitiveness. The problem arises, of course, from the fact that all the causal factors interact in complex ways, with the result that it is difficult to weight their separate importance. While microstudies are potentially illuminating, even here the difficulties remain. Furthermore, firm personnel, even if they are willing to share their 'real' perceptions, frequently give contradictory or incomplete accounts of the causal significance of the factors that have influenced their transformation of inputs and outputs. Accordingly, more attention needs to be given to the theoretical and methodological problems that need to be tackled if we are ultimately to provide more convincing explanations in this area.

NOTES

1. The author would like to gratefully acknowledge financial assistance for undertaking the case study in Taiwan and Japan from The Nuffield Foundation, The Carnegie Trust, The Overseas Development Administration, and The University of Edinburgh. Generous assistance was received from Dr Chaonan Chen and Dr Paul Liu from the Academia Sinica in Taiwan and from Mr James Tsai of the Industrial Technology Research Institute in Taiwan. I am also thankful for the time unstintingly given by the senior personnel interviewed in firms and government offices in Taiwan and Japan. Valuable comments were received from members of the UK Development Studies Association and the European Association of Development Institutes who attended an earlier workshop in Brighton. Needless to say, none of these individuals is responsible for the contents of this chapter.
2. See Fransman (1984) for a more detailed discussion of this view together with an examination of some of the criticisms.
3. See note 7 below.
4. For a more detailed discussion of these determinations and processes see Fransman (1985), section four on the sources of technical change.

5. In an authoritative review Nelson (1981) concludes:

> The premise behind this paper is that the theoretical model under-
> lying most research by economists on productivity growth over
> time, and across countries, is superficial and to some degree even
> misleading regarding the following matters: the determinants of
> productivity at the level of the firm and of inter-firm differences;
> the processes that generate, screen, and spread new technologies;
> the influence of macroeconomic conditions and economic institu-
> tions on productivity growth. (p. 1029)

6. One of the classical studies is Dore (1973).
7. While the discussion has included reference to both international
   competitiveness and comparative advantage, it is necessary to remem-
   ber the difference between these two concepts. While a country may
   enjoy an international competitiveness if it has an *absolute* cost
   advantage relative to other countries, it will only possess a comparative
   advantage if its *relative* costs are lower. Nevertheless, productivity is
   clearly central in both cases.
8. For a more detailed examination see Fransman (1985).
9. In 1974 the practice of allowing all immigrants from mainland China
   to remain in Hong Kong was ended; 'from then on, those arrested on
   arrival were repatriated. However, all others who evaded capture and
   subsequently 'reached base', that is, gained a home with relatives or
   otherwise found proper accommodation, were permitted to stay.'
   From October 1980 the policy was changed and 'no illegal immigrant
   from China was to be allowed ro remain in Hong Kong' (Hong Kong
   Government, 1981, p. 145). The latter change coincided with both
   increased migration from mainland China due to internal events in
   that country, and a reduction in the demand for labour in Hong Kong.
   An indication of the latter is the fact that the real wage index which
   rose from 121 in 1978 to 135 in 1979, fell to 130 in 1980.
10. The trade dispute between US and Japanese machine tool firms, and
    the attempt by the legal representatives of some US firms to get
    information on the Japanese industry, raised some obstacles in both
    Japan and Taiwan regarding information availability.
11. Some perspective is needed on the size figures. In 1978, three-quarters
    of the 450 firms in the Federal Republic of Germany's machine tool
    sector had less than 25 employees and only 15 firms employed more
    than 1000 persons. In the United Kingdom, 60 per cent of the 983
    firms employed 10 or fewer persons and only 17 firms employed
    more than 500 persons (UNIDO, 1984, p. 61).
12. An interesting account of the origins of NC is to be found in Noble
    (1979) although with a dubiously argued central thesis. Noble argues
    that NC was favoured over an alternative technology, record playback,
    in order to wrest control over the production process from factory-
    floor workers. Cost considerations, he argues, played no role in the
    choice of technology.

13. For a cost comparison of auto, turret and engine lathes, but not NC/CNC, see Huq and Prendergast (1983).
14. These and some of the following figures come from *Metalworking*, November 1982.
15. These and the following figures come from *American Machinist*, February 1983.
16. This is an interesting contrast with the mid-1880s when American machine tools swept into Europe. See Floud (1976).
17. This and the following figures come from *Machine Tools* (Taiwan), 1981.
18. *Metalworking*, November 1982, p. 159.
19. It is necessary to bear in mind that the increasing export ratio in Taiwan and Japan noted above reflects structural changes in the international machine tool industry as well as international competitiveness. Thus in a recent study of the world machine tool industry it is noted that a 'general world trend. . . was the increasing importance of exports. . . The ratio of exports to output increased from 28 per cent in 1966 to 43 per cent in 1981 with the highest ratio of 49 per cent in 1979. . . this was the consequence of increasing international specialization between countries in the production of different types of machine tools' (UNIDO, 1984, p. 67).
20. Quoted in Berg (1980) p. 213.
21. The main sources used are *Metalworking*; Chokki (present volume); and Vogel (forthcoming).
22. *Metalworking*, November 1982, p. 192.
23. However, due to the complexity of the phenomenon under discussion, it cannot be assumed that those views are an accurate reflection of the 'true' sources of technical change.
24. It must be remembered that producing firms (a) have to actively seek the information that customers etc. have at their disposal and (b) have to act on the information in order to transform it into improvements.
25. A number of sources have been used in this section. These include: *Metalworking*, information supplied to the author by Houdaille Industries, Chokki (present volume), and Vogel (forthcoming).
26. See Chokki (present volume) for details on the early history of the industry.
27. Information supplied by Houdaille Industries.
28. *Metalworking*, p. 146.
29. For an account of the importance of funding sources, see Chokki (present volume).
30. This section draws heavily on interviews held by the author in Taiwan with various government officials.
31. *Machine Tools*, August 1981, p. 39.
32. Ibid, p. 59.
33. As in South Korea, there is a 'curb market' in Taiwan with rates of interest substantially above the official commerical rate. Compared to the curb market rate, therefore, the subsidy element is increased.
34. See Jacobsson (1984).
35. The assistance of Mr James Tsai of ITRI is gratefully acknowledged in the construction of the indices.
36. These figures were supplied by a senior ITRI official.

REFERENCES

American Machinist. Various issues.

Amsden, A. H. (1979) 'Taiwan's Economic History – A Case of Etatisme and a Challenge to Dependency Theory', *Modern China*, vol. 5, no. 3 (July) pp. 341–80.

Amsden, A. H. (1984) 'The Division of Labor is Limited by the *Rate of Growth* of the Market (or Why Innovation is Faster when Rate of Growth is Faster): The Taiwan Machine Tool Industry Revisited', Barnard College, Columbia University (mimeo).

Berg, M. (1980) *The Machinery Question and the Making of Political Economy, 1815–1848* (Cambridge: Cambridge University Press).

Chokki, T. Chapter 4, present volume.

Chow, S. C. and Papanek, G. F. (1981) 'Laissez-Faire, Growth and Equity – Hong Kong', *Economic Journal*, vol. 91, no. 362, pp. 466–85.

Constant, E. W. (1980) 'A Model for Technological Change', in *The Origins of the Turbojet Revolution* (Johns Hopkins University Press).

Dore, R. (1973) *British Factory-Japanese Factory: the Origins of National Diversity in Industrial Relations* (London: Allen & Unwin).

Dosi, G. (1982) 'Technological Paradigms and Technological Trajectories: A Suggested Interpretation of the Determinants of Technological Change', *Research Policy*, pp. 147–62.

Findlay, R. (1981) Comment in Hong, W. and Krause, C. B. (eds), *Trade and Growth of the Advanced Developing Countries in the Pacific Basin. Papers and Proceedings of the Eleventh Pacific Trade and Development Conference* (Seoul, South Korea: Development Institute).

Floud, R. (1976) *The British Machine Tool Industry 1850–1914* (Cambridge University Press).

Fransman, M. (1984) 'Explaining the success of the Asian NICs: incentives and technology', *IDS Bulletin*, vol. 15, no. 2 April.

Fransman, M. (1985) 'Conceptualising technical change in the Third World in the 1980s: an interpretive survey', *Journal of Development Studies*, vol. 21, no. 4, July.

Fransman, M. and King, K. (eds) (1984) *Technological capability in the Third World* (London: Macmillan).

Hong Kong Government (1981) *Hong Kong 1981* (Hong Kong).

Huq, M. M. and Prendergast, C. C. (1983) *Choice of Technique in Machine Tools* (Edinburgh: Scottish Academic Press).

Jacobsson, S. (1984a) 'Technical Change and Technology Policy – The Case of Computer Numerically Controlled Lathes in Argentina, Korea and Taiwan' (paper prepared for UNCTAD).

Jacobsson, S. (1984b) 'Industrial Policy for the Machine Tool Industries of South Korea and Taiwan', *IDS Bulletin* (April) pp. 44–9.

Johnson, C. (1982) *MITI and the Japanese Miracle: The Growth of Industrial Policy, 1925–1975* (Stanford: Stanford University Press).

Krueger, A. O. (1981) 'Export-Led Industrial Growth Reconsidered', in W. Hong and C. B. Krause (eds), *Trade and Growth of the Advanced Developing Countries in the Pacific Basin. Papers and Proceedings of the Eleventh Pacific Trade and Development Conference* (Seoul, South Korea: Korea Development Institute).

Liebenstein, H. (1981) 'Microeconomics and X-Efficiency Theory: If There is No Crisis There Ought To Be', in Bell, D. and Kristol, I. (eds), *The Crisis in Economic Theory* (New York: Basic Books).

Little, I. M. D. (1979) 'The Experience and Causes of Rapid Labour-Intensive Development in Korea, Taiwan, Hong Kong, and Singapore; and the Possibilities of Emulation', Working Paper No. 1, ILO, Asian.

Machine Tools (1981) (Taipei: Taiwan).

Mansfield, E. *et al.* (1977) *The Production and Application of New Industrial Technology* (New York: W. W. Norton).

Metalworking, Japan. Various issues.

Myint, H. (1981) 'Comparative Analysis of Taiwan's Economic Development with Other Countries', in Institute of Economics, Academia Sinica, *Conference on Experiences and Lessons of Economic Development in Taiwan* (Taipei: Academia Sinica).

Nelson, R. R. (1978) 'Innovation and Economic Development: Theoretical Retrospect and Prospect', *IDB/CEPAL Studies on Technology and Development in Latin America.*

Nelson, R. R. (1981) 'Research on Productivity Growth and Productivity Differences: Dead Ends and New Departures', *Journal of Economic Literature*, vol. XIX (Sept) pp. 1029–64.

Nelson, R. R. and Winter, S. G. (1977) 'In Search of Useful Theory of Innovation', *Research Policy*, pp. 36–76.

Noble, D. F. (1979) 'Social Choice in Machine Design: The Case of Automatically Controlled Machine Tools', in Zimbalistia (ed), *Case Studies on the Labour Process* (New York: Monthly Review Press).

Peck, M. J. and Tamura, S. (1976) 'Technology' in Patrick, H. and Rosovsky, H. (eds) (1976) *Asia's New Giant: How the Japanese Economy Works* (Washington, DC: The Brookings Institute).

Ranis, G., Ohkawa, K. and Fei, J. C. H. (1983) 'Economic Development in Historical Perspective: Japan, Korea, and Taiwan, in Ohkawa, K. and Ranis, G., (eds) *Japan and the Developing Countries* (Oxford: Basil Blackwell).

Rosenberg, N. (1976) *Perspectives on Technology* (Cambridge: Cambridge University Press).

Rosenberg, N. (1982) *Inside the Black Box: Technology and Economics* (Cambridge: Cambridge University Press).

Schumpeter, J. A. (1943) *Capitalism, Socialism and Democracy* (London: Allen & Unwin).

Sciberras, E. and Payne, B. (forthcoming) *Technical Change and International Competitiveness: A Study of the Machine Tool Industry* (London: Longman).

Taiwan (1980) *Ten Year Development Plan for Taiwan, Republic of China (1980–1989)*, Council for Economic Planning and Development, Executive Yuan, Taiwan (March 1980).

Taiwan (1981) *Four Year Economic Development Plan for Taiwan: Republic of China (1982–1985)*, Council for Economic Planning and Development, Executive Yuan, Taiwan (December 1981).

UNIDO (1984) *World Non-Electrical Machinery – An Empirical Study of the Machine Tool Industry* (New York: United Nations).

U.S. Academy of Sciences (1983) *The Competitive State of the U.S. Machine Tool Industry* (Washington DC: National Academy Press).

Vogel, E. (forthcoming) Chapter on machine tools in forthcoming book.

Wade, R. (1984) 'Dirigisme Taiwan-style', *IDS Bulletin* (April) pp. 65–70.

Westphal, L. E. (1978) 'Industrial Incentives in the Republic of China (Taiwan)' (mimeo) (Washington DC: World Bank).

6 The Capital Goods Industry and the Dynamics of Economic Development in LDCs: The Case of Brazil

FABIO STEFANO ERBER

I INTRODUCTION

This chapter is addressed to the discussion of the role of the capital goods industry in the development of an LDC (less-developed country), analysing in some detail the case of Brazil.

The second section reviews the role of the capital goods industry in the processes of capital accumulation and technical progress in an economy whose 'stylized characteristics' are drawn from the example of the advanced capitalist economies. It concludes with the question of whether such conditions are found in LDCs. The rest of the chapter tries to answer this query.

The third section recalls the intellectual background of the 'battle for the industrialization' of the LDCs and the different roles the capital goods industry was ascribed in the development of such countries.

The three following sections analyse the development of the Brazilian capital goods industry during its phases of import-substitution growth and decline (Section IV), the boom of the 'Brazilian miracle' (Section V) and the following crisis (Section VI). Their focus is on the development of local production of capital goods and the role played in such development by the factors suggested by the literature reviewed in Section III as warranting the establishment of capital goods production in an LDC.

Section VII takes up the issue of technological development in the Brazilian capital goods industry and its relationship to exports and, to a much lesser extent, employment.

215

Finally, Section VIII sums up the answers provided in the preceding parts, relating the development of the Brazilian capital goods industry to the more general aspects of its pattern of capitalist development.

Since Brazil is the largest producer of capital goods in the Third World (China excluded),[1] with a domestic content of supply comparable to that of the advanced countries,[2] and is also one of the main exporters of capital goods among LDCs,[3] part of which are attributed to local technological development, its case is relevant not only on its own but for other LDCs as well.

II THE CAPITAL GOODS INDUSTRY AND THE DEVELOPMENT OF ADVANCED CAPITALIST ECONOMIES

The capital goods industry (CGI), i.e. the industry which produces equipment and machinery, holds a distinguished place in the history of development theory. Analysts of the Industrial Revolution, the classical economists, gave it a place of honour in their explanations of both the specificity of capitalist development, of what distinguished it from earlier modes of production, and of the strength of such development.

Among them, Marx is probably the author who carried the analysis of the role played by the machinery industry in the development of capitalism furthest. He argued that only when the production of machines was made by machines, when the capital goods industry was mechanized, did the capitalist mode of production reach its full form as 'modern industry'. Only then, he argued, were capitalists able to subordinate workers to machinery. The social labour process then became 'objectively' run by the logic of capital accumulation without the constraints imposed by the 'subjectivity' of labour. Throughout the whole industrial process, from the production of machines to the 'machinofacture' of wage goods, everywhere workers became 'appendages to machines' and capital imposed its rationale (Marx, 1968a). The latter led to an increase in the use of machinery, raising the productivity of labour but, at the same time, tended to decrease the rate of profit by reducing the share of capital capable of generating a surplus (variable capital) in total capital, a contradictory process which, according to Marx, was typical of capitalism. Moreover, the relationship between the capital goods industry (together with other industries manufacturing producer goods) and the industries producing consumer goods (respectively, Departments I and II of the economy) played a crucial role in the *dynamics* of the capitalist system, as can be seen in Marx's analysis of expanded reproduction (Marx, 1968b).

Kalecki (1977) would later argue that 'several of the modern theories of growth', including the well-known Harrod-Domar model, could be interpreted as 'variations on the theme of the Marxist scheme of expanded reproduction' (p. 6), which can be summarized by an inter-departmental relationship between profits in the sector producing wage-goods and wages in the other sector(s), and by a relationship between the rate of investment and the stock of capital. This type of relationship has in fact been widely used to explain the unstable and cyclical pattern of development of capitalism (see Matthews, 1959, for a review).

Economic development results from the combination of two processes, capital accumulation and technical progress, which are in fact intertwined, and the machinery-producing industry plays a role as important in the latter as in the former. Innovations in the capital goods industry normally lead to an increase in productivity in industries using its products, and innovations in such industries (either in their products or their processes) normally require embodiment in capital goods (which are often modified for such new purposes). Since the machinery produced for one user can be often utilized by others (eventually with adaptations) the capital goods industry acts as the main locus for the diffusion of innovations throughout the economic system.[4] The same role is played in terms of training manpower. Moreover, if we assume that there is technical progress in the capital goods industry and therefore new vintages of machinery are more productive than older ones, new investments benefit from such increased productivity, expanding effective demand and further investment, building up a 'virtuous circle' of capital accumulation and technical progress (Salter, 1960), a hypothesis often put forward to explain the recent development of advanced countries (Dosi, 1982).

Technical progress in the capital goods industry, in its turn, is based on a 'collective process' involving purchasers of machinery, engineering firms, suppliers of parts and components of the machines, and universities and research institutes, besides the actual producers of capital goods. When carried out in a context where there is considerable division of labour this process is characterized by sinergy – i.e. the result is greater than the sum of the parts. Since innovation in this industry is based mainly on design and manufacturing technology improvements, which develop through time, experience at the level of the firm and of the industry is a prime determinant of innovation capability, raising barriers to entry of newcomers. Although computer-aided-design and computer-aided-manufacturing have recently expanded, some of the skills necessary to innovate in the industry (notably in basic design) are person-embodied, learned by experience – and transferred from one enterprise to another by changes in employment. For such reasons important differences may be found between the private and social costs and benefits of innovating in the capital goods industry, requiring state intervention to foster it (Erber, 1977).

The post-war literature on the relationship between innovation and international competition strengthens further the dynamic importance of the capital goods industry. The studies of innovations and of their diffusion suggest that they require the proximity of capital goods suppliers, especially in early stages of introduction of innovations. Producers of capital goods play an important (albeit often poorly documented) role in suggesting improvements in processes and products which play an important role in their customers' competitive position. Moreover, when the innovation is a capital good itself, the proximity to a supplier is necessary to ensure proper technical assistance and maintenance. Thus, the development of technical capability in the capital goods industry is an important asset in international competitiveness.

Furthermore, exports of capital goods themselves have become one of the main items of international trade. For the main developed economies (USA, Germany, Japan, UK) they represented more than 40 per cent of their total exports in 1975, a share which had increased over the decade (Fajnzylber, 1983). Developing countries account for almost all of the export surplus of capital goods from developed economies, and for more than a fourth of total world imports. None the less, trade between LDCs in machinery and transport equipment is increasing: in 1979 about 8 per cent of the LDCs' total imports of such commodities originated in other developing countries, from about 6 per cent in 1975 (UNCTAD, 1982). Exports of capital goods from LDCs to developed economies are still quite limited although they represent an important share for the leading producers.[5] It should be noted that only a limited number of LDCs are exporters of capital goods (Brazil, Korea, Singapore, Taiwan, Yugoslavia and, to a lesser extent, India and Argentina) (UNCTAD, 1982).

However, in order to fulfil the dynamic role discussed above, the development of capital goods technology and production must be accompanied by a parallel development of the financial system, which is able to respond to the investment decisions of entrepreneurs that underlie the purchase of new capital goods. This is a crucial point in understanding the problems of LDCs in this industry, as will be seen in more detail later.

Although he argued that the development of the machinery industry was a necessary condition for the development of capitalism, Marx did not hold that the inverse relationship was true. In fact he seems to have shared the faith of his predecessors that the development of machinery held the promise of alleviating the drudgery and hardship of work, provided the right social relations of production were present. His followers, such as Luxemburg (1961), argued that indeed socialism would increase the use of machinery relative to capitalism. Thus the trend toward an increasing use of machinery in developed economies became so established that some authors interpret it as one of the 'natural trajectories' followed by technical progress in our civilization (Nelson and Winter, 1977). Only more recently, in the wake of the counter-culture movement, has this trend been contested, but with little practical consequence, as far as one can judge.

III THE CGI AND LDCs: THE BACKGROUND

But what about the economies that in the early stages of development of capitalism became part of the system in their role as suppliers of raw materials and primary products? Ricardo's reply was that the law of value and comparative advantages operated in such a way that 'old countries are constantly impelled to employ machinery and new countries to employ labour' (Ricardo, 1973, p. 26). This view of relative comparative advantages was preserved when the neo-classical paradigm became dominant in the present century, in the Heckscher-Ohlin–Samuelson version, and it implied different rates of diffusion of the use of machinery and different rates of development of local production of capital goods.[6]

As regards the Marxist paradigm, Marx himself did not spend much time on the subject. None the less, he seems to have believed that sooner or later capitalism would spread to the former colonies and other less-developed countries and, as part of this process, one can presume, a local capital goods industry would develop.[7] For a while Marxist writers followed his lead and held that imperialism would industrialize the less-developed countries.[8]

None the less, from the 1920s onwards, another strand in Marxist thought prevailed – that capitalism is a fetter on the development of the LDCs. Thus Marxist orthodoxy argued that imperialism, allied to the pre-capitalist landlords and the 'comprador' bourgeoisie of the LDCs, were against the industrialization of such economies, and therefore inimical to the development of a local capital goods industry. Against such an 'unholy alliance' the 'progressive' sectors of society (peasants, workers and part of the enlightened urban middle class) should unite with a national industrial bourgeoisie to industrialize and modernize the economy and society.[9]

This was the intellectual background against which the 'battle for industrialization of the LDCs' was fought in the post Second World War period. Keynes's dictum that behind every politician there is a long-dead economist would prove true once again, with the difference that, in this case, economists were often alive and in the front line too.

Proponents of industrialization of the Third World took as their prime enemy the arguments of the neo-classical paradigm that LDCs' specialization in primary products was conducive to their development. Thus they attacked at the same time both the prevailing international division of labour and the LDC's internal productive structure. Most of them believed that foreign investors would not be interested in the industrialization of the Third World, which would be the 'historic task' of a national bourgeoisie aided by a clairvoyant state, and by a 'modern' middle class with the support of workers and peasants. The majority also shared an optimistic view of the results of industrialization in terms of increasing the rate of growth of output, income and employment and reducing the political and economic inequalities. None the less, they disagreed about which industries should take precedence in re-structuring the economic structure of such countries.

In early proposals of industrialization of the LDCs, such as those put forward by Nurkse (1953) and Rosenstein-Rodan (1961), the international supply of capital goods played a secondary role, since they emphasized the interdependence of consumer's demand and investment in consumer goods industries as the way out of the 'vicious circle of misery' in which LDCs were entrapped. Machinery for the consumer goods industry was to be mainly imported.

Other proposals, such as those of the writers belonging to Economic Commission on Latin America (ECLA) (e.g., Tavares, 1964)[10] and Hirschman (1958), brought the capital goods industry to the forefront. This reversal rested upon two pillars: a foreign exchange constraint, and the dynamic effects of the 'vertical interdependence' between industries producing consumer and intermediary goods and their suppliers of machinery.

IV THE CGI AND IMPORT SUBSTITUTION

The foreign exchange constraint was seen as inherent to the specialization of the LDCs in primary goods; as a structural *datum*, resulting from several causes which the LDCs did not have the power to alter.[11]

The foreign exchange constraint played a double role in the dynamics of import-substituting industrialization, the pattern which prevailed in Latin America. On the one hand, it spurred industrial growth by limiting the amount of goods which could be imported; on the other, it placed a limit on such growth by constraining the imports of capital goods and other inputs that were necessary to produce locally the goods previously imported. Therefore, in order to keep its momentum, the import-substituting model required a local production of capital goods.[12]

Brazil is one of the countries which carried this process furthest, during the second half of the 1950s. According to Lessa (1964), in the period 1955-60 the production of machinery and equipment in general increased by more than 100 per cent and that of heavy electrical machinery by more than 200 per cent. Investment in the sector increased even further: between 1955 and 1959 (the last year of the period for which there is data available) gross capital formation in the mechanical and electrical products industries increased at a yearly rate of, respectively, 43 per cent and 38 per cent in real terms. At the same time, the imported component in total supply of capital goods declined from 46 per cent in the period 1950-55 to an average of 31 per cent in the period 1956-62 (Erber *et al.*, 1974).

None the less, in Brazil, in 1960, the capital goods industry accounted for less than 10 per cent of the value added in manufacturing industry; about a fourth of the share it held in the USA, Germany, Japan, France and the United Kingdom and less than a third of the share of the Italian capital goods sector (see Table 6.1). Indeed, a cross-country comparison taking into account country GNPs suggested that until the early 1960s the output of the Brazilian capital goods sector was below the international 'norm'. Although fourteen years later the share of the Brazilian capital goods industry in total manufacturing had increased faster than that of the more advanced countries, it was still between a half and a third of the share of the capital goods sector in those countries.[13]

TABLE 6.1 Share of the capital goods industry in total manufacturing industry's value added for Brazil and selected developed countries, 1960 and 1974 (in percentage)

Country	1960	1974
United States	38.1	42.7
Japan	31.7	48.5
Germany	38.2	39.0
France	37.3	39.2
United Kingdom	41.1	40.5
Italy	29.9	36.5
Brazil	9.2	14.5

SOURCE Fajnzylber (1983).

The model of import substitution has often been criticised precisely for its assumption of a rigid foreign exchange constraint and for the neglect of export possibilities (e.g., Bergsman, 1970). Moreover, as ECLA's studies warned, the dynamic possibilities of this type of industrialization were limited even in Brazil, since import substitution could be only partially extended to capital goods and intermediate products, where it would sooner or later confront either foreign exchange restrictions, natural-resources scarcities, and/or problems of minimum scale related to the size of the domestic market. In the Brazilian case the same process which had produced the great economic expansion of the 1950s also led to increased political, social and economic imbalances, expressed by highly concentrated income distribution, severe inflation rates and increased political strife.

As is well known, the political impasse was solved by a military coup in early 1964. After a recession during the period 1964-7, the economy was launched back on an expansion cycle, led by industrial growth, which reached its peak in the mid-1970s and lasted until 1980 (see Tables 6.2

TABLE 6.2 Average yearly growth rates of the Brazilian economy: Gross Internal Product and its main sectors, 1968–82 (in percentage)

Period	GIP	GIP per capita	Agriculture	Industry	Commerce	Transport & communications
1968/74	10.93	8.05	5.13	12.20	11.42	12.69
1975/78	6.36	3.79	4.25	7.29	4.85	8.68
1979/80	7.28	4.66	5.65	7.28	7.31	10.71
1981/82	−1.30	−3.64	2.03	−4.10	−3.04	−2.40
1968/82	7.83	4.83	4.55	7.93	7.08	9.93

SOURCE   Malan and Bonelli (1983).

TABLE 6.3 Brazilian industrial production: average yearly real growth rates according to use of products, 1968–82 (in percentage)

	1968/74	1975/78	1979/80	1981/82	Total 1968/82
Total	12.9	6.7	7.0	−5.0	7.9
Intermediary	13.3	8.3	8.3	−5.2	8.6
Capital goods	18.3	6.0	5.8	−14.9	8.3
Durable consumer	22.5	6.0	9.2	−11.3	11.2
Non-durable consumer products	8.8	5.1	4.8	−0.2	6.0

SOURCE   Malan and Bonelli (1983).

TABLE 6.4 Brazil: Production, imports and exports of capital goods, 1970–82 (millions of US $)

Year	Production (1)	Exports (2)	Production for home market (3) = (1) − (2)	Imports (4)	Consumption (5) = (3) + (4)	Percent (2/1)	(2/4)	(3/5)
1970	2499	81	2418	945	3363	3.2	8.6	71.9
1974	8468	375	8093	3135	11 228	4.4	12.0	72.1
1975	9423	551	8872	3944	12 816	5.8	14.0	69.2
1979	16 933	1656	15 277	3779	19 056	9.8	43.8	80.2
1980	18 047	2276	15 771	4384	20 155	12.6	51.9	78.3
1982	13 081	2297	10 784	3278	14 062	17.6	70.1	76.7

SOURCES Production: 1970–79 Erber (1982) 1980–82 Estimated using FIBGE'S growth rates for capital goods Exports: CEPAL (1985) Imports: Malan and Bonelli (1983).

TABLE 6.5 Brazil: Share of capital goods imports and exports in total imports and exports, 1970–82 (in percentage for selected years)

Year	Imports	Exports
1970	37.7	3.0
1971	41.3	n.a.
1975	32.3	6.5
1980	19.1	11.3
1982	16.9	11.4

SOURCES Imports: Malan and Boneli (1983) Exports: Cepal (1985)

to 6.4). As the tables show, in recent years, a recession has, for the first time since the war, reduced the Gross Internal Product.

V THE CGI AND THE 'MIRACLE'

Two elements characterize the boom period of 1968–74 (the 'Brazilian miracle'): internally, the role played by the durable consumer industries, which grew at a yearly rate of 22.5 per cent (see Table 6.3) and, externally, the favourable balance-of-payment conditions, based upon improved terms of trade and the availability of credit.[14] Thus, for the first time in her history of industrialization, Brazil did not face a foreign exchange constraint at a time of expansion. Imports of capital goods were especially stimulated by local fiscal incentives, tariff exemptions,[15] tied-in foreign credit, scarcity of local finance and overvalued exchange rates[16] (Suzigan *et al.*, 1974; Erber, 1977, 1982).

As one would expect under such conditions, imports of capital goods soared – during the 1967–74 period they increased 367 per cent in real terms, a yearly rate of 24.6 per cent, their share in total Brazilian imports (oil included) reaching a peak of 41 per cent in 1971 and 1972 (from 25 per cent in 1965) (Malan and Bonelli, 1983) (see Tables 6.4 and 6.5).

The bias against local production of capital goods implied by the economic policy of the period via prices and credit was consistent with the other main features of the strategy for economic and political development of the regime – to maximize short-term growth (used also as a legitimizing factor) based on the durable consumer goods industry and on foreign credit. In this sense, the surge in imports reflected the economic and political conditions of the period.

However, the increase in imports of capital goods cannot be attributed only to the policies mentioned above. Some of the imports consisted of parts and components to be used in local production. This reflected one of the weaknesses of the Brazilian industrial structure: the undevelopment of the network of suppliers, which leads, on the one hand, to a high degree of vertical integration of the larger firms (see below) and, on the other, to higher imports.[17]

Part of the increase in imports can be attributed to gaps between local design and production capabilities and demand requirements. The latter are, in turn, deeply influenced by the use of imported specifications of equipment by the main purchasers of capital goods – foreign subsidiaries acting in the durable consumer goods and intermediary industry and state enterprises providing infra-structure services and intermediate products. As shown by Mazzuchielli (1977) the former were responsible for the majority of imports of series-produced machinery and the latter for the imports of custom-built capital goods. Part of the imports of subsidiaries can be attributed to their strategy of standardizing their technology world-wide and possibly also to intra-group trade. The specifications of equipment used by state agencies reflect also the relatively low level of development of engineering firms in Brazil, which usually did only the detail engineering activities of the projects, leaving the basic design and equipment specifications to foreign contractors (Ford *et al.*, 1977). This division of labour has been shown (Erber, 1974; Alves and Ford, 1975) to be highly influenced by the financing structure of the projects, with foreign funding (including that by international agencies) biasing choices in favour of imported plant design and specifications, (apart from imported capital goods). Therefore, although pure 'technology-gap imports' certainly exist, as in every economy, some of them are a result of entrepreneurial strategies and economic policies which strengthen the underdevelopment of local production and design capabilities in the capital goods industry and related engineering services, in what amounts to a vicious circle, since the above-mentioned capabilities are developed through experience, which is undermined by imports.

None the less, and this is important to stress, the expansion of imports did not prevent the internal production of capital goods from growing. In fact, during the period 1968–74, the local output of capital goods increased at a spectacular yearly rate of 18.3 per cent, well above the average for all industry. Thus the domestic content supply of capital goods at its lowest point (1975) was 69.2 per cent of total consumption, increasing in later years to about 80 per cent (see Table 6.4).

Such domestic supply ratios are comparable to those of much larger economies such as the Federal Republic of Germany (84 per cent in the same year) and Italy (77 per cent in 1978). Sweden, which has a similar apparent consumption (US$17.6 billions in 1978, compared with US$19.0 billions for Brazil (Lim, 1979), had a much smaller domestic supply ratio: 65 per cent.[18]

Thus the Brazilian case suggests that although a foreign exchange constraint may be a strong incentive to set up a capital goods industry in an LDC, as shown by the period of import substitution in the 1950s, it is not a necessary condition for the further development of the industry, as shown by the period we have just discussed. In the latter the main factor leading to the development of the capital goods industry was the inter-industrial relationships in a process similar to that prevailing in advanced capitalist countries. None the less, as we have seen, the capital goods industry in Brazil is responsible for a much smaller share of industrial output than in those economies (see Table 6.1), in spite of its growth. This *differentia specifica* has received considerable attention in the explanation of the downswing of the cycle in the aftermath of the 'miracle' and we discuss it in more detail in the next section.

VI THE CRISIS: INTER-INDUSTRIAL RELATIONS AND THE NEW FOREIGN EXCHANGE CONSTRAINT

One of the first development economists to focus primarily upon the role played by inter-industrial relationships in the dynamics of industrialization was Hirschman (1958). Building upon the concept of 'backward' and 'forward' inter-industrial linkages and their dynamic effects in terms of inducing investment, he strongly argued in favour of investing in industries which produce intermediate and capital goods rather than consumer goods, since the former presented higher combined linkages and therefore had a greater impact upon investments in other industries.

While Hirschman's argument was essentially of a prescriptive nature, the theme of the inter-industrial investment relationship was revived in the early 1970s, when the pattern of development that had emerged in Latin America after the period of import substitution was critically assessed by the 'dependence' analysts.

Although the battle for industrialization had been won, for many of its combatants it was a Pyrrhic victory. Contrary to the optmistic hopes of the 1950s, the pattern of development was by and large 'perverse': even where capital accumulation had been resumed, as in Brazil (after the recession of 1963–7), it was based upon the production of durable consumer goods and upon an increasingly unequal income distribution, often enforced by authoritarian political regimes. Moreover, it was led by foreign enterprises, backed up by heavy state investments with the national bourgeoisie playing a secondary (albeit profitable) role. This new pattern of development led to a change in the links between hegemonic and dependent economies and, according to the 'dependence' authors, technology, capital goods and finance were now the main links in the new 'web of dependence'.

In an early formulation (Cardoso, 1973), the underdevelopment of the local capital goods industry and the reliance on imported technology were seen as limiting the process of capitalist development of the periphery, since the Department I of such economies (the sector producing means of production) was said to be virtually non-existent, preventing a productive complementarity required by capital accumulation; since the capital goods were supplied by the central economies, those economies benefited from the dynamic stimuli. The Brazilian case showed this to be an over-simplification: an internal technical capability[19] and the production of capital goods developed with the process of industrialization.

Although they are critical of the general framework of analysis of 'dependency theory', some recent studies of the dynamics of capital accumulation in the context of 'late' capitalist development in LDCs have emphasized the role played by the relationship between the capital goods industry and other sectors. Using a Kaleckian scheme to explain the cyclical nature of such development (e.g., Tavares 1978; Tavares and Belluzzo, 1979) such studies argue that the relatively small size of the capital goods sector in such an economy prevents the CGI from playing the dynamic role it fulfils in the developed capitalist economies via the multiplier and accelerator effects and via increased productivity.

In an LDC there is a propensity for the dynamic effects of autonomous investment to be dissipated much earlier than in an advanced economy. Since both in intermediate and consumer goods (mainly durable consumer goods) there is a tendency to invest in capacities which are ahead of demand (because of indivisibilities and/or oligopolistic competition), such economies have a deep-seated propensity for sharp cycles. When autonomous investments occur in consumer and intermediate goods, economic activity increases sharply because of the size of such investments relative to the already installed capacity, only to contract sharply when their first-round effects are over.

In an economy such as Brazil, where the leading sector is producing durable consumer goods using capital-intensive techniques, and at the same time the average income is low, policies of income concentration[20] and this financing of purchases of such goods may foster capital accumulation during the upswing, albeit at a very high social cost, but cannot prevent a sharp downswing. Under such conditions the phase of expansion assumes a 'perverse' form in terms of income distribution and social equity which is aggravated in the recession by unmitigated unemployment.[21]

Although imports of capital goods can be interpreted as a further 'drain' from the dynamic point of view, they are not a necessary condition for this argument – even with autarky in capital goods supply, the dynamics of capital accumulation would be stunted if the relative size of the industry were small.

The argument can be further extended if we look at the characteristics of the network of activities for designing and producing capital goods. The relative underdevelopment in Brazil (and in other LDCs, as shown by UNCTAD, 1982) of the network of suppliers and engineering services reduces inter-industrial linkages and productivity, by encouraging a much higher vertical integration in the CGI in advanced countries. The 'economies of specialization' which are a prominent feature of the industry are thus lost (Rosenberg, 1963).

Finally, this argument draws attention to the problems of financing the production and purchase of locally produced capital goods. If the financial system is unable to provide for such financing, investment may be postponed or not made at all or purchases of capital goods may be diverted abroad. This may happen without a savings constraint, since savings may exist but be redirected to other uses (e.g. the purchase of durable consumer goods).

Such an analysis, which shifts the focus from the foreign exchange constraint to inter-industrial relationships and to the role played by internal financing, was developed for the Brazilian case, but it may be relevant to other LDCs as well. In fact, Fajnzylber (1983) has suggested that the relative underdevelopment of the capital goods industry is one of the main distinguishing traits of the industrialization of LDCs.

Thus, from the perspective of the authors mentioned above, a slowdown in economic growth was to be expected after the leading durable consumer goods industries had completed their expansion by the mid-1970s and, in fact, the growth rates of the two groups of industries show a considerable reduction in the period 1975–8 (see Table 6.3).

The government that took over in 1974 seemed intent on changing the existing industrial structure, since its Development Plan (II PND) gave top priority to the complex of industries producing intermediate and capital goods. According to the Plan this would, at the same time, reduce the foreign exchange constraint[22] by increasing the domestic content of the supply of intermediate products and capital goods and increasing national control of the economy, since state enterprises would supply the intermediate products, directly or in joint ventures – Brazilian private enterprises are important suppliers of capital goods, public works and engineering services.

The story of the period cannot be dealt with in detail here but its main features illustrate the problems of trying to change the productive structure of the economy without changing its financial structure as well.

The capital goods industry, especially the Brazilian enterprises[23] responded to the Plan by increasing their productive capacity sharply – the average fixed investment of projects presented to the Industrial Development Council by enterprises producing capital goods during the period 1974-6 was 2.6 times greater than the average for the period 1971-3. Over the same period the National Development Bank (BNDE) increased its loans to the capital goods industry in the same proportion[24] (Erber, 1982).

However, apart from increasing the funds of BNDE and its subsidiaries, which is the main source of long-term finance to industry in Brazil, no major changes were made in the internal finance system to support the large investments foreseen by the Plan, especially by the state. The financial policy of the period rested upon a mounting public debt, based on open market operations and on a swelling external debt, which increased over five times between 1973 and 1978, most of which was pegged to floating interest rates.[25] As a consequence, internal interest rates tended to increase in real terms over the period, stifling private investment further.

Under the double pressure of rising inflation and foreign exchange constraints (fuelled by increased oil prices and mounting international interest rates) the ambitions of the Plan were abandoned in favour of a stop-go policy, which lasted from 1977 to 1980, strongly influenced by political events.[26] The state curtailed its investments to control inflation and instructed its enterprises to fund as much as possible of the remaining projects from external sources, while internal interest rates were increased to stimulate private enterprises to do the same. State projects which did take off (especially those in the energy sector - hydropower and oil) were instrumental in sustaining the demand for capital goods until the end of the decade. None the less, the Plan left the capital goods industry saddled with a capacity which has been widely underutilized and which holds no prospect of being fully used in the near future.

More recently the foreign exchange constraint has been a prime deter-minant of the recessionary policy followed by the Brazilian Government since 1980 (Malan and Bonelli, 1983). The reduction in industrial activity and public and private investment has been felt especially in the local output of capital goods which declined at an average yearly rate of 15 per cent in the period 1981-2 (see Tables 6.2 and 6.3). Estimates for 1983 show that the reduction in capital goods production has deepened – in August of that year the level of output was estimated to be 18 per cent lower than a year before, and no evidence was available of a recovery.[27] Taking into account only production for the Brazilian market, by excluding exports, the fall is even more severe (see Table 6.4) – the 1982 level is less than two-thirds of the 1979 output. Imports of capital goods also fell, but less sharply (the 1982 imports are 87 per cent of the 1979, after an increase in 1981).[28] This relative inelasticity of imports is probably due to the same causes previously discussed, since the latter have remained largely unaltered.

However, there are three important differences between the present Brazilian situation and the foreign exchange constraint normally treated in the literature of 'development economics'.

First there is the role played by the capital goods industry in the foreign exchange constraint (FEC). Contrary to other situations of FEC, which appear at times of expansion, the present recession has *reduced* the share of capital goods imports in total imports, from the peak of 41 per cent in 1971–2 to 17 per cent in 1982. Moreover, and most important, the trade balance of the capital goods industry has steadily improved – while in 1970 Brazilian exports of capital goods represented 13 per cent of imports, in 1982 they were 70 per cent of imports (see Table 6.4). A recent study (Araujo and Reis, 1981) shows that about a third of such exports were purchased by OECD countries, the rest being sold to other LDCs. The world recession seems to have affected such exports, causing a reduction of their growth rate, but no more than proportional to the drop in total Brazilian exports (see Tables 6.4 and 6.5).

Second, there is the nature of the Brazilian present FEC, which has financial rather than trade roots. As opposed to the traditional FEC in the development literature, the present Brazilian FEC is not to be found at balance-of-trade level, caused by an excess of imports over exports, but caused by the service of debt and by the reduced inflow of capital (see Table 6.6). The nature and magnitude of the Brazilian FEC are such that no improvements in the balance of trade[24] can overcome it, if not accompanied by a drastic change in the conditions that link the Brazilian economy to the international financial system.

Finally, as a consequence, the main influence of the FEC upon the capital goods industry is not exerted via restriction on imports, as it is in the import-substituting model, when it stimulates the local production of goods, but rather through the recessionary effects it has upon the general level of economic activity which reduce the demand for both imported and locally produced capital goods.

TABLE 6.6 Brazil: Balance of payments, 1973–82 (in US $ millions)

	1973	1974	1975	1976	1977	1978	1979	1980	1981	1982
1. Trade	+7	-4690	-3540	-2255	+97	-1024	-2840	-2829	+1202	+778
Exports (FOB)	6199	7951	8670	10128	12120	12659	15244	20132	23293	20175
Imports (FOB)	-6192	-12641	-12210	-12383	-12023	-13683	-18084	-22962	-22091	-19397
2. Services	-1722	-2433	-3162	-3763	-4134	-5062	-7920	-10212	-13135	-17050
Non factors and others	-965	-1533	-1429	-1574	-1576	-1805	-3098	-3591	-3604	-5128
Interests	-514	-652	-1498	-1810	-2104	-2696	-4186	-6311	-9161	-11357
Profits and dividends	-243	-248	-235	-380	-455	-561	-636	-310	-370	-565
3. Transfers	...	1	2	4	...	71	18	155	199	-7
4. Current account	-1715	-7122	-6700	-6013	-4037	-6015	-10742	-12886	-11734	-16279
5. Capitals	+3512	6254	6189	6651	5269	10916	7657	9804	12773	7867
Direct investment	+940	887	892	962	810	1071	1491	1146	1584	986
Loans*	+4495	6961	5933	7761	8424	13811	11228	11070	15554	12517
Repayments*	-1672	-1920	-2172	-2992	-4060	-5324	-6385	-5020	-6242	-6916
Others**	-251	326	1536	920	96	1358	1323	2608	1877	1280
6. Errors and omissions	+382	-68	-439	554	-602	-639	130	-408	-414	-544
7. Superavit/deficit	+2179	-936	-950	1192	630	4262	-3215	-3490	635	-8956
Reserves	6416	5269	5269	4040	7256	11895	9689	6913	7507	3994
Gross debt	12572	17166	21171	25985	32037	43511	49904	53848	61411	69654

* Average and long term.

** Short term included.

SOURCE Malan and Bonelli (1983).

VII EXPORTS AND TECHNICAL PROGRESS

In the course of the recent decade capital goods exports have increased considerably – their value in 1982 was over 28 times greater than in 1970 (see Table 6.4). Their importance for the industry increased with the internal recession (again, see Table 6.4), so that in 1982 they accounted for 17 per cent of total production. They also play a significant role in alleviating the foreign exchange constraint of the economy, accounting in 1982 for 11 per cent of total Brazilian exports (see Table 6.5). In international terms, Brazil has become one of the main exporters among LDCs,[30] although its share in total world trade is still marginal.

Part of this growth may be due to price factors, since Brazilian export prices rose less than the average (see Table 6.7), reflecting both the competitiveness of Brazilian firms and the government fiscal and credit incentives to exports. However, several studies of Brazilian export performance have attributed this success to technological factors (Araujo and Reis, 1981; Araujo *et al.*, 1983; Guimaráes *et al.*, 1983).

Other authors (e.g., Lall, 1982), building upon the experience of Brazil and other NICs (especially Korea and India), argue that the technological development achieved by such LDCs through 'minor innovations' in the capital goods industry and engineering services is an indicator of their dynamic comparative advantage and that a new international division of labour is emerging, in which 'the comparative advantage of developed

TABLE 6.7 Price indexes of capital goods exports from Brazil, Japan, Federal Republic of Germany and the USA, 1970–79

Year	All, except Brazil (1)	Japan (2)	FRG (3)	USA (4)	Brazil (5)	(5/1)
1970	63	68	49	76	68	1.08 (100)
1971	67	71	55	77	67	1.06 (93)
1972	71	77	62	78	69	0.97 (90)
1973	81	87	79	80	76	0.94 (87)
1974	91	97	87	91	90	0.99 (92)
1975	100	100	100	100	100	1.00 (93)
1976	103	98	103	107	105	1.02 (94)
1977	112	104	116	114	110	0.98 (91)
1978	129	126	137	123	116	0.90 (83)
1979	139	124	155	134	121	0.87 (81)

SOURCE Araujo and Reis (1981).

versus developing countries will be determined not so much by skill requirements *in general*, but by skill inputs based on *specific learning processes which cannot be replicated in developing countries*' (Lall, 1982, p. 174, original emphasis).

The technological development of the Brazilian capital goods industry has been studied by many authors (e.g., Cruz, 1983; Erber 1982, among the most recent ones).[31] Such studies show that the Brazilian capital goods industry has acquired considerable mastery over the full set of design and manufacturing technological activities for a range of products, based on the tradition of metalworking in Brazil[32] and on processes of copying-and-adapting. None the less, the evidence available suggests that such trajectory of technological development is limited and that the Brazilian industry tends to rely on imported technology for new and more-complex products.

Part of the shift to the imported technology can be attributed to technical factors, since 'reverse engineering' is difficult to apply when the gap between the previous experience of the firm and current requirements of design and manufacturing are large and time for learning is short. In this sense, the steep upswing of demand in the Brazilian two cycles of the post-war period and the shift of demand from the non-durable consumer goods industry to the durable consumer and intermediate sectors probably created a gap which induced the use of imported technology. This was accentuated by the fact that 'reverse engineering' of machinery by local producers is difficult to perform in the absence of engineering services (plant design and specification) capabilities.

The literature on the capital goods industry (especially Erber, 1977, 1982) has shown that the import of technology does entail the development of a local technological capability – in fact it argues that such capability is *inherent to the licensing relationship*. On the other hand it also shows that such learning is *limited*, so as to preserve the relationship. This should be no cause for surprise if one considers the *rationale* of the exporter of technology.

Exporters of technology have a deep-seated interest in ensuring that their customers possess some technological capabilities, since their earnings are usually pegged to the latter's sales. Furthermore, the responsibilities of licensor and licensee are very difficult to apportion in cases of failure, breakages, etc., which may jeopardize the licensor's international reputation. Thus, the importer of technology must at least be able to manufacture the goods and/or operate the processes according to the specifications, failing which the licensor must teach the licensee how to do it.

Moreover, in order that a product can be manufactured, all its parts and components must be specified in minute detail, and such specification must conform to the available supply of materials, parts and components, as well as to the specific production conditions of the local manufacturer. Therefore, the stage of detailed design[33] is better performed locally, where the product is to be manufactured, than abroad, where the licensor is located. For all parties, then, it is desirable that the licensee should know how to produce detailed designs.

Although manufacturing know-how and detailed design skills are necessary conditions for introducing innovations (as well as for production), they are not sufficient for purposes of innovation: *basic design* skills are necessary for innovation. Moreover, the mastery of the first two skills does not lead necessarily to a basic design capability: although in some products, especially mechanical products, it is often possible to progress from one to the other; in others, notably in products which perform atomic or molecular transformation, there is a discontinuity of knowledge between basic design on the one hand and detailed and manufacturing technology on the other.

Since basic design skills are not necessary for producing the goods, the exporter of technology has no interest in closing the gap; on the contrary, the teaching of such skills could foreclose a future source of revenues and even nurture a future competitor, especially where technical progress is incremental and engineering-based, as in the capital goods sector. The same applies to the skills for the feasibility stage of design. For branches where innovation is not only design-intensive but also science-based, such as electronics the transfer of technology is much more limited.

Thus, licensing does provide for learning but it is *partial* learning – a type of learning which at the same time ensures the licensor's revenues and the continuation of the relationship over time. Such technical control is strengthened by legal provisions: as is well known, technology is not sold, but leased – the owner of the technology does not forsake the property of the technology, but only allows the licensee to use it for a limited duration of time, under certain conditions, some of which may be quite restrictive (export prohibitions, tied-in imports, etc.). Such legal control applies even in the absence of patents, although the latter strengthen control.

Thus the evidence of the literature argues that the transfer of technology is structurally limited on the side of the supplier of technology. Moreover, it is structurally limited on the side of the importer too.

In fact, one of the main questions posed by this literature was: since the local entrepreneurs were aware of such limitations (as shown by the research) and of the costs they entailed (tied-in imports; export prohibitions); threats of being ousted from the market by a subsidiary after the licensor had tested the market; or having to pay for the technology in equity, relinquishing the control of some important decisions), why did they not invest more in their own technology, walking, so to speak 'on two legs'?

The answer showed that many factors were at work, among which six ranked especially high:

(1) *The competition of foreign technology*, which, being easily imported, put a high risk on attempting to develop local technology, especially where lead times were longer and costs higher with the latter. Government policies relating to foreign investment, imports of capital goods (where project financing played a crucial role), and import of disembodied technology were important determinants of such competition.

(2) *The pressure of clients*, which often made the use of imported technology a *conditio sine qua non*, barring thus the possibility of developing local technology. This was especially observed in Brazil for capital goods and engineering services, including purchases by State enterprises.

(3) *The structures of the markets* in which such enterprises operated, which placed a premium on the monopoly they were granted by the licensor, and also allowed them to pass on to the customers the cost of the technology imported.

(4) *The size of the local market*, relative to the expenditures necessary to develop local technology and the lack of protection of such technology.

(5) *The short-term horizon* with which local enterprises operated, in many cases due to the lack of planning by the state.

(6) *The political outlook of local entrepreneurs*, who were more afraid of being controlled by the State than by foreign firms.

Thus, at one level of analysis, the answer was that the dynamics of economic and political forces was such that there was no incentive to the local entrepreneurs (and even less to subsidiaries of foreign firms) to develop a technological capability beyond that provided by technological transfer. This conclusion could be used to justify state intervention to foster such further development – and it often was.

The preceding analysis has, however, further implications. First it is argued that the import of technology (and similarly the import of capital goods) is a necessary condition in phases of fast capital accumulation and structural change. But, second, it is suggested that such technology imports prevent the local capital goods industry from playing the same role in the 'virtuous circle' of growth of the developed economies, since the CGI is unable to generate or fully absorb the whole range of technological capabilities, and the links between the industry, and other activities such as engineering services, are only partially established, creating a 'vicious circle' of underdevelopment.

The same limitations impinge upon the thesis that the NICs could rely upon their technological capability in capital goods and engineering services to break the foreign exchange constraint, fashioning a 'new international order'. Such capability is, as we have seen, structurally limited, and its relevance for the insertion of such countries in the international division of labour is likely to be further reduced in the future.

Although the way out of the present cycle is not in sight, it is clear that it will be associated with a deep change in the technical basis of the world economy, of which some aspects are already visible in the development of electronics and biotechnology, of which the former is especially important for the capital goods industry and related services.

Electronics is based upon large-scale scientific activity on the frontiers of technology and its activities are to a considerable extent aimed at meeting changing needs of high-income, brand-conscious consumers, activities in which the LDCs have no comparative advantages. The resources used for innovation in those industries are highly concentrated in the advanced countries, and the theory and experience of diffusion of innovations strongly suggest that the rate of diffusion of such innovations will be much faster in these countries than in the LDCs. This will widen the gap not only in research and development but also in manufacturing technology.

Moreover, the diffusion of electronics will affect many of the activities in which the NICs could have comparative advantages. This applies, for instance, to the simpler (non-electronics) machine tools and the labour-intensive detailed design services they would sell to the advanced countries (Lall, 1982), which are likely to be replaced by numerically controlled machine tools and computer-aided design,[34] produced more efficiently in the central countries. The latter may also prove to be strong competitors in the markets of the least-developed countries (markets not to be overlooked in the present crisis), since electronics will reduce the costs of adaptation of designs and of scaling-down of process and equipment to suit the specific needs of such countries.[35]

Another cycle-related factor which may reduce the technology exports of LDCs is their capacity to finance them. The present balance-of-payments problems faced by countries such as Brazil, Mexico, Argentina, Korea, will probably undermine further their technology export capability by reducing their capacity to finance such exports in conditions similar to those provided by the more advanced countries.

Finally, the present phase of the cycle may lead to a *reduction* of the technological capability of the LDCs, not only in relative terms (the widening-gap argument outlined above) but also in absolute terms, by two mechanisms. The first is the closure of local firms, unable to resist the international crisis and the restrictive policies introduced by local governments to control inflation and balance the external account (at least in Latin America). The drastic cut-down in public investment in such countries is not compensated by increased exports, since protectionist and/or contractionist policies are spreading, with feed-back effects.[36] The closure of such enterprises means the liquidation of a technical capability which will take long to reconstruct, even when the new upswing comes (Cruz, 1983).

The second mechanism is the shift of manufacturing from LDCs to the central countries by multinational companies. Stimulated by the new possibilities of automation opened up by electronics and by an increased weight attached to product-quality in competition, this seems to be already happening in electronic semiconductor production (Rada, 1982). It is still unclear how extensive this phenomenon will be, but it clearly has adverse implications for the capital goods sector and related services technology and production capabilities of the LDCs.

The conclusion that technological dependence is just part of a specific pattern of development is also important in avoiding some pitfalls of technological determinism. It is not simply by changing the degree of technological self-reliance that this pattern of development will be radically transformed – a 'naive optimism' often found in the literature. The determinants of technological dependence have to be sought not only at the level of the lack of technical and scientific skills in LDC's (although they may be a powerful constraint in some cases), but especially at the level of the economic and political considerations that guide the action of the enterprises and of the state as regards the development of local technical capabilities. This view also leads to a reassessment of the role that explicit science and technology policies may have in changing technological dependence. When such policies do not converge with other policies (e.g., policies related to foreign investment) their efficacy is severely limited, since they alone cannot change the pressures and inducements (some of which were mentioned above) which lead the enterprises to rely mainly on imported technology.

This argument seems also to be applicable to another major strand in the literature, which argues that the development of a capital goods industry in the LDCs is justifiable if such development would lead to the use of more labour-intensive technologies and to the production of goods and services more appropriate to the level of income of the bulk of the population in such countries. Although such use of the technological and manufacturing capabilities of the capital goods industry is highly desirable from the point of view of equity and social welfare, it faces as a necessary condition a drastic change in the political and economic conditions which rule the present pattern of development in Brazil and other LDCs.

VIII THE CGI AND THE PATTERN OF DEVELOPMENT OF LDCs: SOME CONCLUSIONS

The issue of the specificity of the pattern of development of LDCs is one of the most important dividing lines between authors who study the problems of development. Some authors have argued that, if unimpeded, capitalism tends to reproduce itself on a world-wide scale, generating similar productive and distribution structures (e.g., Rostow, 1960). Others have stressed the specificity of the insertion of LDCs in the international division of labour in terms of commerical, investment and financial relationships which, coupled to their internal productive and distribution structures (strongly influenced by their colonial heritage), fashion a pattern of development that is not only specific but more limited than that of the 'central' economies.

The analysis of the Brazilian capital goods industry[37] lends weight to the second group of authors. Although Brazil is the largest producer of capital goods in the Third World, its capital goods industry does not seem able to play the same role in the dynamics of capital accumulation and technical progress as that industry does in the advanced countries, nor to break the foreign exchange constraint of the economy.

The limited development of local capital goods production and technology is the result of many, interrelated, factors, including the financial structure of the economy and inter-industrial relationships. The former has given a new character and strength to the foreign exchange constraint and, thus, to the relationships between Brazil, the advanced countries and the international financial system, which now plays a decisive role in the internal development of the capital goods industry. Inter-industrial relationships are based upon highly skewed income and wealth distributions.

To change both, so that the capital goods industry fulfils the same role it does in advanced countries, would require very deep changes in the economic social and political structures of the Brazilian society and in the way the Brazilian economy is articulated to the international system. Such changes would indeed require a great change in the Brazilian pattern of development and, last but not least, in the way the international economic and political systems are structured and operate.

NOTES

1. UNCTAD (1982) estimates show that Brazil accounted for 13 per cent of capital goods production in the Third World (China included). Those figures probably underestimate the Brazilian share by including in other countries' figures some consumer goods production.
2. See Section V.
3. See Section VI.
4. See Rosenberg (1963) for an extended discussion of the role of capital goods industry in the diffusion of innovations.
5. Especially Korea and Brazil which exported to advanced countries, respectively, two thirds and one-third of total capital goods exports in 1980 (UNCTAD, 1982).
6. The assumptions of continuity and substitutability of the neo-classical paradigm led to an emphasis on *projects* and not on *sectors* (cf. Stewart, 1977).
7. This is an interpretation based on his articles on India, published in the *New York Herald Tribune*, and on his letters to Vera Zazulich (Marx, 1968).
8. See Santi (1973) for a review of the ideas of the 'classics' of imperialism (Bukharin, Hilferding, Luxemburg, Lenin) on the subject. In the 1920s Lenin changed the views he puts forward in 'Imperialism' and supported the idea that imperialism would not lead to the industrialization of the LDCs.
9. See Varga (1963) for a modern restatement of this view.
10. See Rodriguez (1981) for a detailed and critical review of ECLA's theories.
11. Such as the smaller demand – and price – elasticity of primary goods in DCs as compared to the growth of demand for manufactured goods in LDCs; the structure of markets in which primary and manufactured goods were produced and sold; the pattern of technical progress, which tended to economize on raw materials; and the different conditions faced by the two types of countries, influencing their ability to appropriate the results of increased labour productivity due to technical progress. For a full account of such arguments, see Rodriguez

(1981). See also Ellis and Wallich (1961) for the discussion at the Rio de Janeiro meeting of the International Economic Association in 1957.

12. ECLA's argument is well summed by Tavares (1964, p. 6):

> It can be asserted that given the conditions of the import substitution model, it is practically impossible for the industrialization process to proceed from the base to the apex of the production pyramid, that is to start with the more simply processed consumer goods and progress gradually until it includes capital goods. The substitution process might be regarded as a building of which every storey must be erected simultaneously, although the degree of concentration on each varies from one period to another.

13. Our estimates of the share of the capital goods industry in total Brazilian industrial output (12 per cent at the peak in 1977) suggest that the figures in Table 6.1 (which are for value-added) may be overestimated, even bearing in mind that the CGI may have a higher than average value added.

14. Brazilian foreign debt grew from US$3.8 billions in 1968 to US$17.2 billions in 1974.

15. It is estimated that 80 per cent of capital goods in Brazil benefited from incentives or concessional treatment (Castelo Branco, 1976; Tyler 1980).

16. The share of private finance in total finance of capital goods imports rose from 36 per cent in 1970 to 49 per cent in 1978. Local credit conditions for the purchase of capital goods were less favourable than those granted by foreign sources and local funds were available only for a fraction of total local production of capital goods (probably less than 10 per cent) (ibid).

17. According to data from FIPE (1978), imports of components and parts for electrical and non-electrical machinery increased their share in total imports of such products from 16 to 28 per cent between 1971 and 1975.

18. In the United States the domestic supply ratio was 92 per cent in 1977. Data from UNCTAD (1982).

19. See Section VII of this chapter.

20. As is well known, Brazilian income distribution is especially skewed and government policies rendered it worse, especially during the boom period.

21. There are no unemployment benefits in Brazil.

22. The trade balance, which was in equilibrium in 1973, showed a deficit of US$4.7 billion in 1974, caused by a jump in imports from US$6.2 billion in 1973 to US$12.6 billion the next year, a fourth of which were capital goods and 45 per cent intermediary products (oil, another 22 per cent, excluded).

23. Data on direct foreign investment show that the main expansion of foreign enterprises (especially in mechanical machinery and ship-

building) occurred earlier in the cycle – during the 1971–4 period (see Erber, 1982).

24. Only Brazilian firms have access to the Bank's funds.
25. In 1978 (when the net external debt was the US$32 billion) an increase in one percentage point of the LIBOR led to an increase of US$300 million in interest payments by Brazil.
26. E.g., the campaign in the press against the 'excessive' role of the State in the economy.
27. In comparison, during the recession of 1964–7, internal capital goods production continued to grow at a 6 per cent yearly rate (Erber, 1977).
28. None the less the domestic component in 1982 was still high – three-quarters of total supply (see Table 6.4).
29. Capital goods exports accounted for 17 per cent of total Brazilian exports in the period 1980–82.
30. In 1979 Brazilian exports represented 15 per cent of total capital goods exports by LDCs, roughly the same share of capital goods production in the Third World (Araujo and Reis, 1981, and UNCTAD 1982).
31. See Erber (1977 and 1981) for a full set of references.
32. The Brazilian industrial metalworking tradition goes back to the early decades of this century. Comparing the achievements of Brazilian firms to those of other Latin American countries, Cruz (1983) emphasizes the role played by such experience. See also Section I of this chapter.
33. The design of a machine goes through three main stages (Asimov, 1962):

    (i) Feasibility – The design process starts from a need recognition. Such are then converted into the essential functions the equipment must perform and the latter expressed by specific performance requirements (e.g. capacity of containment and support). If, by confronting the resources available to the firm with such requirements and other constraints (e.g. delivery time), the enterprise decides that the equipment is feasible, it may end up with a set of feasible design concepts from which one will be chosen in the next stage.
    (ii) Basic design – Sometimes called 'preliminary design', this is, technically, the most important stage in the design process since it involves not only the choice of the design concept to be implemented but also the specification of the structure of the equipment (the arrangement of its parts) and the definition of the materials, sub-assemblies and components to be used in its manufacture. The main elements which determine the competitive possibilities of a machine (technical performance, cost and delivery time) are defined at this stage.
    (iii) Detailed design – here the main consideration is to provide information for production as each part to be manufactured is drawn in detail with emphasis being placed upon dimensions and tolerances.

The relative importance of the three stages of design will depend largely on the novelty of the product for the enterprise. When the product is well known to the enterprise, the emphasis is on optimization of the characteristics of the product at the preliminary design stage, the importance of feasibility increasing with the novelty of the product.

According to the categories of R & D, used in international definitions (e.g. the Frascatti Manual of the OECD) the feasibility and basic design stages should be included in 'developing', as long as the design is for a new product, but detailed design should be excluded. For a fuller analysis of the design stages and technical references, see Erber (1977).

34. For evidence on the gap of diffusion of electronic-based capital goods between central and peripheral economies, see, among others, UNCTAD (1982), Tauile (1983). For computer-aided design, see Kaplinsky (1982).

35. As is well known, one of the main features of the electronic innovations is that they break the link between automation and large-scale production, allowing for the automation of batch production.

36. For instance, one of the leading manufacturers of machine tools in Brazil recently went into receivership when their Mexican market closed. The reduction of investment of OPEC countries will also reduce the markets for the LDCs' technology exports.

37. The same applies to the related engineering services.

REFERENCES

Alves, S. and Ford, E. (1975) *O comportamento tecnológico das empresas estatais: a escolha de firmas de engenharia, a escolha de processos industriais e a compra de bens de capital*, mimeo (FINEP, Rio de Janeiro).

Araujo Jr, J. T. and Reis, E. (1981) 'Exportações de bens de capital: desempenho recente e perspectivas', mimeo (IPEA/INPES, Rio de Janeiro).

Araujo Jr, J. T. *et al.* (1983) *Exportação de Manufaturados, Concorrência e Mudança Technológica: un estudo da experiência brasileira dos anos 70*, Relatório de Pesquisa (IEI/UFRJ, Rio de Janeiro).

Asimow, M. (1962) *An Introduction to Design* (Prentice Hall, USA).

Bergsman, J. (1970) *Brazil – Industrialization and Trade Policies* (Oxford University Press, London).

Cardoso, F. H. (1973) *Autoritarismo e Democratização* (Paz e Terra Terra, Rio de Janeiro).

Castelo Branco, F. (1976) *Importações de Bens de Capital e Substituição de Importações: algumas considerações sobre o problema recente no Brasil*, MA thesis, Universidade de Brasilia.

Cepal (Commission Economica para America Latina) (1985) *El Comenero Exterior de Bienez de Capital en America Latina*, mineo (Santiago).

Cruz, H. (1983) *Mudança tecnológica no setor metal-mecânico do Brasil – Resultados de estudos de casos*, Tese de Livre-Docência, Universidade de São Paulo, São Paulo.

Dosi, G. (1982) 'La circolaritá tra progresso tecnico e crescita: alcune osservazioni sulla "legge Verdoorn-Kaldor" ', *L'Industria*, vol. III, no. 2.

Ellis, H. and Wallich, H. (1961) *Economic Development for Latin America* (Macmillan, London).

Erber, F. (1974) 'A Empresa Estatal e a Escholha de Tecnologia', *Ciência e Cultura*, vol. 26, no. 12.

——————(1977) *Technological Development and State Intervention: a Study of the Brazilian Capital Goods Industry*, D. Phil. thesis, University of Sussex.

——————(1981) 'Science and Technology Policy in Brazil: a Survey of the Literature', *Latin America Research Review*, vol. SV, no. 1.

——————(1982) *Technology Issues in the Capital Goods Sector – a Case Study of Leading Industrial Machinery Producers in Brazil.* (UNCTAD, Geneva).

Erber, F. *et al.* (1974) *Absorção e criação de tecnologia na indústria de bens de capital*, Série de Pesquisas no. 2. (FINEP, Rio de Janeiro, Brazil).

Fajnzylber, F. (1983) *La Industrializacion Trunca de America Latina* (Editorial Nueva Imagen, Mexico).

Fajnzylber, F. and Tarragó, T. (1976) *Las Empresas Transnacionales – expansión a nivel mundial y proyección en la industria mexicana* (Fondo de Cultura, Mexico).

FIPE (Fundação Instituto de Pesquisas Econômicas) (1978) *Pesquisa complementar sobre substituição de importações*, mimeo (FIPE, São Paulo, Brazil).

Ford, E. *et al.* (1977) *A oferta de serviços de consultoria de engenharia no Brasil*, (FINEP, mimeo, Rio de Janeiro).

Guimarães, E. *et al.* (1983) *O Progresso Técnico e o Desempenho das Exportações Brasileiras de Manufacturados*, mimeo (FUNCEX, Rio de Janeiro).

Hirschman, A. (1958) *The Strategy of Economic Development* (Yale University Press, New Haven).

Kalecki, M. (1977) 'As Equações Marxistas de Reprodução e a Economia Moderna', in M. Kalecki, *Crescimento e Ciclo das Economias Capitalistas* (Ed. Hucitec, São Paulo).

Kaplinsky, R. (1982) 'Trade in Technology: Who, What, Where and When? (International Workshop on Facilitating Indigenous Technological Capability, Edinburgh).

Lall, S. (1982) *Developing Countries as Exporters of Technology* (Macmillan, London).

Lessa, C. (1964) 'Quinze Anos de Politica Econômica', mimeo (Centro CEPAL/BNDE, Rio de Janeiro).

Luxemburg, R. (1961) *The Accumulation of Capital* (Routledge & Kegan) Paul, London).

Malan, P. and Bonelli, R. (1983) 'Crescimento Econômico, Industrialização e Balanço de Pagamentos – O Brasil dos Anos 70 aos Anos 80', IPEA/ INPES, *Textos para Discussão Interna*, no. 60 (Rio de Janeiro).

Marx, K. (1968a) 'Matériaux pour l' "Economie"' in K. Marx, *Oeuvres*, vol. II (Bibliothéque de la Pleiade, NRF, Paris).

———— (1968b) 'Materiaux pour le Deuziéme Volume du Capital', ibid.

Matthews, R. (1959) *The Trade Cycle* (James Nisbet & Co., Cambridge).

Mazzuchielli, F. (1977) *A expansão inconclusa: considerações sobre o setor de bens de capital no Brasil*, MA thesis, Universidade de Campinas.

Nelson, R. and Winter, S. (1977) 'In Search of a Useful Theory of Innovation', *Research Policy*.

Nurkse, R. (1953) *Problems of Capital Formation in Underdeveloped Countries* (Oxford University Press).

Rada, J. (1982) *Structure and Behaviour of the Semiconductor Industry*, mimeo (IMI, Geneva).

Ricardo, D. (1973) *The Principles of Political Economy and Taxation* (Dent, London).

Rodriguez, O. (1981) *A Teoria do Desenvolvimento da CEPAL* (Forense Universitária, Rio de Janeiro).

Rosenberg, N. (1963) 'Capital Goods, Technology and Economic Growth', *Oxford Economic Papers*, vol. 15.

Rosenstein-Rodan, P. (1961) 'Notes on the Theory of the Big Push', in Ellis and Wallich(1961).

Rostow, W. (1960) *The Stages of Economic Growth* (Cambridge University Press).

Salter, W. (1960) *Productivity and Technical Change* (Cambridge University Press).

Santi, P. (1973) 'El debate sobre el imperialismo en los classicos del marxismo', *Cuadernos de Pasado y Presente*, no. 10 (Cordoba).

Stewart, F. (1966) 'Capital Goods in Developing Countries', in Cairncross and Puri (eds), *Employment, Income Distribution and Development Strategy* (Macmillan, London).

Stewart, F. (1977) *Technology and Underdevelopment*, London: Macmillan.

Suzigan, W. *et al.* (1974) *Crescimento Industrial no Brasil: incentivos e desempenho recente*, IPEA/INPES, Relatório de Pesquisa no. 29 (Rio de Janeiro, Brazil).

Tauile, J. R. (1983) 'A difusão de máquinas ferramenta com controle numérico (MFCN) no Brasil e algumas implicações para o desenvolvimento econômico', *Ciência, Tecnologia e Desenvolvimento*, no. 2 (CNPq/UNESCO).

Tavares, M. C. (1964) 'The Growth and Decline of Import Substitution in Brazil', *Economic Bulletin for Latin America*, vol. IX, no. 1.

———— (1978) *Ciclo e crise – o movimento recente da industrialização brasileira*, Tese para Professor Titular, Universidade Federal do Rio de Janeiro.

Tavares, M. C. and Belluzzo, L. (1979) 'Notas sobre o Processo de Indus-
trialização Recente no Brasil', *Revista de Administração de Empresas*,
vol. 19, no. 1.
Tyler, W. (1980) 'Restrições à importação e incentivos fiscais para o setor
de bens de capital no Brasil, 1975/79', *Pesquisa e Planejamento
Econômico*, vol. 10, no. 2.
UNCTAD (1982) *The Impact of Electronics Technology on the Capital
Goods and Industrial Machinery Sector: Implications for the Developing
Countries* (UNCTAD Secretariat, Geneva).
Vaitsos, C. (1974) *Intercountry Income Distribution and Transnational
Enterprises* (Oxford University Press).
Varga, E. (1963) *O Capitalismo do Século XX* (Biblioteca Universal
Popular, Rio de Janeiro).

7 Crisis and Recovery in the Mexican Economy: The Role of the Capital Goods Sector

AJIT SINGH

INTRODUCTION

Since the beginning of 1982, the Mexican economy has been subject to a severe crisis, which because of Mexico's very large debt continues to have world-wide repercussions. Between 1977 and 1981 the country's g.d.p. had expanded at an extraordinary rate of 8 to 9 per cent per annum; however, in 1982, the g.d.p. fell by 1 per cent, and in 1983 it contracted further by 5 per cent. Since the floating of the peso in February 1982, the peso–dollar exchange rate has depreciated to nearly a seventh of its value; the annual rate of inflation had soared from less than 30 per cent in 1981 to about 100 per cent in the first half of 1983. As implied by the size of the fall in g.d.p., there has been a huge increase in unemployment and an enormous under-utilisation of industrial capacity. In 1983, real wages in industry are estimated to have fallen by 25 per cent.

The main purpose of this chapter is to examine the role of the capital goods industry in this crisis as well as in a prospective economic recovery. Section II describes the state of the capital goods industry in Mexico in a comparative international perspective. Sections III to V analyse the current economic crisis and the extent to which the weaknesses of the capital goods industry contributed to the crisis. In Section VI it is argued that further and faster development of the capital goods sector, by deepening the process of import substitution, is crucial to Mexico's economic recovery, particularly in the medium and long term. Section VII reports the main conclusions.

II INDUSTRIAL DEVELOPMENT AND THE CAPITAL GOODS INDUSTRY IN MEXICO IN INTERNATIONAL PERSPECTIVE

Table 7.1 summarises the main features of the long-term structural transformation of the Mexican economy during the period 1950–78.[1] The following aspects particularly deserve attention. First, Mexico is a high growth economy whose trend rate of growth of production over the quarter century 1950–73 has been about 6 per cent per annum. The rate of growth of productivity over the same period has averaged at 3.5 per cent p.a. Consequently the economy has undergone enormous structural change. By 1978, the contribution of agriculture to g.d.p. had fallen to a mere 9.2 per cent, although agriculture still employed a third of the country's labour force. Manufacturing industry had expanded at a rate of 8 per cent p.a. between 1960 and 1973; by 1978 it accounted for nearly a quarter of the total output and employed about a fifth of the country's labour force.

The rapid expansion of Mexico's manufacturing sector over the last three decades is reflected in its comparative international standing (see Table 7.2). As Table 7.2 shows, during a period when manufacturing in the third world, particularly among the NICs, has expanded very fast, Mexico has increased its share of third-world manufacturing production. By 1980, the country accounted for more than 10 per cent of total third-world manufacturing output. The table also indicates that although the absolute size of Mexico's manufacturing sector is about half that of Brazil, it is bigger than that of India and nearly twice as large as that of Korea.

Table 7.3 compares the economic structure of Mexico with that of Brazil and Argentina, as well as that of the advanced countries such as Japan, France and the USA. There are notable differences in the structures of the developing and the developed countries in this table, particularly with respect to the share of agriculture in national production and, more important, in relation to the share of primary commodities in merchandise exports. Of the three Latin American countries, the economic structures of Mexico and Brazil are broadly similar, with the one major difference that that Mexico has a much less developed capital goods industry than Brazil. Taking the machinery and transport equipment industry as a proxy for the capital goods sector, it accounts for only 19 per cent of total manufacturing production in Mexico compared with 30 per cent in Brazil (and 24 per cent in Argentina).

Another indication of the relatively low level of development of Mexico's capital goods industry, compared with the other NICs, is given by Dahlman and Cortes (1984). They compare the 'domestic procurement ratios' –

TABLE 7.1 Mexico: Output, employment and productivity in the long term: by sectors of activity, 1950-78 (per cent)

	Average annual growth rate[2]				Structure		
	1950-60	1960-68	1968-73	1973-78	1950	1968	1978
Output	5.52	7.12	6.21	3.96	100.00	100.00	100.00
Agriculture	4.52	3.58	1.44	2.58	17.82	12.39	9.21
Mining	1.70	2.20	4.16	2.69	1.70	1.23	1.09
Oil	9.45	8.50	5.32	11.97	1.67	2.66	3.70
Manufacturing	6.02	8.98	6.91	4.37	18.79	22.61	23.83
Construction	7.34	10.02	9.91	4.49	4.18	6.14	7.48
Electricity	12.79	13.04	9.57	7.76	0.22	0.67	0.93
Transport	5.52	6.49	6.78	6.63	2.15	2.05	2.39
Commerce[5]	6.16	7.60	6.43	3.02	27.05	29.78	28.76
Other services[5]	4.81	5.59	5.82	3.17	18.97	15.81	14.93
Government	4.37	8.92	8.32	5.01	6.46	6.61	7.68
Employment[3]	2.70	2.65	2.66	n.a.	100.00	100.00	100.00
Agriculture	1.27	0.22	0.23	n.a.	54.85	39.39	33.06
Mining	3.24	−1.46	−1.55	n.a.	1.05	0.80	0.59
Oil	5.63	7.20	3.18	6.93	0.37	0.70	0.76
Manufacturing	4.71	5.18	3.34	2.79	12.82	18.90	19.60
Construction	6.12	3.94	4.56	2.99	3.01	4.61	5.39
Electricity	5.08	4.38	5.48	6.47	0.28	0.40	0.47
Transport	3.92	2.97	2.87	4.88	2.63	3.04	3.10
Commerce[5]	2.84	3.49	3.32	5.10	9.79	10.60	10.77
Other services[5]	4.47	4.71	4.76	4.43	10.92	16.20	17.11
Government	3.80	6.50	7.00	5.46	4.27	6.37	9.16
					Relative index[4]		
					1950	1968	1978
Productivity	2.75	4.35	3.46	n.a.	100.00	100.00	100.00
Agriculture	3.21	3.35	1.20	n.a.	32.30	31.46	27.58
Mining	−1.76	4.07	5.80	n.a.	256.78	160.60	191.70
Oil	3.62	1.21	2.07	4.71	445.03	379.31	374.62
Manufacturing	1.25	3.61	3.46	1.54	146.61	119.68	118.19
Construction	1.16	5.35	5.12	1.85	138.86	133.13	141.75
Electricity	7.33	8.30	3.87	1.21	79.78	166.19	171.88
Transport	1.53	3.42	3.80	1.67	81.55	67.41	72.12
Commerce[5]	3.22	3.97	3.02	−1.98	276.23	281.01	280.15
Other services[5]	0.33	0.83	1.01	−1.21	173.62	104.01	89.81
Government	0.55	2.27	1.23	−0.43	151.30	103.77	80.47

NOTES 1. The years selected for the different periods correspond to peak points of the economic cycle. 2. Growth rates of output are calculated on 1975 prices data. 3. Employment is defined as the remunerated economically active population. 4. The productivity index is calculated by dividing output per worker employed in each activity by the corresponding national average. 5. Commerce and services include workers in unclassified activities.

SOURCES Secretaría de Patrimonio y Fomento Industrial, Dirección General de Politica e Inversiones Industriales. *Estadisticas Annuales de Producción y Empico por Rama de Actividad Economica, 1980*: and Secretaría de Programmción y Presupuesto, Coordinación General del Sistema Nactional de Información, *Encuesta Continua de Mano de Obra*, several quarters.

Reproduced from Brailovsky (1981).

TABLE 7.2 Ten developing countries with the largest share of manufacturing value added (MVA) of the Third World*, 1963, 1973 and 1980

1963		1973		1980	
Country	Share of MVA	Country	Share of MVA	Country	Share of MVA
Brazil	17.42	Brazil	20.62	Brazil	22.66
Argentina	13.69	Argentina	13.79	Mexico	10.85
India	13.00	Mexico	10.70	Argentina	9.86
Mexico	9.86	India	8.76	India	8.27
Venezuela	3.59	Turkey	4.18	Republic of Korea	4.46
Turkey	3.46	Venezuela	2.91	Turkey	3.73
Chile	2.97	Iran (Islamic Republic of)	2.76	Iran (Islamic Republic of)	3.02
Peru	2.75	Republic of Korea	2.71	Venezuela	2.61
Phillippines	2.73	Philippines	2.36	Philippines	2.51
Egypt	2.08	Peru	2.25	Thailand	2.01
Total	71.55	Total	71.04	Total	69.98

*Excluding China and a few other Asian socialist countries.
SOURCE   UNIDO (1984)

the percentage of capital goods consumption which is supplied locally – for Mexico, Korea, Brazil and India. This comparison for the latest year available showed that Mexico had the lowest ratio (56 per cent), followed by Korea (61 per cent), Brazil (78 per cent), and India (87 per cent). Dahlman and Cortes also note that unlike Korea, Mexico also had a very low export ratio for capital goods. These ratios for the four countries were as follows: India (4 per cent), Mexico (7 per cent), Brazil (18 per cent), and Korea (25 per cent).

During the course of the veritable industrial revolution which has been taking place in the third-world countries in the last two decades,[2] they have not only become exporters of manufactures and simple capital goods, but many of them have also themselves become significant exporters of technology. The so-called technology exports of the third world's leading industrial countries have recently attracted a great deal of attention from economists as well as policy-makers.[3] The technology exports are very important, although by no means the only indicator of the development of technological capabilities in these countries. There are serious difficulties in obtaining comparable inter-country data in this area, but

TABLE 7.3   Indicators of economic structure in developing and advanced countries in 1978

	Mexico	Brazil	Argentina	Japan	France	USA
1 GNP per capita (dollars)	1290	1570	1910	7280	8260	9590
2 Distribution of GDP (per cent)						
(a) agriculture	11	11	13	5	5	3
(b) industry	37	37	45	40	37	34
(c) manufacturing	28	28	37	29	27	24
(d) services	52	52	42	55	58	63
3. Distribution of value added in manufacturing						
(a) food and agriculture	21	15	17	8	13	12
(b) textiles and clothing	13	10	13	7	6	8
(c) machinery and transport equipment	19	30	24	36	35	31
(d) chemicals	14	12	13	11	8	12
(e) other	33	33	33	38	38	37
4 Share of primary commodities in merchandise exports in 1977	71	74	76	3	33	–

SOURCE   Casar and Ros (1983).

Lall (1984) has carefully assembled the best available information on technology exports of the leading NICs; this is reported in Table 7.4. The table shows that in industrial project exports, the leading exporter is India, followed at a large distance by Korea and Brazil. In non-industrial civil construction project exports, by far the most important country is Korea, followed by India and Brazil. Mexico's performance in these respects is quite poor relative to that of India, Korea or Brazil.

Table 7.5 provides information on the comparative development of the machine tools industry in the leading NICs. This key industry in the capital goods sector is rightly regarded as crucial to a country's technological development. The statistics in Table 7.5 again show clearly that the machine tools industry is much less developed in Mexico than in the other countries. Whereas countries like Argentina, Brazil and India export about 10 per cent of their production, the comparable figure for Mexico is less

TABLE 7.4 Summary of technology exports by NICs (cumulative values)* (US $ million)

T. E.	Country						
	Taiwan	Korea	India	Mexico	Brazil	Argentina	Hong Kong
A. *Industrial*							
Industrial project exports (contract values)	n.a.	[< 802]	2200–2500	n.a.**	>285	106	–
Direct investment (equity stake)	83	67	95	238	n.a.	49	1800
Licensing, consultancy and technical services							
i. Actual receipts	n.a.	n.a.	322	51	n.a.	0.3	n.a.
ii. Contract values	n.a.	472	[> 500]	n.a.	>357	22	n.a.
B. *Non-industrial*							
Civil construction project exports (contract values)	n.a.	43 953	6024	984	>4284	696	–
Direct investment (equity stakes)	18	256	21	n.a.	252	n.a.	n.a.

n.a. signifies positive but not available.
– signifies nil.
Figures in square brackets are estimates.
*For a full discussion of the definitions and qualifications to the figures, see Lall (1984).
**It is estimated that the total value is very small.

SOURCE Lall (1984).

TABLE 7.5 Measures of market penetration for machine tools, by country 1966–67, 1970–71, 1974–75 and 1979–80[a]

Countries and territories	Exports as a percentage of the sum of gross output and imports, annual average				Imports as a percentage of the sum of gross output and imports, annual average			
	1966 1967	1970 1971	1974 1975	1979 1980	1966 1967	1970 1971	1974 1975	1979 1980
Developing countries and territories								
Argentina	4.61	4.59	11.68	13.63	35.59	43.96	40.89	61.59
Brazil	4.05	5.80	4.16	9.97	36.33	51.38	53.56	30.59
China[b]	—	2.61	1.26	5.04	46.68	52.74	26.56	24.34
India	1.32	4.34	7.10	11.06	59.41	43.26	27.24	29.10
Mexico	0.14	0.07	—	0.88	93.16	92.89	98.65	92.89
Republic of Korea	—	...	...	3.95	100.00	...	...	71.33
Singapore	...	...	...	28.99	...	...	...	74.97
Taiwan Province	...	13.12	27.23	49.01	...	39.17	60.12	32.69

[a]All calculations based on data in current US dollars.
[b]Excluding Taiwan.

SOURCE UNIDO (1984).

than 1 per cent. Similarly Mexico has the highest import penetration ratio among all the developing countries and territories reported in Table 7.5; this ratio has remained at over 90 per cent since the mid-1960s. These data provide further evidence of the paradox that despite the very large absolute size of the Mexican industrial sector (the second largest among the third-world countries[4]) and its very rapid rate of growth over the three decades 1950–80, its capital goods industry and technological capacity appear to be considerably less developed than that of the comparable NICs.

Finally, it is important to note the significant role of the foreign multinationals in the Mexican capital goods industry. Dahlman and Cortes (1984) point out that a very large part of Mexican capital goods exporting is by subsidiaries of multinational companies. Power machinery and equipment constitute 25 per cent of these exports (most of which consist of internal combustion engines exported by multinationals to the USA and European plants). Another 8 per cent are commercial vehicles (most of which go to Latin America), and another 10 per cent is office machinery (mostly typewriters exported by multinationals to Latin America). Dahlman and Cortes note that relatively few exports are by Mexican firms, and these appear to be concentrated in equipment for the petroleum industry, glass-making machinery and some agricultural equipment.

III OIL AND LONG-TERM ECONOMIC AND INDUSTRIAL STRATEGIES

The Presidency of Jose Lopez Portillo started in 1976 in the midst of a major economic and currency crisis, financial instability and an IMF stabilisation programme. However, these negative aspects were very soon to be far outweighed by the international recognition of Mexico's enormous oil reserves. The availability of these huge reserves, among the world's largest, totally transformed the prospects of the economy. The central policy issue was how to translate this oil into economic development, to ensure that the oil was an addition to total national wealth on a long-term basis, rather than substituting for the existing sources of wealth as had been the experience of many oil-producing countries, both rich and poor.[5]

For this purpose Mexico was essentially presented with two kinds of long-term strategies for the development of the economy. One, which was best articulated by the World Bank (1979), but which had many influential adherents in Mexico, consisted basically of seeking closer integration of the Mexican economy with the world economy and, *inter alia*, fast development of Mexico's oil resources. More specifically, some of the major features of this policy programme were as follows: (a) fairly rapid dismantling of import controls and opening up of the economy so that the forces of world competition might compel Mexican industry to become more efficient; (b) reliance mainly on variations in the exchange rate for whatever level of protection Mexican industry might require in the interim; (c) lowering the growth of real wages and changing labour laws, as well as adopting other measures to induce employers not to substitute capital for labour, thus increasing employment; (d) encouragement of foreign investment. This set of policy measures clearly had a certain internal logic and coherence.

However, an alternative 'nationalist' long-term strategy for Mexico was pressed by a section of the party and the government, notably by the Secretaria de Patrimonio Y Fomento Industriale (Ministry of Industry). This alternative strategy contained the following main elements: (a) in the context of a world economy which was likely to grow much more slowly than it had in the past, retaining import controls and relying on fast growth of internal demand and domestic competition to induce productive efficiency; (b) relatively slower development of hydrocarbon resources (with a strict limit on their exports), and the use of oil revenues principally for investment in domestic agriculture and industry; (c) deepening the process of import substitution, particularly in relation to capital goods industries, and encouraging exports, both by means other than exchange rate variations; (d) increasing employment essentially by faster growth of manufacturing industry. The latter would not only increase employment directly but also lead indirectly to the creation of more jobs in other sectors; it would also bring about desirable long-term changes in the structure of the economy.[6]

The analyses underlying each of these two strategies are very different. From the standpoint of economic policy, the choice between them was clearly significant.[7]

IV THE ECONOMIC BOOM AND THE CRISIS

In the event, neither of the strategies outlined above were fully implemented.[8] Right from the beginning, as a part of the agreement with the IMF (which had stepped in to provide assistance in the economic crisis of 1975–6), the government embarked on a large-scale programme of import liberalisation. It was intended that the programme would be implemented in two stages: in the first stage, import quotas would be replaced by tariffs yielding equivalent protection; and subsequently tariffs would be gradually reduced. In fact, liberalisation occurred at a much faster pace than planned. By 1980, over three-fifths of the tariff items – representing approximately 40 per cent of the value of imports – were exempted from licenses. Not only had the import license requirement been removed from many of the manufactured consumer products, but in terms of value it had also been removed from almost 40 per cent of intermediate and over 50 per cent of capital goods. With respect to controlled items, there was also evidence that the criteria for granting licenses had been made relatively lax. Furthermore, as Brailovsky (1981) notes, it was common practice for large public enterprises to ignore tariffs and quantitative controls on imports. Brailovsky also estimated that in 1979 the average tariff rates in Mexico with respect to the total value of imports was only 6.2 per cent, partly because of a large number of exemptions.

Nevertheless, in relation to economic policy, the economists at the Patrimonio had two significant victories: one real and the other symbolic. The real gain was that President Lopez Portillo, in his State of the Union address to the Congress on 1 September 1980, fixed a limit on oil exports. He enunciated the government's oil policy which envisaged that sufficient oil would be produced to meet the needs of the domestic economy, but that oil exports should not exceed 1.5 million barrels per day. The symbolic victory was that the government accepted the Patrimonio's advice and did not join GATT, a proposal which was being vigorously advocated by most other economic ministries. However, this signal against Mexico's closer integration with the world economy was contradicted in practice. The government continued with its policy of import liberalisation, which only started to be reversed in the second half of 1981 as the economic crisis mounted.

Tables 7.6, 7.7 and 7.8 provide evidence on the actual behaviour of the economy: both real (Tables 7.6 and 7.7) and the financial economy (Table 7.8). As can be seen, between 1977 and 1981 the Mexican economy expanded rapidly. Even the non-oil g.d.p. achieved an extraordinary rate of growth of 8 per cent per annum at a time of significant deceleration in world economic growth. Instead of increasing unemployment, which most industrial countries experience during this period, in Mexico, at a conservative estimate half a million new jobs were being created each year. Towards the end of the period, revised figures indicate that nearly a million new jobs were being created annually. Similarly, as Table 7.7 shows, after the economic crisis of 1976 investment in plant and equipment recovered strongly. By 1980, gross fixed capital formation as a proportion of g.d.p. was nearly 25 per cent.

However, as Table 7.8 shows, the health of the financial economy was not so robust. After a sharp fall from its 1977 level of 30 per cent, to

TABLE 7.6   The performance of the real economy: Mexico 1976–81 and 1971–76

	1976	1977	1978	1979	1980	1981	Average 1976–81	Average 1971–76
Growth of GDP [*] (% p.a.)	4.2	3.4	8.2	9.2	8.3	8.1	7.4	6.5
Growth of non-oil GDP (% p.a.)	4.2	3.3	8.0	9.0	7.9	7.9	7.2	6.5
Growth of employment[1] (thousands)	154	385	416	503	622	627	491	n.a.
Memorandum: growth of occupations[2] (thousands)							811[3]	446

[1] Refers to economically active population.
[2] This figure is for the number of persons employed, but involves double counting of persons with multiple occupations and therefore higher than the figure for economically active population.
[3] Average for 1976–80.
[*] at constant prices.

SOURCES   *Sistema de Cuentas Nacionales de Mexico*, SPP, SEPAFIN Industrial Model.

17 per cent in 1978, the rate of inflation (measured by the g.d.p. deflator) in 1980 was again 28.7 per cent, and in 1981, 26.3 per cent. But the most important indicator of the deterioration of the financial economy was the continuing increase in the current account deficit which by 1981 had reached a colossal figure of $11.7 billion. This was despite the nearly 30-fold increase in oil revenues, which rose from $0.5 billion in 1976 to $14.4 billion in 1981 (see the bottom half of Table 7.8). This disjuncture between the financial and the real economy was directly responsible for the economic collapse which followed in 1982.

There were three main reasons for the huge increase in the current account deficit over the period 1977 to 1981: (a) a massive increase in manufactured imports which quadrupled in nominal value and tripled in terms of volume over the five years 1976 to 1981; (b) relatively poor performance of non-oil exports, which was to an important extent due to the US and world recession; (c) interest payments on public debt which also increased rapidly. Of the three, (a) was an avoidable act of public policy, while (b) and (c) were less so since they depended to a large extent on the USA and world economic activity and interest rates. An analysis of (b) and (c) lies outside the scope of this chapter but in the following section (a) will be examined in some detail particularly in relation to the imports of capital goods.

TABLE 7.7 Fixed gross capital formation 1976–80

	GDP	Fixed gross capital formation (thousand million 1960 pesos)*					Investment to GDP (percentage)
		Total	Buildings	Plant and equipment		Other	
				Domestic production	Import		
1970	398.6	88.1	45.5	24.9	16.6	1.1	22.1
1977	411.6	80.7 (−8.4)	44.6 (−2.0)	23.7 (−4.8)	11.4 (−31.1)	1.1	19.6
1978	441.6	93.5 (15.9)	50.5 (13.2)	28.6 (20.7)	13.2 (15.8)	1.2	21.2
1979	476.9	110.5 (18.2)	57.6 (14.1)	33.6 (17.5)	18.5 (40.2)	0.9	23.2
1980	516.5	127.8 (15.7)	65.0 (12.9)	38.1 (13.3)	23.7 (28.1)	1.0	24.7

*Per annum percentage growth rates (shown in brackets).

SOURCE Eatwell and Singh (1981b).

TABLE 7.8 The financial performance of the Mexican Economy 1976–81 (all figures in thousands of millions of US dollars except where stated otherwise)

	1976	1977	1978	1979	1980	1981
% change in GDP deflator	19.6	30.4	16.7	20.3	28.7	26.3
Balance of payments current account	−3.069	−1.623	−2.693	−4.856	−6.761	−11.7
(a) Balance of goods and non-factor services	−1.190	0.360	−0.310	−1.542	−1.808	−4.1
(b) Balance of factor payments	−1.879	−1.983	−2.383	−3.314	−4.953	−7.6
Memorandum						
Interest on external public/debt	1.266	1.542	2.023	2.888	3.958	5.5
Oil exports	0.543	1.029	1.799	3.861	10.305	14.4
Merchandise imports	5.427	5.150	7.376	11.380	17.174	23.1
% change in unit value in dollars of manufactured imports[1]	7.4	8.0	10.5	12.7	15.2	17.0
% change in unit value in dollars of oil exports (dollars)	8.4	6.7	0.5	47.2	55.2	8.0

[1] Figure is for all imports.

SOURCE *Sistema de Cuentas Nacionales de Mexico*, SPP, Informe Annual de Banco de Mexico, various years.

V IMPORTS, STRUCTURAL CHANGE AND THE CAPITAL GOODS SECTOR

In the early 1950s, the ratio of imports to g.d.p. in Mexico was around 15 per cent. During the phase of import-substitution industrialisation in the 1960s, the economy, and particularly the manufacturing sector, performed exceptionally well (see Table 7.1), and by the early 1970s the import ratio had fallen to 10 per cent of g.d.p. The crude elasticity of manufactured imports with respect to growth of manufacturing production between 1960 and 1973 was appreciably less than 1, about 0.8. However, during 1977–81, which saw a quantum leap in imports, imports as a percentage of g.d.p. increased by 5 percentage points and the elasticity of manufactured imports with respect to manufacturing production increased to 4. Even with a large increase in oil exports, such an elasticity was unsustainable.[9] It is also interesting to note that despite (or as some would say because of) the enormous increase in imports the rate of growth of manufacturing production during 1977–81 was only about 6 per cent per annum; the latter figure is lower than the corresponding rate of growth of g.d.p. and, equally important, it is also less than the long-term trend rate of growth of manufacturing production over the period 1960–73, which had been about 8 per cent p.a. (see Table 7.1).

What were the reasons for the large increase in imports between 1977 and 1981? This is a complex subject which has provoked a big debate among students of the Mexican economy (see, in particular, Barker and Brailovsky, 1983; Schatan, 1981; Jimenez James and Schatan, 1982; Taylor, 1983). The following factors, either singly or in combination with each other, may be regarded as the most important in accounting for the surge in imports:

(1) Structural change in the economy towards the development of more import-intensive sectors.
(2) The rate of growth of domestic demand.
(3) A faster increase in Mexican prices and costs relative to those of foreign goods.
(4) Liberalisation of imports, noted in Section IV.
(5) Short-term bottlenecks or shortages of capacity which may have existed in certain sectors.

It is not the purpose of this chapter to join the general debate on Mexican imports and to examine the relative contribution of the various factors such as import liberalisation. However, in keeping with the main theme of the chapter, it will be useful to analyse (1), (5), and the role of the capital goods sector in this process. In view of the weaknesses of the Mexican capital goods industry outlined in Section II, it might be expected that the observed growth of imports may have been caused by structural changes in a rapidly expanding economy. Eatwell and Singh (1981b) investigated this hypothesis and the results are reported in Table 7.9.

In this table the rate of growth of imports is decomposed in such a manner so as to illustrate the effect on imports of two factors: (a) the changing structure of the Mexican economy, i.e. the increase in imports due to the relative expansion of import-intensive sectors; and (b) the effect of increased penetration, i.e. the increase in imports due to the rise in the propensity to import over the previous year. Thus, over the period 1960–70 when imports grew at a rate of only 3.2 per cent p.a., the influence

TABLE 7.9 Structural change and market penetration effects on the real growth rate of manufacturing imports, 1960–80 (average per annum percentage growth rates)

Domestic demand for manufactures		Manufacturing imports		
		Total	Without structural change	Without market penetration change
1960–70	8.2	3.2	0.7	8.5
1970–75	6.0	10.3	7.7	6.1
1975–80	7.3	15.0	13.5	9.2
1977–78	10.5	30.8	24.4	16.9
1978–79	12.2	36.0	30.0	18.2
1979–80	11.6	38.4	35.8	14.3

SOURCE　Eatwell and Singh (1981b).

of structural change was in fact considerable, for without such change their rate of growth would have been even less, i.e. 0.7 per cent. In the same period import propensities changed in such a way as to diminish import growth. If they had not imports would have grown at 8.5 per cent. In sharp contrast in 1979–80 structural change had again had a positive, but relatively much smaller effect on import growth. However, import penetration had now risen to such an extent that it was this alone which accounted for a difference in the growth of imports of between 14.3 per cent and 38.4 per cent. So the key element in explaining import growth in the late 1970s was increased penetration.

Although because of import liberalisation there had been a massive increase in import penetration in the consumer goods sector (including food – the share of consumer goods in total imports over the period 1976 to 1981 increased from 5 per cent to 10 per cent), *90 per cent of Mexico's imports during the economic boom consisted of capital and intermediate goods*. As Table 7.10 shows, the deterioration in the trade balance of this sector played a very important role in the balance-of-payments crisis in the economy. It will be recalled from Table 7.8 that the total current account deficit in 1981 was $11 billion; the deficit in the capital and intermediate goods in that year was nearly $10 billion. In 1982, as a consequence of the balance-of-payments crisis and a very sharp recession in the economy, Mexico ran a trade surplus of nearly $7 billion, but the capital and intermediate goods were in deficit by $5 billion.

A significant part of the capital goods imports during the years 1976 to 1981 indeed consisted of the requirements of Pemex (the national oil company) for its programme of construction of oil platforms. However, as

261

TABLE 7.10 Trade balance and the balance on capital and intermediate goods: 1975–83 (US dollars millions)

	1975	1976	1977	1978	1979	1980	1981	1982	January 1982	June 1983
Trade balance	−3637.0	−2644.4	−1054.7	−1854.4	−3162.0	−2178.7	−4510	6744.5	105.7	6463.3
Balance on capital and intermediate goods	−2100.9	−1987.4	−1755.1	−2234.6	−4052.4	−6506.8	−9922.6	−4911.9	−2899.2	−703.4

SOURCE NAFINSA/UNIDO (1984).

Brailovsky (1981) shows, such imports constituted in 1976, 1977 and 1979 only a small proportion (a little over 10 per cent of the total imports of industrial goods). Even in 1978 when Pemex had to greatly increase its imports to construct a gas pipeline to the USA in a very short period, the Pemex imports comprised less than 20 per cent of the total.

A very important question raised by the foregoing discussion is what would have been the consequences of reducing the level of capital goods and other imports in the period of the economic boom so as to avoid the balance-of-payments crisis? This is not just a matter of being wise after the event, but the issue of import controls had been raised at a serious policy level at the time. The impending economic crisis had been foreseen by many economists, and Eatwell and Singh (1981a) had argued for a re-imposition of a strict regime of import controls in order to bring about a *rapid* improvement in the current balance.[10] Apart from reducing the imports of inessential consumer goods, such a programme would also have involved a much lower level of capital goods imports.[11] Would this decrease in capital goods imports have lowered the rate of capital formation, increased capacity shortages and reduced the growth of production? Eatwell and Singh had suggested that a planned reduction in imports would have a positive rather than a negative effect on manufacturing production and the growth of g.d.p. It will be recalled that during the economic boom of 1977–81, despite the fact that the rate of growth of domestic manufacturing demand was over 10 per cent p.a., manufacturing production expanded at a lower rate (at 6 per cent p.a.) than its long-term trend (8 per cent p.a. between 1960 and 1973). Eatwell and Singh further noted that the economy was not constrained by capacity shortages, not least because of the strong investment programme of the previous years. They also called attention to the *growing under-utilisation* of industrial capacity since 1979.[12] They therefore argued that a lower level of imports of many categories of capital goods would not only help restore current account balance, but also positively aid domestic manufacturing production.

The relationship between imports, capacity utilization, the balance-of-payments position and economic growth may be illustrated by examining a specific case: the situation of Mexico's steel industry during the boom. Table 7.11 shows that between 1978 and 1980, although steel capacity had been nearly 10 million tons, production had only been about 7 million tons. In 1980, steel imports had amounted to 3 million tons. Whatever the truth about dumping, industry sources indicated that a main reason for the large excess capacity was that older plants were being phased out while production was being shifted to new plants. If the old plants had been kept in production, the domestic costs of production would have risen but steel imports would have been much reduced. To the extent that the

TABLE 7.11 Production, capacity utilization and imports in the Mexican steel industry 1975–80

	Capacity (in tons)	Production (in tons)	Capacity utilization	Imports (in tons)
1975	6.39	5.27	82.5	0.702
1976	7.14	5.30	74.2	0.544
1977	8.40	5.60	66.7	1.732
1978	9.50	6.81	71.7	1.613
1979	9.66	7.01	72.6	1.53
1980	9.66	7.02	72.7	3.003

SOURCE Eatwell and Singh (1981b).

Mexican economy was being constrained by balance of payments during this period, the domestically produced steel, even at higher costs, would have been cheaper from the national point of view and therefore well worth producing.

There is reason to believe that the case of steel was by no means unique in the Mexican capital goods sector during the economic boom.

VI ECONOMIC RECOVERY AND THE CAPITAL GOODS INDUSTRY

In normal times, the size of the economic task facing any government in Mexico is, indeed, daunting. The country's labour force, despite some recent fall in the rate of growth of population, is expected to grow at a rate of 3.5 per cent per annum during the next decade. The long-term rate of growth of productivity in the Mexican economy has been about 3.5 per cent per annum (see Table 7.1). Thus the economy needs to expand at a long-term rate of about 7 per cent p.a. simply to provide jobs to new entrants to the labour force, let alone help reduce the current high rates of unemployment and underemployment.

As the experience of the last six years has shown, such high rates of growth are compatible with external balance only if there is a very sharp reduction in the overall *propensity to import* (from the levels which prevailed during the boom). As a major oil producer, *in principle* Mexico is, indeed, fortunate in having before it the alternative of achieving external balance by expanding oil exports. However, as Brailovsky (1981) has demonstrated, such a course would in economic terms be most unwise, as Mexico would run out of oil reserves in a comparatively short span of time at the end of which the economy would be in a much worse position than before.[13] In the short to medium term, an expansion of oil exports may also be infeasible because of the nature of the world oil market.

Further if the world economy is going to grow at a slower rate in the future than it did in the post-war golden age of high growth which lasted from 1950 to 1973,[14] the *long-term* rate of expansion of Mexico's non-oil exports would also be lower. In these circumstances, the requirements of external balance would necessarily impose extremely stringent conditions on Mexico's propensity to import if the country is to achieve the socially required rates of overall economic growth. During the 1960s, as noted earlier, when Mexico had high rates of economic growth the import elasticity of Mexico industry was only 0.8. Despite oil, in the changed circumstances of the world economy the value of this elasticity in the future would most likely need to be even lower.

It will be recalled that in the period of the economic boom the crude imports elasticity of output in the Mexican manufacturing sector had been of the order of 4. Therefore, a crucial task before Mexico's policy-makers is to help reduce this figure over time to 0.8 or less in a planned and systematic way. In the short term, because of the slump, the level of imports has fallen dramatically. The dollar value of Mexico's imports fell by 70 per cent between the first quarter of 1982 and the first quarter of 1983 (World Bank, 1984). This has, however, been accompanied by a sharp fall in the level of production because of the non-availability of complementary imported inputs. As the country moves out of the slump, the medium- and the longer-term task for the economic planners is to restructure the productive system in such a way that the import elasticity (of g.d.p.) is permanently lowered so as to enable external balance to be obtained at high overall rates of economic growth.

As the bulk of Mexico's imports consists of capital goods, the development and growth of the indigenous capital goods industry must play a central role in this endeavour. It was noted in Section II that Mexico's capital goods industry is not as well developed as that of the other leading NICs. A significant issue is, what factors have impeded the development of capital goods production in Mexico in the past? More important, is the country capable of expanding this industry substantially and rapidly in the future? It will be useful in this context to consider two of the most important potential constraints on the development of the industry: (a) on the demand side, the size of the market; (b) on the supply side, technological capacity and skills.

As far as the size of the market is concerned, the absolute level of Mexico's industrial production is greater than that of either India or S. Korea (see Table 7.2), both of which have a far more advanced capital goods industry than Mexico. Further, as NAFINSA–UNIDO (1984) point out:

(a) The Mexican purchases of petrochemical and refining equipment amount to 10–15 per cent of the Western world's sales of these products.
(b) Imports of gas turbines by Mexico represent 30 per cent of the world market of gas turbines.
(c) Mexico, despite the current recession is the second largest buyer of US transport equipment; the country is also the second largest buyer of the US earth-moving equipment.

Turning to Mexico's technological capacity and skills, by third-world standards Mexico possesses a large and skilled labour force and a significant technological and scientific infrastructure. It was noted in Section I that Mexico is not as important an exporter of technology as the other semi-industrial countries like India, Brazil or Korea. Nevertheless, the country has impressive research and technical institutes with an international reputation in many fields. Dahlman and Cortes (1984) call attention to the activities of the Mexican Institute of Electrical Research and the Mexican Petroleum Institute (IMP), which are linked to the state-owned companies Commission Federal de Electricickl and Pemex respectively. The former has an international reputation in the field of geothermia and has provided technical assistance to many Latin American countries. The latter (IMP) is concerned with the development of engineering and technologies required by the Mexican oil industry, and has developed about seventy products used in perforation, industrial wastes, a number of catalyzers used in refining, and various petrochemical processes. By the end of 1981, IMP had obtained twenty different foreign patents in various countries and seventeen more were pending. There are similar examples of technological development and technology exports by Mexican firms in a variety of industries, all of which indicate that Mexico's *potential* technological capacity for producing sophisticated capital goods should certainly be no less than that of the other leading NICs.

The main reason for the comparatively low level of development of the capital goods industry in Mexico has been the country's proximity to the USA, and the lack of a co-ordinated policy on imports and domestic production of capital goods. In view of the ready availability of capital goods from the USA, the Mexican public sector institutions in particular have in the past freely imported their requirements without much thought for the development of the domestic industry (see Nafinsa/UNIDO, 1984; Brailovsky, 1981). In future, it will be essential to follow a more rigorous and clearly delineated programme of import substitution in the capital goods sector and the purposive increase of domestic demand to assist the development of the domestic industry. Such a programme of protection for capital goods production is essential, both on the conventional infant industry argument and on the longer-term balance-of-payments consideration outlined above. Nafinsa/UNIDO (1984) make a number of useful proposals for a planned medium-term programme of protection and development of the various categories of capital goods in Mexico. These proposals deserve careful study.

VII SUMMARY

The most important points of this chapter may briefly be summarised as follows.[15] First, although the Mexican economy has had rapid industrial expansion over the three decades 1950-80 and has undergone enormous structural change, its capital goods industry is much less developed than that of countries like Brazil, India or S. Korea. Second, the chapter analysed the economic boom and crisis of the period 1977-82 and it was argued that the extraordinary growth of imports which occurred between 1977 and 1981 played a major role in causing the balance-of-payments disequilibrium that led to the crisis. Third, an analysis of imports indicated that much the larger part of the observed increase was due to a rise in import propensities rather than a structural change in the economy towards more import-intensive sectors. Capital and intermediate goods accounted for 90 per cent of imports, and the huge increase in this category of imports made a very significant contribution to the current account imbalance. It has been argued that rigorous controls over these imports (and those of consumer goods) would not only have helped to avert the balance-of-payments crisis but would also have positively aided domestic manufacturing production and capacity utilisation. Finally, it has been suggested that as the Mexican economy moves out of the present slump, the socially necessary higher rates of economic growth will be feasible in the medium and longer term only if there is a very substantial reduction in the import elasticity of industrial production. This would require far-reaching changes in the productive structure. The development and expansion of the capital goods industry, through a planned programme of import substitution, must constitute an essential component of this transformation. Mexico has a large enough internal market and possesses the necessary skills in its labour force as well as a technological capacity for such a programme to be potentially fully viable.

NOTES

1. The last subperiod 1973–8 shown in Table 7.1 spans the years of an earlier economic crisis which occurred between 1975 and 1977. See further, Section III of this chapter.
2. See further, Singh (1984).
3. For an up-to-date and comprehensive review of the subject, see the 1984 special issue of *World Development* on technology exports of the developing countries.
4. See Table 7.2. The 'third world' as defined in the UNIDO statistics reported in Table 7.2 excludes China and a few other Asian socialist countries.
5. See Kaldor (1981).
6. The best analysis of this strategy is contained in Brailovsky (1981) and in The National Industrial Plan, produced by the Secretaria de Patrimonio y Fomento Industrial. For a critical general analysis of the World Bank Strategy, see Singh (1981).
7. For a further examination of these issues, see Singh (1983).
8. See further, Barker and Brailovsky (1983).
9. This issue is fully explored in Brailovsky (1981).
10. There was also a major debate at the time about the best means of achieving a current account improvement – by devaluation, deflation or by import controls. See further, Eatwell and Singh (1981a).
11. A large part of capital goods imports was being done by the public sector. Eatwell and Singh had suggested establishment of commissions of officials from the relevant ministries and nationalised and private industry to bring about a planned reduction of imports in various categories in the short as well as the medium and longer term.
12. See also Barker and Brailovsky (1983) who provide evidence that overall capacity under-utilisation in Mexican industry was greater in 1981 than in 1980; in 1980 it had been greater than it was in 1979. Eatwell and Singh (1981a) as well as Brailovsky and Barker also discuss the effects of reduced imports and of the degree of capacity utilisation on inflation. On the latter point see also Ize and Salas (1985)
13. On the basis of the estimated potential oil reserves and the observed economic relationships (in particular the high values of income elasticity of demand for imports), Brailovsky concluded that if a high oil exports strategy was adopted Mexico's oil reserves would reach 'a critical level' within seven years. See Brailovsky (1981). See also Singh (1983).
14. See Singh (1984).
15. For the necessary qualifications to these conclusions, the reader must refer to the preceding sections.

REFERENCES

Barker, T. and Brailovsky, V. (eds) (1981) *Oil or Industry?* (Academic Press, London).

Barker, T. and Brailovsky, V. (1983) 'La politica economica entre 1976 y 1982 y el plan nacional de desarrolo indsutrial', paper presented at the Seminar on Mexican Economy at El Colegio de Mexico, 8–10 August.

Brailovsky, V. (1981) 'Industralisation and Oil in Mexico: A Long Term Perspective', in Barker and Brailovsky (1981).

Casar, J. I. and Ros, J. (1983) 'Trade and Capital Accumulation in a Process of Import Substitution', *Cambridge Journal of Economics*, vol. 7, no. 3–4.

Dahlman, C. J. and Cortes, M. (1984), 'Technology Exports from Mexico as a Starting Point in the Study of Technological Capability', *World Development*. vol. 12, no. 5–6.

Eatwell, J. and Singh, A. (1981a) 'Is the Mexican Economy 'Overheated': An Analysis of Short and Medium Term Issues in Economic Policy', *Economia Mexicana*, no. 3.

Eatwell, J. and Singh, A. (1981b) 'Is the Mexican Economy Overheated?: A Further Note on Imports and Capacity Utilisation', *Economia Mexicana*, no. 3.

Ize, Alain and Javier Salas (1985) 'Prices and Output in the Mexican Economy: Empirical Testing of Alternative Hypotheses', *Journal of Development Economics*, vol. 17, no. 3.

Jimenez Jaimes, Felix O. and Claudia Schatan (1982) 'Mexico: la nueva politica comercial y el incremento de las importaciones de bienes manufacturados en el periodo 1977–80', paper presented to a seminar on the external sector, CIDE, (Mexico, DF), July.

Kaldor, N. (1981) 'The Energy Issues', in Barker and Brailovsky (1981).

Lall, S. (1984) 'Exports of Technology by the Newly Industrialising Countries', *World Development*, vol. 12, no. 5–6.

NAFINSA/UNIDO (1984) 'La industria de bienes de capital en la situacion economic actual', Mexico D.F., April.

Schatan, Claudia (1981) 'Efectos de la liberalizacion del comer cio exterior en Mexico', *Economia Mexicana*, no. 3, pp. 79–108.

Singh, A. (1981) 'The Mexican Economy at the Crossroads: Policy Optionn in a Semi-Industrial Oil Exporting Economy. A Comment on Brailovsky', in Barker and Brailovsky (1981).

Singh, A. (1983) *Employment and Output in a Semi-Industrial Economy Modelling Alternative Policy Options in Mexico*, paper prepared for the Technical Workshop on Forecasting Models and the Employment Problem (ILO, Geneva) (September).

Singh, A. (1984) 'The Interrupted Industrial Revolution of the Third World: Prospects for Resumption', *Industry and Development*, no. 12.

Taylor, L. (1983) 'The Crisis and Thereafter: Macroeconomic Policy Problems in Mexico', paper presented at the Conference on Economic Problems of Common Concern to Mexico and the USA, University of California, Santa Cruz, 10–12 November.

UNIDO (1984) *Industry in a Changing World* (New York).

World Bank (1979) *Mexico, Manufacturing Sector: Situation, Prospects and Policies* (Washington, DC).

World Bank, (1984) *World Debt Tables* (Washington DC).

Index

269